Responsibility and Desert

Responsibility and Desert

MICHAEL MCKENNA

OXFORD
UNIVERSITY PRESS

Oxford University Press is a department of the University of Oxford.
It furthers the University's objective of excellence in research, scholarship,
and education by publishing worldwide. Oxford is a registered trade mark of
Oxford University Press in the UK and in certain other countries.

Published in the United States of America by Oxford University Press
198 Madison Avenue, New York, NY 10016, United States of America.

© Oxford University Press 2024

All rights reserved. No part of this publication may be reproduced, stored in
a retrieval system, or transmitted, in any form or by any means, without the prior
permission in writing of Oxford University Press, or as expressly permitted
by law, by license or under terms agreed with the appropriate reprographics
rights organization. Inquiries concerning reproduction outside the scope of the
above should be sent to the Rights Department, Oxford University Press, at the
address above.

You must not circulate this work in any other form
and you must impose this same condition on any acquirer

CIP data is on file at the Library of Congress

ISBN 9780197679968

DOI: 10.1093/9780197679999.001.0001

Printed by Integrated Books International, United States of America

for Coen

Contents

Acknowledgments	ix
1. Introduction	1

PART I. THE VIEW

2. Directed Blame and Conversation	15
3. Basically Deserved Blame and Its Value	45
4. Punishment and the Value of Deserved Suffering	77

PART II. CLARIFICATIONS AND FURTHER DEVELOPMENTS

5. The Free Will Debate and Basic Desert	105
6. Fittingness as a Pitiful Intellectualist Trinket?	135
7. Guilt and Self-Blame	172

PART III. INTERROGATING THE PROPOSAL

8. The Attenuated Role of the Hostile Emotions	197
9. Power, Social Inequities, and the Conversational Theory	225
10. Wimpy Retributivism and the Promise of Moral Influence Theories	248
11. Conclusion	271

Appendix: The Signaling Theory of Blame as a Competitor Proposal	287
Bibliography	299
Index of Authors	313
Index of Topics	317

Acknowledgments

I owe many people a great deal for help in the years it has taken me to develop the main theses in this book. A few, however, deserve special mention.

I am especially grateful for the support I have received from Derk Pereboom. More than any other philosopher, Derk's views are most directly opposed to the views I advance in these pages. Yet, as I have developed them, he has been nothing short of generous and even enthusiastic about my arguments. He's commented on multiple drafts of every chapter in this book, saving me from many errors or other shortcomings. In fact, Derk is the one who convinced me that the views I had developed in a series of articles over roughly the past decade merited treatment in a monograph. Thank you, Derk.

I am also grateful to David Shoemaker. He, too, has had an oversized influence on much of what I have developed in this book. Dave has been one of my very best and most cautious critics. He commented on an earlier completed draft of this manuscript, offering me much needed help.

Randy Clarke has also had such a strong influence on my work. He has been so generous with his time, commenting carefully on everything I have written in these pages. I remain indebted to him for teaching a graduate seminar on responsibility years ago at Florida State University, permitting me to sit in. Randy's lectures were so clear and fascinating that he was the inspiration for my 2012 book, *Conversation and Responsibility*. That inspiration and what I learned from him then also helped fuel this book.

Dana Nelkin has been extremely supportive in helping me with the arguments in this book. Her work is certainly as important as anything written on these topics, and it has been as influential on

X ACKNOWLEDGMENTS

my own as anybody's. I am always amazed when somehow, charitably, she sees the best in my proposals but still manages to place her finger on just that spot where my best critics will resist.

For over a decade now, ever since my arrival here at Arizona in 2010, Carolina Sartorio has been the very best of colleagues. Carolina never fails to read with great care every damn thing I write. I confess, I feel I owe her an apology since I think she tolerates more than enjoys all this work on the ethics of responsibility. She's all about the metaphysics. Despite that, she'll work through it all to help me. Thank you, Carolina.

I must also send out a special thank you to Paul Russell. If there is anyone who initially got me interested in these topics, it was Paul back in the 1980s, when I was a graduate student at Virginia. As a visiting professor, Paul taught a seminar linking Hume on freedom and responsibility to P. F. Strawson's work. Since then, he has been quite generous, always offering excellent comments on whatever I am working on.

Over the years, I have now worked on various book-length projects with Peter Ohlin of Oxford University Press, either as an author or as an editor of a collection. On every occasion he has shown impeccable judgment. Thank you, Peter, for supporting this project.

There are several other philosophers who have been a great help to me in the past decade as I have been developing the views set out in the pages to follow. So, for the philosophical help and genuine friendship a sincere thank you goes out to Mark Balaguer, Gunnar Björnsson, David Brink, Ish Haji, Terry Horgan, Tim Kearl, Jeannette Kennett, Ellie Mason, George Sher, Michael Smith, Mark Timmons, Manuel Vargas, Steve Wall, Robert Wallace, Brandon Warmke, and Michael Zimmerman.

Within the past year I have had two wonderful opportunities to discuss an earlier draft of my completed manuscript with impressive audiences. One of these was organized by Paul Russell and Andras Szegiti in Lund, Sweden, sponsored by the Lund

ACKNOWLEDGMENTS   xi

Gothenburg Responsibility Project at Lund University in October 2022. I am indebted to Paul and Andras; my three critics, Yuliya Kanygina, Daniel Telech, and Patrick Todd; as well as members of the audience. Another was organized by Jeannette Kennett in Sydney, Australia, and sponsored by the Centre for Agency, Values, and Ethics (CAVE) at Macquarie University in June 2022. I am grateful for the feedback I received from the members of the CAVE community.

Because this manuscript began as a set of previously published papers, I also want to thank all who gave me comments on much earlier drafts. So, thank you Santiago Amaya, Carla Bagnoli, Macalester Bell, Christopher Bennett, Nathan Biebel, Alex Bisbo Basto, Olle Blomberg, Daphne Brandenburg, Jan Bransen, Eric Brown, Joe Campbell, Justin Capes, Andreas Carlsson, Gregg Caruso, Justin Coates, Justin Caouette, Phoebe Chan, Tom Christiano, Randolph Clarke, Justin D'Arms, Alison Denham, Austin Duggan, Anton Emilsson, Christel Fricke, Michael Gill, Carl Ginet, Bob Hartman, Doug Husak, Katrina Hutchison, Terry Horgan, Ishtiyaque Haji, Daniel Haas, Chris Howard, Dan Jacobson, Sofia Jeppsson, Marta Johansson, Robert Kane, Erin Kelley, Jeannette Kennett, Matt King, Naomi Kloosterboer, Noa Latham, Keith Lehrer, Andrew Lichter, Max Kramer, Catriona Mackenzie, Coleen Macnamara, Kate Manne, Ben Matheson, Victoria McGeer, Kristin Mickelson, Mark Migotti, Per Milam, Elijah Milgram, Wade Monroe, Eddie Nahmias, Dana Nelkin, Shaun Nichols, Marina Oshana, Carmen Pavel, Derk Pereboom, Ingmar Persson, Guido Pincione, Abelard Podgorski, Doug Portmore, Travis Quigley, Wlodek Rabinowicz, Piers Rawling, Philip Robichaud, Daniel Russell, Paul Russell, Nicholas Sars, Carolina Sartorio, David Schmidtz, Matthe Scholten, Stephen Schwartz, Seth Shabo, David Shoemaker, Marc Slors, Saul Smilansky, Angela Smith, Daniel Speak, Helen Steward, Jada Strabbing, Andras Szegiti, Victor Tadros, Matt Talbert, Neal Tognazzini, Jason Turner, Alexander Velichkov, Kadri Vihvelin, and Michael Webber.

xii ACKNOWLEDGMENTS

I am also grateful to three anonymous referees for Oxford University Press. All offered very helpful advice.

Finally, I am indebted to Danielle Steffey, my wonderful wife, for her loving support and natural philosophical instincts.

* * *

This book is dedicated to my son, Coen Steffey McKenna. Coen, I cannot thank you for your support in writing this book. That's because you offered none. In your case, I wrote it despite you rather than because of you. These first twelve years of your life have been nothing but a distraction for me. It is a wonder I have been able to get any serious philosophical work done at all. All the same, you have been a distraction I'd not trade for anything in my life. Every adventure with you, every ski run, every bike ride or meandering hike, every quiet night reading to you, getting you off to school in the morning, or fixing you supper is far more important than any damn thing I could write. I love you with my every breath. I'm only hopeful that we can share the next dozen years with even more of the wildness this life throws at us. One day when I am long gone, read these words and know that I am loving you from the stars. Anyway, this book is for you son.

—Michael McKenna
December 4, 2023

1

Introduction

What is the relationship between desert and moral responsibility? More specifically, what is the relationship between desert and various responsibility responses, including blame and praise, resentment and gratitude, guilt as well as (some forms of) pride, and reward and punishment? The most immediate answer is that desert supplies a distinctive normative basis for appropriate instances of these responses; it is appropriate to blame when blame is deserved, to praise when praise is deserved, to reward when reward is deserved, and so on. But this tells us little unless we gain some sense of the nature of these responses—what such things as blame and punishment are—as well as the nature of the normativity distinctive of desert. An adequate theory of moral responsibility needs to illuminate these issues, or, if it rejects this burden, it owes us an explanation. The need to get clear on these matters also bears importantly on the free will debate. Many philosophers, myself included, characterize free will in terms of the control condition necessary for moral responsibility and then, to specify matters further, in terms of *basically deserved blame*. Well, what is that? What is basically deserved blame? Surprisingly, many who adopt this way of theorizing about free will have had little to say about either the nature of blame or the nature of desert, basic or otherwise. This book is devoted to the interface between desert and various responsibility responses, especially blame, but also punishment, and a range of reactive emotions intimately connected to both blame and punishment, such as resentment, indignation, and guilt.

Two themes feature centrally in the pages to follow. One involves further developments of the conversational theory of moral

Responsibility and Desert. Michael McKenna, Oxford University Press. © Oxford University Press 2024.
DOI: 10.1093/9780197679999.003.0001

2 INTRODUCTION

responsibility that I advanced in an earlier work, *Conversation and Responsibility* (2012). There, I argued that moral responsibility, and especially our responsibility responses that are involved in holding others morally accountable, have not only an expressive (Feinberg, 1970) and communicative (Duff, 2001 Watson, 1987), but also a conversational character. Or at least there is a useful analogy with a speaker's conversational responses when engaged in meaningful conversation with other competent speakers of a shared language. To overtly and directly blame or praise someone—in word, deed, or recognizable attitudinal modification—carries a meaning analogous to the meaning one conveys to another speaker when she responds to a prior conversational contribution by that other speaker. Blame, praise, reward, and punishment, as well as various emotional expressions outwardly directed, like resentment or gratitude, thus have a meaning or significance of a sort comparable to the Gricean notion of nonnatural meaning.

Unique to my communication-based proposal is the contention that these meaningful responsibility responses are responses to *prior* contributions by a morally responsible agent whose conduct also has a kind of interpretive meaning. On my proposal, a responsibility response of blame, for instance, is not, then, the initial point where we have a communicative element in a theory of moral responsibility—that is, the communicative element does not just initially appear at the stage of holding another morally responsible. It appears also at the stage of *being* morally responsible. The morally responsible agent's act itself, say a blameworthy one, also has interpretive significance. It has a meaning—agent meaning—that I have compared to Gricean speaker meaning. On the proposal as I have developed it, and building on P. F. Strawson's (1962) understanding of moral responsibility, that meaning is a function of an agent's discernible quality of will as manifested in acting as she does. Responses like blame or praise, characteristically expressed via the medium of resentment or gratitude, are then meaningful further interactions in something like an unfolding conversation.

INTRODUCTION 3

This first theme, which is about the *nature* of moral responsibility, leads to a second regarding the *normativity* of moral responsibility. Given the nature of responsibility responses like blame and praise, justificatory considerations immediately arise. A blaming response, for instance, expressed via a blamer's resentment, can be inappropriate because it misrepresents the quality of will of the agent blamed. Or in some other way, the mode of blaming might not be meaningful or intelligible as a response to culpable wrong. Thus, norms of veracity as well as intelligibility can apply. Just as some conversational responses might be unintelligible, so, too, a blaming response might not be apt in response to a blameworthy agent's poor conduct. So, I contend, once we appreciate blame's nature according to the conversational theory, normative considerations—about the appropriateness of blame or punishment—arrive on the scene. But norms of veracity and intelligibility, perhaps characterized in terms of fittingness, are inadequate to supply the normative resources needed to justify treatment that can be quite costly and harmful for a culpable party. Blaming can hurt, and of course punishment can hurt. We need a kind of normativity with the heft to justify a practice that can be harmful to persons. What sort of normative evaluation will do the trick? Many have thought that it is desert. No doubt, there are competitors, like fairness (Wallace, 1994), or contractualist notions of reasonability (Scanlon, 1998), or utility (Smart, 1963), or a more cautious form of consequentialism (Vargas, 2013). But desert has been widely recognized by many as the most plausible candidate for the normativity at the heart of our shared conception of moral responsibility. So, a second theme of this book is to come to a clear understanding of what desert in the sphere of moral responsibility comes to—as opposed to, for instance, the desert that pertains to prizes or grades and so on (cf. Feinberg, 1963).

My plan is to unite these two themes. A constitutive ingredient of what a morally responsible person deserves when she is blameworthy is that others communicate with her via blaming or even

4   INTRODUCTION

punishing practices. The expressed blame, including conveying the content communicated in blaming, *is* what is deserved, or at least it is among the things deserved. It is not as if it is merely an instrument to dispense something else that is deserved. Or so I will argue.

It bears mentioning before we proceed that I am only interested here in moral responsibility in the accountability sense. Gary Watson (1996) and then David Shoemaker (2015) have both argued convincingly that there are different kinds of moral responsibility. The accountability sense is the sense wherein we hold one another to account for our morally significant conduct. In this sense, culpable moral wrongdoing then justifies others in holding the guilty to account by potentially burdensome forms of blaming behavior and also by way of punishment. Other kinds of moral responsibility do not directly implicate the prospects of hard treatment, and my focus here will be on desert as the normative relation that serves to justify such practices.

Here is a roadmap of what is to come.

* * *

The book divides into three parts. The first sets out the basic view about the nature and norms bearing on both blame and punishment. The second clarifies and further develops the view. The third criticizes it, showing the potential weaknesses and exploring alternatives and limitations.

Part I: The View

Chapter 2, "Directed Blame and Conversation," sets out and develops further my (2012) communicative account of blame. I treat blame as a response to an ongoing meaningful interaction between a morally responsible agent as the blamed party and a member of the moral community holding that person to account by blaming her. Two important points get special attention. One is to clarify and defend my methodology of focusing on only prototypical cases of blame when it is overt and directly targeted at a blamed party. I reject the project of offering necessary and sufficient conditions for the full extension of blame. Instead, I contend that by understanding these crucial central cases, we can then account for other cases of blame, like private (merely attitudinal) blame. A second point is devoted to explaining the extreme variability in felicitous modes of directly blaming one who is blameworthy. Two different parties might directly blame a blameworthy person in ways that are perfectly apt, and yet their modes of expression might be wildly divergent. How then can we make sense of a unified notion—blame—and then attend to normative assessments of it? I argue that the variability is a function of two things. First, different meaningful responses can arise from one blamer rather than another due to the fact that different blamers might stand in different meaningful relations with the one blamed. Just as different interlocutors in conversation might use different contextual considerations to convey meaning in a conversation by exploiting various implicatures and shared pragmatic background conditions, so, too, different blamers might be differentially suited and so blame by differing means. Second, blame is targeted at blameworthiness, and blameworthiness is an evaluatively complex assessment of an agent's conduct. It involves an assessment of the deontic status of an agent's act as, say, right or wrong; an assessment of the agent's attitude or quality of will, where this involves axiological appraisal of the worth (badness) of her attitude toward her objectionable action; and there is also often a related aretaic assessment of the agent who performs the blameworthy act insofar as her character is (often) also impugned. Apt blame can therefore vary by focusing on and being a response to these different dimensions of blameworthiness.

Chapter 3, "Basically Deserved Blame and Its Value," shows how it is that desert is a unique normative basis for justifying blame. In

6 INTRODUCTION

this way, it aims to clarify how desert is different from appeals to normative considerations such as utility (Smart, 1963) or fairness (Wallace, 1994). In doing so, I distinguish between nonbasic and basic desert theses. Nonbasic desert embraces evaluations of blame in terms of deservingness. But it then offers some further normative justification for desert. Basic desert does not, and it is then challenging to say much about it that is informative insofar as it is basic. I attempt to make some progress by understanding what sort of normative appraisals are entailed by desert. Does basic desert entail that it is good for a culpable wrongdoer to get what she deserves, including the harms attendant with blame? How can it ever be good to harm a person when the good at issue is not merely instrumental? Or does desert not entail any axiological assessment but just license a deontic assessment regarding the permissibility of or an obligation to blame? I defend the more challenging thesis—that desert claims encompass judgments regarding the noninstrumental goodness of the blameworthy receiving blame and, along with it, the harms that can characteristically come with being blamed. The main challenge for this view, as I see it, is to defend the highly controversial thesis that it ever can be noninstrumentally good to harm a person.

Chapter 4, "Punishment and the Value of Deserved Suffering," builds a theory of basically deserved punishment from the conversational theory of moral responsibility by drawing upon the account of basically deserved blame advanced in Chapter 2. Treating basically deserved punishment as a central tenet of retributivism, I argue that the harm in deserved punishment, like the harm in deserved blame, can be noninstrumentally good. However, I also argue that the range of deserved punishments is far more limited than what is often on offer by other retributivist theories of punishment. What is deserved, I argue, in punishing a culpable wrongdoer for her criminal activity is limited to eliciting a proper degree and kind of guilt in (punishing) conditions conducive to experiencing that guilt as a fitting response to her criminality. The focus here,

INTRODUCTION 7

similar to the view advanced by Anthony Duff (2001), is on the conversational aim of engaging a culpable wrongdoer, encouraging her to respond to our unwelcome treatment of her in a way that is an expression of her accepting responsibility for her crimes. A crucial element of this proposal is the far more modest upper limits on what might be a deserved form of punishment.

Part II: Clarifications and Further Developments

Chapter 5, "The Free Will Debate and Basic Desert," is devoted to the question of whether basic desert is essential to our understanding of the free will debate. Of course, many metaphysicians writing about free will contend that we can engage in the free will debate without any reference to moral responsibility at all (e.g., Vihvelin, 2015; van Inwagen, 2008, 2017). These philosophers will have little interest in this chapter. However, many others think that we should get a purchase on the free will at issue in the field of metaphysics by attending to the sort of freedom or control that seems to be central to our moral responsibility judgments and practices, especially when we focus just on the accountability sense of moral responsibility. It is this sense that is at issue when we hold others to account and expose them to the risks of costly blaming and punishing forms of treatment. Some philosophers, such as Derk Pereboom (2001, 2014), contend that when we focus on free will in this dialectical context, the *only* sort of normative basis for blaming or punishing that matters is basic desert. Why? Competitor proposals meant to justify our blaming and punishing practices—like appeal to consequentialist considerations—are clearly compatible with determinism; there just is no metaphysical puzzle left that is worth tending to. I resist this contention. I argue that we do not need the notion of basic desert to sustain the debate about the metaphysics of free will. Other normative bases for justifying blame and punishment also can bring with them robust freedom

8   INTRODUCTION

requirements that render it an open question whether blame and punishment so understood are compatible with determinism. It bears mentioning here that my motivation for advancing this thesis is that I am not prepared to embrace unqualifiedly basic desert as a legitimate normative basis for blame and punishment. Perhaps for some reason it is benighted. My aim in this book is to examine basic desert and offer the best case for it playing a role in a theory of moral responsibility. But I think it remains an open question whether it should after all be endorsed. If not, I say, the free will debate remains a live controversy, even assuming we *do* need to theorize about free will by linking it to the control condition for moral responsibility.

Chapter 6, "Fittingness as a Pitiful Intellectualist Trinket?" uses P. F. Strawson's disparaging assessment of libertarians' appeal to an intuition of fittingness as a way, first, to understand what fittingness is and, second, to scrutinize the relationship between fittingness and desert. Just about the time Strawson penned those dismissive words, Joel Feinberg (1963) instead wrote approvingly of fittingness as a way to help us understand desert as the normative basis for assessing, among other things, blame and punishment. I argue that Strawson's dismissal of fittingness was only in response to a very specific appeal to it that he alleged was made by libertarians of his day. One question worth considering is whether his characterization of these philosophical adversaries was anything more than caricature. But that aside, I argue that Strawson actually needed the notion of fittingness as Feinberg appealed to that relation since, otherwise, Strawson was without resources to explain how the reactive attitudes could do the work he alleged they could do. He claimed that by tending to them, we could fill a justificatory gap between morally blameworthy behavior (roughly, acting with ill will) and our practices of blaming and punishing (expressing in our treatment our resentment or indignation). But how exactly? I argue that the how is by way of fitting attitudes. When someone acts toward us or others with ill will and is blameworthy, our angry responses

INTRODUCTION 9

expressing our resentment or indignation are justified response because, at the very least, they are fitting. Once we see this, we can then ask if, as Feinberg suggested, they are also deserved, since, on Feinberg's view, desert is a species of fittingness. Putting the matter in these terms brings into relief the need to get clear on just what fittingness and desert are in the arena of moral responsibility. How are they related? I argue that desert is indeed a species of fittingness and that, when a moral responsibility response such as resentment or indignation is not only fitting but deserved, it helps to justify forms of hard treatment.

Chapter 7, "Guilt and Self-Blame," takes up the question of how we are to understand self-blame within the conversational theory of moral responsibility. An apparent problem arises, since on its face it seems implausible to treat self-blame with the resources provided by communication. A self-blamer does not need to communicate or converse with herself to blame herself. The same point applies to guilt as the emotional expression or vehicle for self-blame. Guilt, unlike second- or third-personal resentment or indignation, seems not to be a form of anger directed at oneself in blaming. There are, moreover, philosophers like Andreas Carlsson (2019) who argue that guilt is the fundamental grounds for being morally responsible: One is blameworthy for an action just in case and because one deserves to feel guilty for performing it. A conversational theory better have a convincing way to account for self-blame and guilt, or it looks as if the theory simply cannot capture the grounding or fundamental features of moral responsibility. Rejecting my earlier efforts to account for self-blame and guilt (2012), I argue that both self-blame and guilt can be better understood as desired responses to others were they to blame the blameworthy person. They are thus potentially responses to the meaningful forms of the blame of others. In developing the view, I also argue that the relation between blame—both self-blame and other-directed blame—and pertinent reactive attitudes is, as I put it, deep but contingent. Self-blame does not *essentially* require guilt, nor does guilt require self-blame.

10   INTRODUCTION

Part III: Interrogating the Proposal

Chapter 8, "The Attenuated Role of the Hostile Emotions," examines the role of moral anger in a theory of moral responsibility. One issue concerns the importance of moral anger for moral blame. Many philosophers following (what they take to be) Strawson's lead assume that pertinent reactive attitudes of resentment and indignation are essential to what moral responsibility is, at least in the negative case regarding our blaming practices. I refer to this as the *essentialist thesis*. A different thesis, typically adopted by abolitionists about angry blame and retributive punishment is that this moralized sort of anger is problematic since it favors hostile treatment of the culpable. I call this the *hostility thesis*. Because, it is argued, this emotion is benighted, and because it is thought to be so closely tied to blaming, some argue that our moral responsibility practices of holding the blameworthy responsible by blaming and punishing them cannot be justified. This in turn provides an incentive for skepticism about moral responsibility, at least when the responsibility at issue is framed in terms of basic desert. I argue that both theses are false. The reactive attitudes are only contingently albeit deeply connected to our blaming practices. It is possible for blame to persist in the absence of the role of moral anger. At least it is possible for beings that are differently emotionally equipped than most of us are. Moreover the case for the excessively hostile features of moral anger is far overstated, and, properly modulated, moral anger need not have the deleterious effects that it is alleged to have. These effects can be properly modulated with other virtuous traits of character when engaging in appropriate and proportionate blame. Also, expressing moral anger in blaming is consistent with sustaining compassion for those whom one holds to account and even adopting a nurturing attitude toward them, helping them as one can with the aim of moral improvement.

Chapter 9, "Power, Social Inequities, and the Conversational Theory," scrutinizes the seemingly innocent remark by Strawson that in general we all demand a reasonable amount of good will on behalf of others. This is just not true. Some members of the moral community, in striking contrast to others, are so poorly positioned in terms of social standing that it never dawns on them that they might be entitled to demand good will from others—especially those from more privileged circumstances. Indeed, it seems that these disparities are baked deeply into our moral responsibility practices, so much so that they often go entirely unrecognized. Does this corrupt our responsibility practices? Possibly. But the goal of this chapter is just to make vivid how thoroughly our responsibility practices can have unjust inequities and asymmetric relations of power embedded in them. Note that, as the conversational theory makes clear, our practices of interpreting the good and ill will of others, as well as our practices of signaling blame and praise, are all built up out of interpretive resources regarding what counts as a signal of good rather than ill will. The pertinent standards for settling these matters will be shaped by who among others are socially positioned to settle what counts as a reasonable degree of good will and what behavior signals compliance or departure from these standards. It is an advantage of the conversational theory, I argue, that it supplies the resources for bringing these often-unrecognized considerations to light. Still, a weakness of the theory is that it also is silent regarding proper modes of correcting pertinent injustices.

Chapter 10, "Wimpy Retributivism and the Promise of Moral Influence Theories," returns to the topic of retributivism discussed in Chapter 3. Two theses work together to generate a view I playfully call *wimpy retributivism*. The first thesis begins as an exploration of how minimal theories of basically deserved blame and punishment might be while remaining respectable theses at all. I argue, drawing on my proposals earlier on, that the blame and the punishment the culpable might deserve could be quite limited by comparison with other proposals. But then, exploiting the fact that reasons of desert for blame and for punishment are only *pro tanto*, I consider reasons that weigh against ever acting on those

12   INTRODUCTION

reasons. One set of reasons has to do with skepticism about the severity of our blaming and punishing responses. Might we underestimate how harmful they might be? If so, we have reasons to blame or punish less harshly or not at all, lest we risk harming a person far more than she deserves. A second set of reasons turns on our epistemically limited resources for assessing the freedom and the moral competence of those whom we hold responsible. What, for instance, if free will skepticism is true and no one has free will? Even free will realists like me have to register that they could be wrong. Maybe no one has free will, and it is false that wrongdoers deserve blame and punishment. Or maybe the domain of those we take to act of their own free will is just far more limited than we believe it to be. These two sets of concerns might drive the minimal retributivist to a kind of quietism, too wimpy to ever act on *pro tanto* reasons of desert. Hence, we arrive at wimpy retributivism. The second thesis is that a moral influence theory of moral responsibility of the sort advanced by Manuel Vargas can be used as a supplement to reasons of desert. Typically, such consequentialist theories, in the fashion of J. J. C. Smart (1963), are opposed to desert-based theories. But I argue that the wimpy retributivist can seek an alliance with a moral influence theory and supplement reasons of desert with further consequentialist resources. This, I argue, can save the wimpy retributivist from quietism.

In Chapter 11, I close the book with a comprehensive review of the terrain covered, drawing together various lessons and highlighting a few themes that have animated my arguments throughout.

PART I
THE VIEW

2

Directed Blame and Conversation

What is blame's nature, and what are its norms? According to the conversational theory of moral responsibility, blame—at least a distinctive kind of blame—can be accounted for in terms of its communicative role in an interpersonal exchange between members of a moral community. The view I defend is broadly Strawsonian insofar as a restricted class of emotions plays a pivotal role. Nevertheless, it also departs from Strawsonian orthodoxy insofar as these emotions are not essential to blame. Ultimately, I shall offer an account of blame's norms that makes room for the familiar thought that the blameworthy deserve blame.

2.1 The Challenge of Theorizing about Blame

Despite the pervasiveness of the phenomena in ordinary life, blame is an elusive phenomenon. It is maddeningly hard to nail down a theory that gets the extension even close to right.[1] This is shown by the diversity of strikingly different views about its nature. On some views, to blame is just to engage in a kind of punishment (Smart, 1963). On others, to blame is most fundamentally to register a criticism of an agent's free conduct (Zimmerman, 1988) or, instead, to protest how she exercised her judgment-sensitive capacities

---

An earlier draft of this chapter was originally published in 2013, as "Directed Blame and Conversation," in *Blame: It's Nature and Norms*, ed., Justin Coates and Neal Tognazinni, New York: Oxford University Press.

[1] See also Brink (2021: 122–3), Fricker (2014), and Shoemaker and Vargas (2019), who make a similar point.

Responsibility and Desert. Michael McKenna, Oxford University Press. © Oxford University Press 2024.
DOI: 10.1093/9780197679999.003.0002

16 THE VIEW

(Hieronymi, 2004; Smith, 2005; Talbert, 2012). On yet others, it is a matter of altering one's relationship with the blamed party in light of that party's wrongful impairment to the relationship (Scanlon, 2008). Another option has it that to blame is to believe that a person has acted badly or has a bad character, and to desire that this not be so (Sher, 2006). Or instead, to blame is to perceive that a person acted wrongly and with ill will, and to do so from the standpoint of caring about morality (Arpaly, 2006). In a similar vein, it is to adopt an aversive attitude toward a person in response to the belief or judgment that a person is blameworthy (Brink, 2021). A recent intriguing addition to these views is that to blame is to respond to norm violations by engaging in costly signaling of one's commitment to those norms and to a commitment to enforcement of them (Shoemaker and Vargas, 2019). Then, of course, there is the Strawsonian view that blaming just is a matter of reacting to the one blamed with a pertinently charged emotion, such as resentment or indignation. This list is far from exhaustive.

The task of accounting for blame is made all the harder given that there are different notions of responsibility. It's not just that there are different theories of what responsibility is; it's that there are different kinds of responsibility to theorize about and a multiplicity of theories directed at these different kinds. As one member in the family of responsibility concepts, blame is caught up in this mix. This makes it especially challenging to focus on the proper range of phenomena and the attendant concept(s) of blame.

There is, furthermore, a wide variability to the permissible modes of manifesting blame. This complicates matters even more. You and I might both be entitled to blame a colleague for some bit of scandalous conduct, and yet we might fittingly do so in ways that are wildly divergent. I might refuse to speak to him, whereas you might invite him to your house for drinks and have a stern conversation. Moreover, you might be exercised primarily by the wrong thing he did, whereas I might be more concerned with what his behavior suggests about how little he cares for a mutual

DIRECTED BLAME AND CONVERSATION   17

colleague. How, then, might one get an account of blame up and running?

I will proceed by focusing on prototypical cases of blame. I'll seek a means of explaining just these and will forgo any attempt at an exhaustive account of blame. Nevertheless, the central cases of blame I will focus upon are representative of what many have in mind when reflecting upon blame. My hope is that other cases of blame—cases within, so to speak, the extension but closer to the periphery of the concept—can be explained at least in part by reference to my treatment of the prototypical cases (cf. Fricker, 2014).

2.2 Some Preliminary Considerations Regarding the Nature and Norms of Blame

Consider first responsibility. I am only interested in blame as it bears on questions of moral responsibility, as opposed to, say, legal responsibility. As for moral responsibility, many philosophers have argued that there is more than one sort (e.g., Fischer and Tognazinni, 2011; Haji, 1998; Scanlon, 1998; Shoemaker, 2011, 2015; Watson, 1996; Zimmerman, 1988). Here, I will focus just on moral responsibility in the accountability sense, as featured in Jonathan Bennett's well-known essay, "Accountability" (1980). Moral responsibility in this sense involves the possibility of holding an agent to account for her conduct and thereby seeing her as properly capable of being responsive to our various demands, expectations, and sanctions. Such an agent is one who can be expected to acknowledge and comply with others' moral expectations. When she falls short, she is taken to be justly liable to burdensome modes of response from those who are warranted in holding her to account.

Now consider blame. Moral blame as it bears upon accountability involves a negative evaluation of an agent's conduct in a manner that is in some way linked to the appropriateness of

18 THE VIEW

holding her to account for what she does. The natural thought, when focusing on this sort of blame, is to attend to cases in which a person is held directly to account by another who openly blames her as a direct means of making moral demands, expressing expectations, reprimanding, or something similar. But care needs to be taken at this point since accountability-blame is *not* limited to such cases. We often blame others—in the pertinent sense—in their absence. Also, we sometimes conceal our blame from anyone. Given this observation, it is useful to distinguish between *private blame*, *overt blame*, and *directed blame*. Private blame involves adopting a blaming attitude toward someone but without any of the outward behavioral manifestations. Overt blame involves adopting such an attitude and making it manifest in one's conduct. This can be done in the absence of the blamed. Obvious examples involve blaming the dead. *Directed blame* is overt blame manifested in the presence of the blamed party. Indeed, it is outwardly directed *at* the blamed party.

Instances of directed blame are relatively rare by comparison with private blame and overt blame that is not directed. Nevertheless, I will focus just on directed blame. Why? In my estimation, it's the more fundamental notion.[2] Hence, despite the

---

[2] Readers might want something more than assertion here, as both David Brink and Gunnar Björnsson have noted in correspondence. *Why* are cases of directed blame more fundamental? Why, for instance, aren't the private episodes of pertinent emotional responses not more fundamental? Aren't the outward expressions of directed blame causally downstream from the private case, as Brink might put it (2021: 124)? In reply, as I see it, causal order is not the best way to identify fundamentality when it comes to theorizing about blame. My case for the fundamentality of the public cases of blame rests mostly on the overall plausibility of treating directed blame as fundamental and as a guide to helping account for other cases of blame, so I ask for my readers' patience. Hear me out. But two further points bear noting here. First, as regards causal order, the private cases of blame, and especially their manifestation in episodes of reactive emotions, are, I contend, intelligible as blaming responses only insofar as they involve pertinent action tendencies, and I have argued elsewhere (2012). Those tendencies are best understood in terms of directed blaming responses. Second, at least in terms of explanatory aims, an account of blame as it bears on *accountability* is most fundamentally about blame when it serves the functional role of holding to account those who are blameworthy. Those are the directed cases.

relative rarity of directed blame, it is best to treat such cases as prototypical and then explain other cases, like cases of private blame, by reference to our understanding of the more fundamental cases.[3] Key to this approach is accounting for these more peripheral cases by way of proximity to the central cases. In this respect, the strategy I will adopt is not a proper analysis of blame. It is at least consistent with treating the full extension of blame as vague at the boundaries. Departure from the prototypical cases is to be understood in terms of family resemblance.

Thus far, I have engaged in preliminary conceptual spadework in the service of getting clear on the question of blame's *nature*. But what of its *norms*? Here we can distinguish three questions. The first concerns the normative warrant for blaming someone. What justifies its being the case that a person ought to be blamed? The second concerns the standing one has who is rightly positioned to blame the party who is blameworthy. What makes it permissible (or obligatory) for this person or that, but not some other, to do the blaming? While the first of these two questions naturally points to the agent who is to blame, the second points to the one who does the blaming. A third question concerns the normative force of blame—the sting it putatively ought to have when directed at one who is blameworthy. Why and how ought a blamed person regard as burdensome the blame directed at her? In my estimation, this question naturally points to the relationship between the blamer and the blamed; when blame stings, it puts pressure on one's relations with others.[4] The first of these questions we can call the question of *normative warrant*, the second we can call the question of *normative standing*, and the third we can call the question of *normative force*.

---

[3] For an effort to offer a unifying functionalist account that still captures the importance of directed blame, see Björnsson (2022). There might not be much daylight between Björnsson's proposal and the present strategy given that the central work of normative expectations on his view is cashed out in terms of dispositions to publicly blame.

[4] Pamela Hieronymi (2004) disagrees. For her, the force comes from the realization that one has done wrong.

20 THE VIEW

In this chapter and the next, I'll direct my attention just to the topic of normative warrant.

As to the question of normative warrant, it will be granted on all sides that one pertinent norm is a matter of veracity. Is the agent who is blamed for something or other in fact blameworthy for it? Did she, for example, perform the action, or did someone else do it? Was what she did morally wrong or instead morally objectionable along some other dimension, or is this instead a matter of dispute? Did she do it under duress or in some other manner that compromised her freedom? Was she nonculpably ignorant in doing it? In considering whether an agent ought to be blamed, these questions of fact need to be settled. The relevant norm of veracity is that, at least as a *pro tanto* consideration, an agent ought to be blamed only if she is in fact blameworthy. The more challenging topic as regards the question of normative warrant is why, once it is settled that an agent is blameworthy, there is reason to blame that agent.

2.3 Blame as a Response to Quality of Will

I turn to blame's nature. P. F. Strawson (1962) remarked that we care a great deal for the regard others have for us, especially when that regard is revealed in how they act toward us. He then proceeded to account for the phenomenon of blaming in terms of responding to such regard. On the Strawsonian view I endorse, blaming another for something she has done is primarily a matter of responding in a distinctive fashion to the perceived morally objectionable quality of an agent's will as manifested in her blameworthy behavior. In short, blameworthiness is settled primarily, albeit not exclusively, in terms of quality of will.

What is meant by the expression "quality of will"? On my view, it is *not* about identifying a distinct faculty—a will—and attending to some particular property of it. The relevant synonym for

DIRECTED BLAME AND CONVERSATION   21

"quality" is not "property" but rather "value." It is a matter of the worth of an agent's regard for another person, or for other salient considerations (2012: 57–63).[5] This value can be good, ill, or indifferent. It can also be further qualified as moral or nonmoral. So understood, the moral or nonmoral worth of an agent's regard for another can be manifested in the content of her intentions or her reasons for action. But it also can be revealed by her failure to show due regard for someone whom, or something that, she should have, and thus in her failure for this to figure in her intentions or reasons at all.

One important factor in assessing the moral quality of an agent's will has to do with the moral status of her action—for instance, whether the agent acted morally wrongly and so violated a moral obligation. Another is whether she did so freely. A third is whether she did so either knowingly or from culpable ignorance. Note that we have here three variables. One concerns some moral evaluation of the agent's action. A second concerns a control or a freedom condition. And a third concerns an epistemic condition. Each can contribute to an assessment of the moral quality of an agent's will. Although controversial, I do not think these factors are always sufficient to discern the quality of an agent's will as it bears on blameworthiness. In many cases they will be. But I have argued that it is possible to imagine cases in which an agent freely and knowingly does something morally wrong, and yet she does not act from a morally objectionable quality of will. Suppose, for instance, that she is acting in the context of a moral dilemma. (Think of Sophie from *Sophie's Choice*.) Or, she might be acting under some sort of duress that does not exempt her from her obligations or take her freedom from her. In these kinds of cases, she might very well not act from any objectionable lack of regard for moral considerations.

---

[5] The qualification "other salient moral considerations" is meant to allow for morally objectionable behavior that does not necessarily involve harm to another person but instead to, say, nonhuman animals, or the environment, or perhaps a value or ideal.

22 THE VIEW

Indeed, she might be pained by the thought of acting as she does. If so, I contend, she is not blameworthy (2012: 14–20).[6]

As the preceding discussion shows, blameworthiness involves different sorts of evaluative considerations. As a form of moral appraisal, one evaluative ingredient of blameworthiness is focused on *the action* performed by the blameworthy agent.[7] This is settled by, for instance, determining that the agent acted morally wrongly. Here, the evaluative focus is on the *object* of moral responsibility, and, at least in most familiar cases, the evaluation is cast in deontic terms. But a distinct evaluative ingredient, I contend, is focused on the *agent* in relation to her action. Her regard for others and for salient moral considerations (such as the fact that she does morally wrong) is a *further* evaluative ingredient. In this case, the focus is on the *subject* of moral responsibility. Note that modifiers of "good," "ill," or "indifferent" as pertaining to an agent's will are axiological, not deontological terms. Of course, insofar as the value or worth of an agent's regard for others—that is, her quality of will—also casts light on her *character*, there is, at least often, an aretaic dimension as well. Hence, appraisals of blameworthiness can be evaluatively complex, encompassing deontic, axiological, and aretaic judgments.

Our focus is the nature of blame, not the nature of blameworthiness. So, granting the preceding characterization of blameworthiness, why is it important as regards blame? Because blaming is most fundamentally a response to perceived blameworthiness. It is useful to get a clear sense of what it is to which blame is aptly

---

[6] For an intriguing attempt to specify a unified quality of will condition encompassing all of the conditions specified here, see Björnsson (2017). Björnsson might well protest that these various conditions involve more theoretical complexity than is needed. A countervailing worry, however, is that the more fine-grained approach better tracks the different sorts of excusing and justifying pleas in response to charges of blameworthiness.

[7] Of course, omissions, as well as consequences (of actions or omissions) are also candidate objects of blameworthiness. I restrict attention here just to action solely for ease of exposition.

DIRECTED BLAME AND CONVERSATION 23

sensitive. Indeed, there is an important lesson about blame close at hand: Variability in the fitting modes of blaming is liable to be a function of the variability in the evaluative cocktail that is embedded in a judgment of blameworthiness. We'll return to this point below.

As for the evaluative component of blameworthiness involving the object of responsibility, some contend that moral blameworthiness is limited in its potential objects to moral wrongdoing and so to violations of moral obligations. On this view, what an agent can be blameworthy for must be limited to the sphere of this sort of deontic assessment—a strict violation of a moral requirement (e.g., Darwall, 2006; Wallace, 1994). Naturally, blame is limited accordingly.[8]

Although I wish to remain officially neutral on this point, my impression is that this is unnecessarily restrictive. Consider the category of the suberogatory, as this has been clarified by Julia Driver (1992), among others. Why are actions that can only be negatively evaluated in axiological or instead aretaic terms not even potential objects of blameworthiness? I fail to see why exactly a person cannot be blameworthy for acts that involve no violations of any moral obligations and so are not, strictly speaking, morally wrong, but are nevertheless morally bad, or instead unvirtuous. It may be that the mode of directly blaming that is fitting as a response to such acts is different. Perhaps it is weaker than that which is called for when an agent does something that is straightforwardly morally wrong. But blameworthiness for such acts, and thus the prospect of blame directed at the agents who perform them, should be left as a live option.

More recently, Terry Horgan and Mark Timmons (2022) have also argued that the deontic categories need expanding to include

---

[8] Some (e.g., Haji, 1998; Zimmerman, 1988) deny that blameworthiness requires moral wrongdoing, but they preserve a conceptual connection between blameworthiness and wrongness: moral blameworthiness involves acting with the belief that one is doing something that is objectively morally wrong.

24 THE VIEW

the expected as distinct from the required. Failing to do what is expected is not to be thought of as violating a requirement, and so as violating an obligation, yet it can still be negatively evaluated in deontic terms. Here, too, we have a candidate for a kind of blameworthiness and so an apt basis for directed blame.

2.4 The Mode of Response Constitutive of Directed Blame

Grant that blaming is primarily a matter of responding to the morally objectionable quality of an agent's will as manifested in her behavior. Grant also that blameworthiness is evaluatively complex and that blaming is liable to be sensitive to that complexity. The question remains, what sort of negative response is constitutive of blaming? More specifically, what sort of negative response is constitutive of directed blame? Is it primarily a matter of belief? Desire? Some combination? Along with other Strawsonians, I contend that it is most useful to understand moral responsibility and its cognate notions, blame being among them, by reference to a range of morally reactive attitudes. A reactive attitude is an attitude in response to the perceived attitude of another.[9] The reactive attitudes at issue are not (merely) cognitive or conative, but also are affective. They involve emotions, in this case *morally* reactive emotions, and they pertain to the stance of holding morally responsible. Central to the current topic are those morally reactive attitudes directly implicated in blaming. These particular reactive emotions are best understood as a species of moral anger, often picked out by the terms of sentiment "resentment" and "moral indignation."[10]

---

[9] There are as well reactive attitudes that are self-referential, such as guilt. Here I shall focus on reactive attitudes had by one that are directed at others. I take up guilt in a subsequent chapter.

[10] There is some disagreement about how resentment and indignation differ. As I see it (2012: 66), resentment is at play when one is directly affected or targeted by the

R. Jay Wallace (1994: 25–33) made an important contribution to the reactive-emotions account of blaming by developing a normative interpretation whereby we can make good sense of a reactive emotion being appropriate or inappropriate. The idea is to understand the emotional dimension of a phenomenon like blaming not merely in terms of a disposition to have and act from an emotion of a certain sort, but also in terms of when it is apt to have one, and so when it is apt for one to respond to another in a blaming manner motivated by such an emotion. According to Wallace, these attitudes have certain propositional objects at which they are directed. This allows us to make sense of how it is that these attitudes might be misdirected.

Wallace limited the relevant propositional attitudes to beliefs involving failures to comply with obligations or expectations. A blaming attitude of moral indignation, for instance, is inappropriate when the one at whom it is directed did not after all fail to comply with any obligation to which the one blaming held her. Or instead, it is inappropriate when it is unfair to hold such a person to an expectation of this kind (perhaps she is severely mentally disabled and is just incapable of grasping or complying with such demands). While I agree with Wallace's strategy regarding the normative interpretation of these reactive emotions and their place in blaming, I prefer a more inclusive and open-ended treatment of the range of objects which bear on considerations of propriety. By restricting the relevant morally reactive attitudes to beliefs about obligations, Wallace explicitly limits the domain of moral responsibility, and so the domain of blame's target, to the deontic sphere of moral right and wrong (1994: 63). As in keeping with my remarks in the previous section, I contend that it is better to characterize the reactive attitudes of resentment and moral indignation so that they are sensitive to a person's having acted in a manner that is subject to

---

objectionable behavior eliciting the emotion. Indignation is at play when it is another who is wronged, harmed, or in some way affected by the eliciting behavior.

26 THE VIEW

some sort of moral criticism, either in deontological terms, but also, at least possibly, in axiological or aretaic terms.

On the view I propose, the species of moral anger distinctive of resentment and moral indignation is directed at a more complex sort of object as in comparison with Wallace's fairly lean—and admittedly more elegant—proposal.[11] This species of moral anger, I contend, is aptly responsive to all of the following: an agent having acted freely; an agent having acted knowingly or from culpable ignorance; an agent's act being morally criticizable in some manner (was morally wrong, morally bad, or vicious); and, *most prominently*, an agent's acting from a morally objectionably quality of will, either by acting with ill will or by acting in the absence of a sufficiently good will.

Strawson himself (1962) discussed the reactive attitudes in the context of their central role in adult interpersonal life and, most notably, in our complex web of social practices. This is highlighted by Gary Watson's (1987) observation that, for Strawson, holding someone morally responsible *means something in practice*. Blaming via resentment or indignation reveals itself in the altered means of interacting with the one blamed. Normal courtesies are withheld, patterns of conduct are changed, expected social plans and arrangements are altered, and particular means of expressing one's moral anger in word and deed are found to be common in ways that are sometimes fitting and sometimes not. Although those discussing Strawson's work often note this point, in my opinion it has not been fully appreciated. A focus *just* on the range of emotions and their aptness invites the misleading thought that what matters most fundamentally in the affective dimension of a phenomenon like blaming is the attitudinal part that can be privately experienced and concealed. In my estimation, this is backwards. As I have

---

[11] I leave aside the controversial issue as to whether reactive attitudes are best understood via a cognitivist construal, as Wallace has it, or whether there is some other way to capture the representational content implicated in them. Here I take on a cognitivist framework merely for means of exposition. But I mean to be ecumenical.

argued elsewhere (2012: 69–72), the more fundamental cases of emotions like resentment and moral indignation—at least insofar as they play a role in our blaming practices—are those that encompass their characteristic behavioral manifestations in ways that reveal their place in our interpersonal lives. We are able to understand privately experienced resentment or indignation as a mode of blaming by reference to the public cases.

To help illustrate the way these emotions are manifested in practice, I have focused on a simple case of blame between two friends and coworkers, Daphne and Leslie, who meet at a local shop for an afternoon coffee (2012: 68–9). In response to what she took to be an offensive racist joke about Hispanics, Daphne becomes morally indignant toward Leslie, angrily tells her she does not welcome the remark, and then storms out of the coffee shop. Daphne then alters future plans with Leslie, not inviting Leslie to a lunch date with another coworker, who is Hispanic, and in various other ways makes fitting alterations to her means of interacting or not interacting with Leslie. Further, Daphne takes there to be limits to the modes of blaming Leslie. For example, she does not let it affect her judgments about whether to offer Leslie some extra work. The point of calling attention to these details is to help show that these different ways that Daphne acts, from her angry verbal confrontation to her altered lunch plans, are not distinct from and so simply caused by her blaming Leslie; they're constitutive of her blaming Leslie. They express her moral indignation and so are not *merely* motivated by her moral indignation. The role and presence of the emotion is infused in the altered social practices themselves, giving them a salience or meaning that they would otherwise not have.

Watson (1987) has claimed that the morally reactive attitudes are incipiently forms of communication. This is dead right. It is shown especially by focusing on cases of directed blame like the case of Daphne and Leslie. When the focus on the morally reactive attitudes is on their manifestation in our social practices and as directed at those blamed, we can see how it is that an episode of

28 THE VIEW

resentment or indignation can communicate moral demands and expectations. It can, as well, communicate an altered regard for the one held to blame, an indication of the likely means of future treatment, further expectations about means of redress, moral atonement, compensation, and so on.

2.5 Directed Blaming and Conversation

On the conversational theory of moral responsibility, the actions of a morally responsible agent are potential bearers of a species of meaning, *agent-meaning* (2012: 92–4). As bearers of agent-meaning, such actions function as (fallible) indicators expressive of the quality of will with which agents act. When one directly blames another, she responds to the agent in light of this species of meaning. Her blaming response, via an overt manifestation of a pertinent reactive attitude such as resentment, communicates her regard for the blamed agent and that agent's action in light of the quality of will that is presumed to be manifest in it. A natural way to understand what is communicated, at least in many cases, is a matter of protest, as philosophers like Pamela Hieronymi (2001), Matthew Talbert (2012), Angela Smith (2013), and Derk Pereboom (2021) have argued.[12]

Just now I characterized actions as bearers of a species of meaning expressive of an agent's quality of will and of directed blaming via the morally reactive attitudes as playing a communicative role. But

---

[12] Some are committed to the thesis that what is protested in blaming is a *claim* implicit in a blameworthy agent's act that a wronged party can be treated a certain way (Hieronymi, 2001). But this is too restrictive. Sometimes an agent acts from weakness of will and there is nothing in what they do that would signal a commitment to any such claim. Also, there seem to be cases of protest that do not involve blame, as Shoemaker and Vargas have argued (2019: 584). But if, as Pereboom argues (2021: 44), the sort of protest involved in blaming is suitably agent-directed, a reasonable version of the protest view complements the conversational theory as I have developed it. (See also Adrienne Martin's [2010] related discussion of forgiveness, which complements Pereboom's proposal.)

DIRECTED BLAME AND CONVERSATION   29

I have proposed a bolder thesis (2012). The notions of meaning, expression, and communication thus far enlisted do not fully capture the distinctive interanimation between blameworthy agent and those blaming, at least when the kind of blame is directed. More mileage can be gotten out of Watson's insight that the reactive emotions as manifested in practice have a communicative role. The relation between a morally responsible agent and those who hold her to account for her blameworthy conduct can be usefully illuminated on an analogy with a conversation.

When a blameworthy agent acts, she understands that her actions are liable to interpretation. How so? Members of the moral community might assign a salience or meaning to her mode of acting as indicative of one kind of quality of will or other. As a morally responsible agent, when she acts, she is aware that her actions can take on meaning. Hence, when her acts are pertinently morally charged, we can understand her *as if* she were introducing, or risking the possibility of introducing, a meaningful contribution that is a candidate for a conversational exchange with others. I have called this stage *Moral Contribution*. When one holds another morally responsible by blaming her, what she communicates can be understood on analogy with engaging in a conversation with the agent who initiated that exchange. This second stage, the stage wherein one blames, I have called *Moral Address*. It is then open to the blamed agent to extend the "conversation" further by means of offering an excuse, a justification, an apology, and so on. This third stage, I have labeled *Moral Account*. It is then open to those holding morally responsible by blaming to extend the conversational analog further, by, say, forgiving, or punishing, or simply ending the exchange and moving on, and so on. This sort of interaction, which we might call a *moral responsibility exchange*, is modeled on analogy with a conversational exchange between competent speakers of a natural language.

Understood in this way, moral responsibility should be most fundamentally understood as playing a role in a dynamic process.

30 THE VIEW

It relates those who are and those who hold morally responsible in a fashion structurally analogous to the sort that unfolds between competent speakers of a natural language when involved in a conversational transaction. The nature of blaming, and specifically directed blaming, is a distinctive move in that kind of social practice, a practice of holding co-members of a moral community to account. The conversational role of particular instances of blaming will arise within the framework of patterns of social life wherein variation from expectations will have a certain salience. For example, were Leslie not typically involved in lunch outings with Daphne, Daphne's failure to invite her could not take on the meaning it does.

Theorizing about moral responsibility in general, and blame in particular, as I have thus far, has a payoff in terms of extending the analogy with features of literal, linguistic conversational exchanges. Speakers of a natural language engaged in the give and take of conversational transactions rely upon complex expectations of shared background assumptions that allow for successful implicatures and related modes of conveying meaning that cannot be captured simply by attending to the strict semantic content of what is said between interlocutors. Innuendo, sarcasm, things discretely not said, or not even indirectly insinuated, all figure into our understanding of the delicate interactions of individuals engaged in felicitous (and infelicitous) conversations with each other. Pragmatic context takes center stage here. A structurally analogous point applies to the nature of blaming understood as functioning like a move in a conversation. An altered pattern of behavior by one person as a means of manifesting her indignation could very well be taken to have a salience by a blamed party that it would not and could not have for another person. That other person's interactions and relations with the blamed party might be quite different, or might involve different roles (say, boss or spouse rather than mere acquaintance or casual friend). Hence, there is a sufficiently complex web of social interrelations between persons to make sense of something analogous to phenomena like implicatures in the modes of blaming that are available to members of a moral community. This helps to explain an observation made early on—that two individuals might very well blame another in ways that are equally fitting, but do so in wildly divergent ways.

What of the modal status of claims about the relation between blaming and the morally reactive emotions? I began this chapter by contending that the reactive attitudes should play a pivotal role in theorizing about responsibility but that, despite that, they are not essential. Admittedly, this is puzzling. Let me explain. What I take to be *essential* to moral responsibility is that it is deeply interpersonal, at least in the prototypical cases I focus upon here. It relates those who are morally responsible agents to those who hold morally responsible, who themselves are also morally responsible agents. This relation is essential to the nature of being morally responsible. This is in contrast to, for example, a ledger theory (e.g., Haji, 1998; Zimmerman, 1988). On a ledger theory, being morally responsible is, so to speak, metaphysically settled irrespective of any of the phenomena related to holding morally responsible. So, I contend (2012: 80–8) along with other Strawsonians, we cannot make good sense of being morally responsible in the absence of some understanding of the standpoint of holding morally responsible. (Just like we cannot understand competent speakers of a natural language without understanding the nature of the audience to whom such speakers address themselves.) But are emotions required for this? Well, that depends on how strongly we understand the modal force of "required." Is it a metaphysical or a conceptual necessity that blaming involves an episode of a reactive attitude like resentment or indignation, as it seems philosophers like R. Jay Wallace understand it (Wallace, 1994: 2)? This goes too far and is unnecessary to account for the phenomenon at hand. At the very least, it is conceptually possible that there could be beings who engage in social practices whereby they hold each other to account for their morally significant conduct but are emotionless beings

32 THE VIEW

altogether. Of course, qua agents who act at all, they would be *motivated* beings; they'd have a conative structure, but it would be devoid of affect. (I will develop this point in Chapter 8.)

Strawsonians might protest that their essentialist claim about the place of the reactive attitudes is indexed to beings like us, to human persons. Referring just to humans, the claim might be, the morally reactive emotions are essential to accounting for moral responsibility in general, and the nature of blaming in particular. A yet weaker claim involves picking out not humans, but instead just *our* practices—moral responsibility as *we* understand it—and then claiming that it is necessary to those practices and this way of life that the moral emotions play a role. Perhaps this is correct, but I see no motivation to make any of these modal claims involving some kind of necessity, even the weakest of them. Why can't the relation between these emotions and the social practices I have highlighted here be contingent but nevertheless deeply embedded, so much so that we just would not get a credible theory of blame without attending to the role of these emotions? At any rate, on the view I defend, the morally reactive attitudes need only be thought of as contingently related to the nature of blaming (2012: 110–4). Regardless, they are deeply embedded in our blaming practices, and we would not understand our blaming practices, such as they are, without reference to them.

Set aside the modal issue. What of the relation of priority or grounding between being and holding morally responsible? Many Strawsonians (e.g., Bennett, 1980; Shoemaker, 2015; Wallace, 1994; Watson, 1987) contend that the nature and norms of holding morally responsible are more fundamental than the nature of being morally responsible.[13] The latter is not to be thought of as having a metaphysical standing to which the former must comply, but rather vice versa. I disagree. This is shown by how I have approached the

---

[13] I am not convinced that this is Strawson's view. The textual evidence seems pretty thin.

topic of blame's nature in this and the two preceding sections. To get clear on blame, I have first attended to what it is to which blame is a response. Thus, I have focused on features of the agent who is morally responsible (by attending to quality of will considerations) as a way of helping to understand blame as a mode of holding morally responsible. It might be thought that I am forced into the opposing camp of those who would regard being morally responsible as the more basic or fundamental thing (e.g., Brink, 2021; Brink and Nelkin, 2013; Fischer and Ravizza, 1998). But, on my view, the mistake is to think that either is more basic than the other (2012: 50–5). There is a relation of mutual dependence that cannot be eliminated—much like the way that we cannot make sense of what it is to be a competent speaker of a natural language without reference to the standpoint of a speaker's audience of potential interpreters who seek to understand the speaker, an insight central to Grice's account of meaning (1957).

2.6 Directed Blaming and the Question of Normative Warrant

Now consider the question of normative warrant. What justifies blaming a blameworthy agent? Moreover, how ought an agent be blamed? There are at least two identifiable norms that bear on these questions. One, as previously noted (Section 2.2), has to do with veracity. Is it true to the facts that the alleged blameworthy agent was actually blameworthy? Did she act freely? Did she act with knowledge or culpable ignorance in doing what she did? Was what she did morally wrong, bad, or unvirtuous? Did she act from a morally objectionable quality of will?

A second norm arises from what the conversation theory tells us about the *nature* of directed blame. This has to do with meaningfulness or intelligibility—what makes sense as a sort of conversational response to the agent in light of her blameworthy action

34 THE VIEW

(2012: 90). Just as in literal conversational transactions between competent speakers of a natural language, so, too, with blaming, there can be more and less sensible or intelligible responses to a meaningful contribution. In literal conversations, some conversational replies are infelicitous—complete nonstarters. This happens when, for instance, there is a breakdown in communication, perhaps because one misheard what another said or did not pick up on an intended implicature. But other contributions can be felicitous and still be, on a scale, more apt than others. Sometimes, as in comparison with another conversationalist, one knows "just what to say." Even here, there's no reason to think that there was, literally, just one correct way to contribute to or continue the conversation. Likewise, I contend, for blaming. Some modes of blaming are infelicitous; they miss their target altogether and just do not make sense as a fitting response to one who is taken to be blameworthy. But as for those that *do* make sense—those that are meaningful ways of communicating with a blameworthy party—there is no regimented way this must be done. Daphne blamed Leslie in, we can grant, a fitting manner by manifesting her moral indignation as she did. But we can equally well imagine that she could have done so by other means that made just as much sense. Here again, we have a further explanation of why quite different modes of blaming can be regarded as equally suitable.

Norms of conversational intelligibility or meaningfulness also help call to attention a further feature of the permissible variability of blaming. In literal linguistic conversations, a contribution by an interlocutor is often pregnant with meaning so that there are different aspects or dimension to what the speaker means. It is open to another conversing with the speaker to carry the conversation in a range of different ways, depending on which aspects of the original contribution this interlocutor wishes to focus upon. Likewise for blaming as a "conversational" response to the perceived agent-meaning of a blameworthy party's act. Recall that judgments of blameworthiness are evaluatively complex. They can encompass deontological, axiological, and aretaic ingredients. If so, then it is open to one who replies to the blameworthy agent to attend more to one rather than another element in this evaluative cocktail.

As I have argued elsewhere (2012: 150–4), the two norms just countenanced—the norms of veracity and conversational intelligibility—are not adequate to account for the normative warrant of blaming. Directed blaming is liable to harm, and the norms canvassed thus far do not account for why it is that it is at least permissible to harm by directly blaming those who are blameworthy. What further norm will fill this bill? To answer this question, we need a clearer sense of just what about blaming constitutes the (potential) harm in it. Here we first must settle on what is meant by "harm" and then return briefly to the topic of directed blame's nature.

As for the matter of harm, I follow Joel Feinberg in thinking of harm in terms of a setback to one's interests (Feinberg, 1986: 33–4). Feinberg held that the many different kinds of interests available to persons can be sorted into two general categories: welfare interests and ulterior interests. *Ulterior interests* concern aspirations and ultimate goals of the sort that figure in writing a novel or seeking a cure for cancer. *Welfare interests* are those more fundamental interests that serve as a foundation for one's pursuing ulterior interests. Among these welfare interests Feinberg listed continuance of one's life into the future, physical health, integrity and functioning of one's body, absence of absorbing physical pain and grotesque disfigurement, emotional stability, the capacity to engage normally in social intercourse and enjoy and maintain friendships, minimal income and financial security, a tolerable social and physical environment, and a certain amount of freedom from interference from others (37).

Now return to directed blame's nature. Due to blame's communicative and conversational role, it is liable to impose on the one

36   THE VIEW

blamed in particular ways.[14] Anger, shunning, and alienation as expressions of morally reactive attitudes are often conveyed in blaming, and there is an expectation that the one blamed ought to reply by offering an apology or an explanation, revising modes of behavior, and so on. This can be emotionally taxing. It can compromise a person's welcomed relations with others. It can also cost her in terms of psychic energy and the freedom to live her life without having to pay the interpersonal costs of altered relationships and unpleasant demands and expectations put to her by those holding her to account. These conversational burdens placed upon her—even if she wishes to shrug them off—come at a cost to her, or at least they are liable to do so for all but the most hardened and indifferent among us. But notice that these costs are restricted to just *some* of the welfare interests Feinberg mentioned, in particular:

- the capacity to engage normally in social intercourse and enjoy and maintain friendships;
- freedom from others' interference; and
- emotional stability.

So, in directed blaming, a distinctive, albeit limited, class of welfare interests is liable to be compromised. A setback to these interests constitutes the unique harm(s) in directed blaming (McKenna, 2012: 134–41).

What further norm might account for the warrant to harm in ways that are distinctive of directed blaming? Desert is often considered the clear contender, although not without considerable dissent. So, we can distinguish between *desert theorists* and *nondesert theorist*. Nondesert theorists might instead seek, for instance, contractualist grounds (Scanlon, 1998), fairness (Wallace,

---

[14] My treatment in what follows of the harm and also the normative warrant for blaming share affinities with an especially penetrating treatment of the topic by Christopher Bennett (2002).

DIRECTED BLAME AND CONVERSATION 37

1994), or consequentialist considerations (Dennett, 1984; Smart, 1963; Vargas, 2013) as the normative basis to justify directed blame. Desert theorists can be parsed into basic and nonbasic desert theorists. The latter contend that considerations of desert are themselves grounded in some more basic normative facts.[15] Others advancing a basic desert theory contend that the pertinent ground does not derive from more basic normative considerations; its desert claim is basic.[16]

Efforts to account for the normative warrant to blame *either* by way of a nondesert theory *or* by way of a nonbasic desert theory are promising (McKenna, 2012: 154–64). Each is worth exploring. Some desert theorists disagree, taking these alternatives to be on their face inadequate to the task of justifying our moral responsibility practices, at least as they bear on accountability. Others, such as Derk Pereboom (2009: 179–81), are more cautious. They acknowledge that these approaches offer accounts of bona fide senses of moral responsibility. But they reject the accountability senses of responsibility and blame that are in dispute in areas such as the free will debate, where they contend that *only* basic desert can do the requisite normative work. I disagree with Pereboom and others on this point. As I will argue in Chapter 5, one can get the normative warrant for blaming in the accountability sense by means other than appeal to basic desert—even while retaining a commitment to a robust notion of what free will comes to. Nevertheless, relying upon the conversational theory, formulation of a defensible basic desert thesis for blame's warrant is a live option. I develop this thesis in Chapter 3, and the proposal offered there will set the stage for the remainder of our inquiry.

---

[15] This seems to be the view that some like Ayer (1954), Hobart (1934), and Schlick (1939) endorsed. A more refined version, and an especially plausible one, as I read him, is found in Lenman (2006).

[16] For example, see C. Bennett (2002), Pereboom (2001), and Sher (2006). Of course, as is well known, Kant endorsed a version of this view.

2.7 The Ethics of Blame and a Challenge for Emotion-Based Views

I have drawn on the conversational theory of moral responsibility to offer an account of blame's nature, and as well gesture in the direction of what is at stake regarding blame's norms. I have done so by limiting the relevant notions of blame and of moral responsibility just to the accountability sense, and then to prototypical cases of blaming in the form of what I have called directed blame. While I have argued that moral anger is *not* necessary for either blame or an account of moral responsibility more generally, I nevertheless contend that the role of this sort of emotion is deeply connected to our moral responsibility practices. We therefore do need to attend to these emotions if we want an informative account of the phenomena. But this creates problems for our understanding of the ethics of blame.

One dimension of directed blame's nature has to do with its relation to the voluntary. Curiously, few critics of emotion-based theories have raised worries about the control a blamer can be expected to exercise over her blaming. But there is a worry that needs addressing. For the most part, except in fairly esoteric contexts, the mere experiencing of an emotion is not under an agent's direct voluntary control.[17] If so, it looks like emotion-based theories of blaming risk the objection that one who blames is not in a position to settle freely on whether to blame or not. This objection need not be developed in terms of a blamer's having *no* control over whether she experiences an episode of a blame-constituting emotion. There is the notion of nonvoluntary control of the sort competent rational agents exercise in belief formation and retention. An agent who resents someone for wrongdoing can, for instance, exercise

---

[17] Of course, there are indirect methods. One can avoid conditions in which she might have occasion to experience the emotion, or can have a stiff drink ready at hand, and so on.

DIRECTED BLAME AND CONVERSATION 39

rational control over her emotion. She can do so to the extent that she can assess the truth as to whether, for instance, that agent really did wrong. But this being the case, she is not able simply to choose directly whether, with these matters settled, she undergoes the emotion. Agents can't directly voluntarily control their emotions in the requisite way.

If those advancing an emotion-based theory of blame were not able to say more about the control an agent can exercise in blaming, this would create problems accounting for the relation between the nature of blaming and its norms. Some of these norms concern questions of whether an agent ought to be blamed, and not just whether it is true to the facts that she is blameworthy. But if merely by having an episode of a pertinent reactive emotion one thereby blames, it appears that one cannot comply with relevant judgments about whether, all-things-considered, an agent *ought* to be blamed. As might be expected, the way out for the emotion-based theorist is by tending to features of blaming that *are* within an agent's voluntary control. The outward manifestation of blaming practices in modifications to interpersonal relations involves acts and omissions that, it can be argued, are within a blamer's control. Here we have further reason to attend to the (I say) more fundamental prototypical cases of blame outwardly directed at the blamed. Doing so makes clear that the relevant norms of blame—and the expectation that blamers can comply with them—are not defeated merely by the fact that blame's nature has an emotional and so nonvoluntary dimension.

2.8 Closing Reflections on Methodology

Some will resist a conversational theory, or more generally any communication-based theory, because it seems too easy to generate counterexamples, a point highlighted by Shoemaker and Vargas (2019) and also Michael Zimmerman (2022) in their recent

40   THE VIEW

assessments of communicative theories generally. There are cases in which an agent is morally responsible for some act, and there is no conversational analog that takes place. Or, instead, it will be protested, in cases of private blame or blaming the dead, we have blame but no communication at all. Hence, a theory such as the one I have advanced tends to some special range of cases but not others. Scanlon, for instance, has objected to Watson's contention that blame is to be understood in terms of its communicative role. Why? Because a person can blame while not communicating anything (Scanlon, 2008: 233–4, n. 54).

Scanlon's objection assumes that a proper theory of moral responsibility, along with attendant notions like blame, should be cast in terms of necessary and sufficient conditions *ala* a proper classical analysis. But, as noted above, I reject this way of proceeding. Phenomena such as blaming are too diffuse in their extensions, and our intuitions about them are too contested in a wide range of cases, to hope that we can get anything like a proper analysis of the full extension of these concepts, at least not one that is informative rather than trivial. Rather, it is best to proceed by focusing on central cases, ones that are of immediate concern as regards questions of normative warrant, standing, and force. If we can account adequately for the nature and norms of these, then the other cases can be explained by reference to these prototypical cases.

Along with my earlier efforts to argue in this way (2012, 2013a), Miranda Fricker (2014) has also adopted the same strategy. She offers a forceful answer to those who question why one should not adopt a more traditional approach by analyzing blame in terms of necessary and sufficient conditions. In an especially insightful passage, she writes,

> analysis—understood as the attempt to achieve necessary and sufficient conditions—is not an appropriate method for any subject matters which have philosophically important features that

DIRECTED BLAME AND CONVERSATION 41

are not necessary conditions. Such features will not figure in any strict definitions, for the requisite trial by counter-example will ultimately defeat them. And yet if these are explanatorily basic features, they are just the sorts of thing that needs to be preserved in a philosophical account that aims to explain the nature of the practice in all its internal diversity. Successful analysis delivers the highest-common-denominator set of features of X; but where X is an internally diverse practice there is significant risk that the highest common denominator will turn out to be very low, delivering an extremely thin account. In particular, it will not be capable of illuminating how the different forms of the practice are explanatorily related to one another. (2014: 166)

The conversational theory of moral responsibility advanced here attends most directly to our adult interpersonal relations with each other, and the ways these do alter, and give good reason to alter, our moral relations with those who are capable of morally significant action. I propose that the most significant cases of blame—those that bears on moral responsibility in the accountability sense—are best understood by adopting this strategy. Other cases of blame can then be explained by way of family resemblance to these central cases.[18]

David Brink and Dana Nelkin have recently offered a promising account of blame that offers theoretically illuminating necessary and sufficient conditions for blame.[19] At the same time,

---

[18] As Derk Pereboom has helpfully pointed out in correspondence, following Frank Jackson (2010), some might protest here that appeal to prototypes is consistent with conceptual analysis in the fashion of offering necessary and sufficient conditions, as in *x is F just in case x is sufficiently similar to prototypes for F*. Of course, others, such as William Ramsey (1992), contend that appeal to prototypes is incompatible with conceptual analysis. I leave it as an open question whether an appeal to prototypes and a similarity relation permits of conceptual analysis proper. Regardless, it is not of the classical variety that offers a decompositional set of distinct necessary and jointly sufficient conditions for every instance falling within the extension of the concept. I assume that it is *this* way of thinking about the pertinent responsibility concepts animating the criticisms of Scanlon, Zimmerman, and others.

[19] See Brink (2021: 122–6) and Brink and Nelkin (2022).

42 THE VIEW

they also offer resources to capture the sort of diversity that both Fricker and I contend seems to defy any such analysis. According to Brink and Nelkin, blame has a core that can be characterized in terms of necessary and sufficient conditions and an attendant syndrome that is, as they put it, downstream from this core. Blame's variability highlighted in this chapter is, on their account, part of the nonaccidental syndrome. As Brink writes in his recent *Fair Opportunity and Responsibility*,

> The core [of blame], which is both necessary and sufficient for blame, is an aversive attitude toward the target that is predicated on the belief or judgment, perhaps tacit, that the target is blameworthy. (2021: 123–4)

About the pertinent aversive attitude, Brink explains,

> There may be no single emotional response common to all case of blame, but they all seem to involve some negative or aversive emotional reaction, if only a mild one. (125)

Features of blame, such as its communicative role and the openness to dialogue, are to be explained in terms of a nonaccidental syndrome that is downstream from this core (124).

Brink and Nelkin's proposal appears to avoid the indictment Fricker leveled against attempts to offer proper analyses of blame. They identify a core in terms of necessary and sufficient conditions. It does appear to be informative, and so thick rather than "thin," as Fricker's challenge would have it. And they explain the communicative and other features by way of this downstream nonaccidental syndrome. Moreover, of prototype proposals, such as the ones Fricker and I have developed, Brink claims that they fail "to explain what unifies the elements of the prototype" (2021: 123). So, Brink and Nelkin have offered an appealing explanation of the heart of blame, and, as well, features that are central to the conversational

DIRECTED BLAME AND CONVERSATION   43

theory, wherein the latter are downstream of what is really central to blame.

How to respond? One is to be entirely concessive. It's not incompatible with the account of blame offered in this chapter that there might also be some core that is captured by a proper analysis. But perhaps this response risks being too concessive. Brink concedes that, as part of his analysis, there may be no emotional response that is common to all cases, but, he contends, there must be some "negative or aversive emotional reaction" (2021:125). Isn't this too generic, or, as Fricker would put it, too thin? Moreover, without further clarification, Brink and Nelkin's proposal is open to counterexamples. To invoke a style of example I have used elsewhere (2012), suppose Satan has placed a bet with his evil buddy Homer that Flanders will not be tough enough to do evil to Grandpa. Flanders, Satan thinks, is too much of a goody-goody. When Flanders is evil to Grandpa, Satan believes Flanders is blameworthy. Moreover, Satan *does* have a negative or aversive attitude toward Flanders; he is frustrated with Flanders for causing him to lose his bet with Homer. Clearly, Satan does not blame Flanders. Yet by Brink and Nelkin's lights, Satan *does* blame Flanders. At the very least, it is not clear on their view why he does not.

To identify the sort of nonaccidental negative attitude that will do the heavy lifting for Brink and Nelkin, we need some sense of what is distinctive about these aversive attitudes that informs us about blame and so help to distinguish Satan's non–blame-constituting aversive attitude from an attitude that *is* blame-constituting. Here is a proposal: They are the sorts of attitudes that, were they acted upon or expressed in outward behavior, would render fitting means of communicating some blame leveled against the presumptive blameworthy party. If this is correct, Brink and Nelkin cannot so easily set aside communicative or conversational elements as (causally) downstream of the core they identify. Rather, as a conceptual matter, we get the thick—rather than thin—characterization of the pertinent attitudes in their analysis by way

44 THE VIEW

of tending to prototypical cases. Given this proposal, we also have a response to Brink's complaint that any prototype strategy cannot explain what unifies the range of cases that fall to the periphery of the central ones. The central ones, as I have featured with directed blame, help make sense of other cases, like ones that just involve Brink and Nelkin's proposed core. Is this a refutation of Brink's proposal? Not at all. But it does show that, without supplementation, Brink and Nelkin's Attitudinal-Core-Plus-Syndrome Theory of Blame is on equal footing with the conversational theory as I have set it out here.

3

Basically Deserved Blame and
Its Value

How should we understand basic desert as a justification for blaming? Many philosophers account for free will by identifying it with the control condition for *basic desert-entailing moral responsibility* (e.g., Fischer and Ravizza, 1998; McKenna, 2013b; Mele, 1995; Pereboom, 2001, 2014; Sartorio, 2016). On such a view, a blameworthy person deserves blame just because of how she acted—for instance, because she knowingly and freely acted morally wrongly. Crucially, the justification provided by desert is *not* rooted in any other normative consideration, such as fairness, utility, or instead the reasonableness of entering into a contract with others (e.g., Feinberg, 1970; Pereboom, 2001, 2014; Scanlon, 2008). But what precisely does basic desert come to? And what is it about blame that makes it the thing that a blameworthy person deserves? Moreover, how is any particular instance of blame fitted properly—rather than ill-fitted—for a blameworthy person's particular act so that it is the thing that is deserved? As it turns out, there are challenges to understanding basic desert for blame, challenges having nothing to do with skepticism about free will. One concerns whether the only good in harming a person by blaming her is exclusively instrumental. Another concerns traditional worries about retributivist theories of punishment that might threaten deserved blame, too. Given these challenges, there may be reason to reject

An earlier draft of this chapter was originally published in 2019, as "Basically Deserved Blame and Its Value," *Journal of Ethics and Social Philosophy* 15 (3): 255–82.

Responsibility and Desert. Michael McKenna, Oxford University Press. © Oxford University Press 2024.
DOI: 10.1093/9780197679999.003.0003

46 THE VIEW

desert-based conceptions of the justification of blame for reasons altogether distinct from any worries about free will.

In this chapter, I develop the view that blame is to be justified in terms of basic desert. I have three interrelated aims. One is to account for the fittingness of blame on analogy with the fittingness of a move in an actual conversation between competent linguistic practitioners of the same language. Another is to explain the desert-relation regarding what is deserved by the blameworthy in a way that helps to avoid traditional worries about retributive theories of punishment. The third is to defend the controversial thesis that the harm involved in blaming can be good in a way that is not merely instrumental.

I offer an account of basic desert-entailing moral responsibility that is neutral between free will realists and free will skeptics. This should prove useful in helping to adjudicate the debate between those realists and skeptics who agree that what is in dispute between them is the freedom required to deserve blame in a basic sense. I'll restrict myself just to blameworthiness and blame, leaving aside praiseworthiness and praise, as well as moral responsibility for conduct that is neither praiseworthy nor blameworthy.

I begin with two preliminary qualifications. First, the instances of blame I take to be of interest, and the role basic desert plays in justifying them, have to do with *directed blame* (as specified in Chapter 2). Second, I assume that, at least in paradigmatic cases, directed blame harms the person blamed. For this reason, I will assume that one cannot justify the goodness in blaming a person unless one can also justify the harms that attend blame.

3.1 Basic Desert

What is basic desert? Given what has already been stated, we know that it is basic at least in the following negative way: The normative warrant it provides is *not* supported by any more fundamental normative principles or values (e.g., see Feinberg, 1970: 56; Pereboom, 2014: 2; or Scanlon, 2008: 188). But that's not saying much. What more can be said to give more content to our understanding of it? I'll restrict my attention to deserved moral blame. I'll not concern myself with basic desert in other domains, like the desert for winning a prize or being treated with respect as a person.

To begin, desert offers a distinctive way of specifying *the sense of aptness* in a judgment that blame is appropriate (Feinberg, 1970: 56–7). Mere aptness on its own simply reports *that* some normative warrant exists; it gives no content to the kind of warrant on offer. Desert does so, not by appealing to considerations of utility, or principles of fairness, or the elements of a reasonable contract, but by appealing exclusively to a "desert-base" that makes fitting that which is deserved (Feinberg, 1970: 58–61). So understood, desert is a distinctive species of *fittingness*.[1] As regards deserved blame, the desert-base for a blameworthy act involves only salient features of *the agent* and *her act*, features that make the agent blameworthy for it. As I have argued, this consists in an agent's knowingly and freely doing something that is morally criticizable from a morally objectionable quality of will. Here we have four ingredients contributing to the desert-base: one concerns the agent's state of knowledge, another concerns the agent's relation to the act as a free one, a third concerns the moral status of the act itself, and a fourth concerns the attitude of the agent in relation to her so acting. These features provide the desert-base for a response that is fitted for the agent's act—in particular, a blaming response.

The blaming response is meant to fit the act in relation to the features of the desert base in some unique, case-specific manner, one that is especially difficult to specify. (I offer a proposal below, and I develop it further in Chapter 6.) There is, furthermore, as noted above, a widely shared presumption that blaming is negative in a way that involves exposing the one blamed to the liability

---

[1] I assert this here without argument, but I deliver one in Chapter 7.

48 THE VIEW

of certain harms; it has a characteristic sting or force. Crucially, blame's being basically deserved supplies resources that can *exhaust* the requisite positive normative warrant for exposing the blameworthy agent to such harms.

Why say that basic desert is able to exhaust the *positive* normative warrant for blaming? On a credible version of a basic desert thesis, the complete normative warrant for actually blaming an agent, one yielding an all-out judgment, also requires the *negative* condition that there are no competing and overriding normative considerations, like those of overall utility or simple prudence, speaking against blaming. Hence, basic desert only provides *pro tanto* reasons. It therefore does not immediately follow that if it is true that a person deserves blame, then, in the all-out sense, the right thing for someone (or other) to do is blame that person.

To help give further content to judgments of deserved blame, it is useful to consider whether they involve only the right or instead also the good.[2] There is no consensus on this point. Some have in mind an exclusively deontic rendering. For example, as Joel Feinberg put it, "That a subject deserves X entails that he ought to get X in the *pro tanto* sense of 'ought'" (1970: 60). For Feinberg, there is no further entailment from its being deserved to its being *good* that a blameworthy wrongdoer is blamed and thereby harmed. To offer another example, in developing his own "desert-based view," Scanlon explicitly denies any such thesis:

---

[2] In what follows, I seek an elucidation of basic desert by considering whether a claim of basic desert entails a judgment that is either deontic or instead axiological. One might be skeptical of this strategy. My proposed strategy, one might object, does not appear to answer a question: What is basic desert? An entailment of basic desert is identified, but identifying an entailment of it is not saying what it is. Basic desert, so the objection goes, seems to be left as a something-or-other that entails this value. In response, I do not think this is right. While it is true that in some cases we do not learn what x is by learning what is entailed by x, sometimes we do. We learn something about a dolphin when we learn that it is a mammal, and so it is informative to learn that "Flipper is a dolphin" entails "Flipper is a mammal." The salient feature of my philosophical strategy is to seek some nonreductive means of elucidating desert when it is regarded as basic and so not grounded in any more basic normative notion. I am treating the entailments identified here as markers of essential features of desert wherein desert is the ground for either the rightness or goodness of the deserved thing.

The fact that someone has behaved wrongly can make it appropriate to withhold certain attitudes and relationships, and withholding these things may make the person's life worse. But withholding them is justified, in my view, by the fact that they have become inappropriate, not by the fact that withholding them makes the person worse off. Ceasing to hope that things go well for a person can be one element of blame, but as I have emphasized, this does not involve thinking it to be good that things not go well for him. (2008: 188)

On a strong version of an exclusively deontic desert thesis, blaming one who deserves blame would be construed as a duty or an obligation. On a weak rendering, it would be cast simply as something that is permissible (e.g., Scanlon, 2008: 188–9).

Others favor an axiological thesis that supplies the basis for a deontic judgment. On such a view, the goodness of the harm in blaming provides a justification for, at a minimum, the permissibility of doing so (e.g., Bennett, 2002; McKenna, 2012: 133). In advancing such a view, Christopher Bennett writes,

I shall show the extent to which our participation in the reactive attitudes [ones expressive of blaming] betrays a commitment to retribution, to the thought that it is a non-contingently good thing that those who have done wrong should undergo some form of suffering. (2002: 147)

Without defending the view, R. Jay Wallace characterizes the thesis of retributivism similarly as

the view that it is intrinsically good that wrongdoers should suffer harm, and that therefore we have a positive duty to inflict such harms on them. (1994: 60, n. 13)

Here, I take Wallace's formulation of retributivism, like Bennett's, to be an instance of an axiological basic desert thesis.

50 THE VIEW

In what follows, I advance a variation on an axiological thesis. A weak version would treat the goodness of blaming as a justification for the mere permissibility of blaming (e.g., Bennett, 2002; McKenna, 2012), whereas a strong version would have it as a moral requirement, as for example it is expressed in the preceding quotation from Wallace (1994: 60, n. 13). A middle ground, which I now endorse, is that the goodness of the harm in blaming provides a practical reason *favoring* blaming.[3] Favoring practical reasons are of an intermediate strength as between reasons issuing from requirements and the merely weak reason supporting permissibility. As I understand them, all that is provided by considerations of permissibility is simply that nothing *prohibits* a certain course of action. Favoring reasons for blaming seem best suited for a thesis about desert. How so? Contending that those positioned to blame have a moral duty to blame is overly demanding to account for our sense of the optionality of blame in a wide range of cases. But mere permissibility does not capture the force of our reasons *to* blame. Favoring does. It is plausible, granting the axiological assumption that, if it is in some way good to harm a person by blaming her, then the goodness counts as a reason favoring such a course of action while at the same time not requiring it.

But why adopt *any* axiological desert-based account of blame? Why not commit to an exclusively deontic version, as for example Scanlon does? Because the latter commits to less—in particular, because it makes no commitment to the goodness of the harm in blaming—isn't it philosophically easier to defend? Here is an argument. A strong version of an exclusively deontic thesis is a non-starter for blame. Requiring others to blame directly the blameworthy places unreasonably high demands on members of the moral community, and most notably those who have been wronged. So the only credible exclusively deontic thesis, at least for blame, is a weak one involving only permissibility. But a weak

---

[3] I am indebted to Ingmar Persson for this suggestion.

version only establishes that one would do no wrong to blame. This provides no positive reason *to* blame. It offers nothing that favors blaming as one of the constitutive features of a desert-based intuition. Insofar as directed blame involves harm, this sort of normative warrant for directed blaming remains silent on why anyone *should* do this harm-causing thing. But if blaming involves harming, it seems one should *not* blame unless she has a good reason to do so; the harming would itself seem to offer a reason *against* blaming, even if it is permissible to harm. Hence, a culpable person's deserving blame would never outweigh a would-be blamer's reasons to refrain from blaming. That can't be right. An axiological version that favors blaming *because* it is good supplies the sort of reason at issue and so avoids this problem.[4]

Dana Nelkin has recently developed a powerful argument for a related thesis (2019b). She focuses on deserved feelings of guilt brought on by blaming, Set aside the matter of guilt for the moment. Nelkin first considers an axiological thesis according to which the reason to give a person the harmful thing she deserves by blaming her is supported by the goodness of doing so. This is the axiological thesis that I endorse here. Nelkin argues against this view (I'll take

---

[4] Wouldn't a deontic thesis cast in terms of *pro tanto* duties do work similar to what I contend is best done by favoring reasons on an axiological approach? Wouldn't these weaker duties give rise to a weak deontic thesis, one that would not be any different from my proposed axiological proposal? No. *Pro tanto* duties are still duties, and duties are requirements that, when one fails them, involve wrongdoing. Of course, being *pro tanto*, they can admittedly be overridden. But absent overriding factors, they are still binding as duties. They are thus not optional for the blamer in a way that is best suited to most instances of warranted blame. Perhaps the preceding is too quick, as Mark Timmons noted in conversation. There are further avenues a deontological theorist might consider. For instance, following a suggestion by David McNaughton (1988), one might distinguish moral oughts that are requirements from moral oughts that are simply recommendations. McNaughton's proposal has affinities with Horgan and Timmon's recent proposal (2023) to include the expected as distinct from the required as a deontic category; perhaps supplying a person with deserved blame can be expected, and that itself is sufficient to supply the sorts of reasons needed here. I grant that this is an alternative one might pursue. If viable, the argument I have offered here would fall short. But this alternative proposal would need to be developed. Regardless, I'll not pursue the matter here.

52 THE VIEW

up her arguments against this thesis below). But then she considers a thesis whereby any goodness, and so favoring reason, flows *from* the mere rightness (or permissibility) of harming by blaming. Here she finds this thesis "even less intuitively plausible" (2019b: 186). The heart of her argument is drawn from a gripping thought experiment. She writes,

> Imagine that you have a special power (call it "The Look"). By looking at another person in the right way, you can bring about feelings of guilt. The other person culpably wrongs another—it is not a trivial offense, but neither is it the worst possible. Imagine that she betrays the confidence of a friend and as a result the friend has a bad day. You now have a chance by looking at the offender in the way that you have mastered so well to bring about guilt feelings in her. It would be the easiest thing, requiring nothing in the way of effort or sacrifice. But now imagine that there is no further good to come from your exercising this power you have. The offender has already resolved not to do the same sort of thing again, no one else is around to experience the results, and the relationship is either already irreparably damaged no matter what, or all has been forgiven so there is no benefit to the relationship to be had, and so on. Would you be making a mistake, or leaving a reason on the table, so to speak, by taking a pass on inducing this painful feeling? (186)

Nelkin reports that she does not have the intuition that one would be making a mistake in passing on blaming in this case by using The Look (186). I agree. Indeed, I would add, as I just set it out above, not only is there no mistake made in passing, but insofar as harming a person itself supplies a reason to avoid harming, there seems to be a reason *not* to give The Look. And so, if there is any mistake, it would seem to be a matter of giving a person what she deserves.

One might protest that my argument relies upon a mistaken assumption about what normative work an appeal to basic desert should do. Basic desert only needs to justify a wrongdoer's receiving blame. It need not provide the good reasons one blaming has *to* blame the person who deserves it. Those reasons, it might be argued, are supplied by other factors, such as a wronged person's need to give voice to her own feelings of anger, to aim at deterrence, or perhaps some other consideration. Perhaps one could regard these as favoring reasons. As such, one might argue, a strictly deontic version merely rendering it permissible to blame *could* make room for favoring reasons and so, supplemented by further reasons, provide the practical reasons a blamer might have to do the blaming. But on such a view, strictly speaking, the desert itself, being an exclusively deontic notion, would *not* issue from or be the ground of those favoring reasons. Nelkin's own positive proposal for a desert thesis is perhaps best understood as a version of this approach. She argues that we can understand a desert thesis in terms of conditional reasons (2019b: 189–90). If there are other factors in play, such as having to decide between causing harm to a culpable person rather than an innocent person, desert favors harming the culpable person. The key here, however, is that there must be reasons *beyond* considerations of desert alone that do the justifying work of blaming a blameworthy person.

I find the preceding defense of a deontic version an unsatisfying way to understand the role that judgments about basically deserved blame play in our moral responsibility practices. In particular, the reasons favoring blaming when someone deserves blame in a basic sense are dependent on factors that go beyond those bearing on the desert itself. However, I'll not pursue the matter any further here. Perhaps after all an exclusively deontic desert thesis *is* the philosophically wiser option insofar as it does commit to less. It must be granted that it would avoid the seemingly paradoxical issue to be discussed below: that harming itself could be

54 THE VIEW

good in a way that is not merely instrumental. Nevertheless, in what follows, I will develop a favoring version of an axiological thesis.[5]

I offer two motives for pursuing this option, motives that remain even if the preceding argument proves unsuccessful. First, there are some whose folk intuitions about desert include a consideration about the goodness and not just the rightness of a blameworthy person getting what she deserves. It is worth examining whether such a view can withstand careful scrutiny even if doing so is not strictly required to make sense of a basic desert thesis for blame. Second, consider those philosophers who theorize about free will in terms of the control required for basic desert-entailing moral responsibility. What at least some have in mind is a thesis about the *value* of agents getting what they deserve when, acting of their own free will, they knowingly do morally wrong, and do so from ill will (e.g., see Pereboom, 2021: 29). I am interested in engaging these philosophers and in developing for them a clear specification of what basically deserved blame comes to.

3.2 Zeroing in on a Principle of Basic Desert

To illustrate the sort of view I will explore, here is a first pass at a principle restricted to morally wrong acts:

---

[5] In an insightful paper, Leonhard Menges (2023) has recently argued for a *claim forfeiture* theory of deserved blame. According to him, deserving blame in the basic desert sense entails that one has forfeited one's right not to be blamed and that there is a reason to blame that person. He denies that this reason implicates any claim of value. On this view, there is a reason *simpliciter* supplied by desert. Menges's view is intriguing. He gets something right in characterizing the deontic sphere not just in terms of permissibility, but in terms of the forfeiture of rights by a deserving blamee. That's promising! But I struggle to understand the assertion that there *is* a reason to blame when that reason competes with the harm caused by blaming, and, by hypothesis, the reason involves no noninstrumental good. It might well be that Menges and I differ in our brute intuitions regarding the role of reasons. I leave the matter unsettled, but I commend Menges's paper as a viable alternative to mine.

Desert (D): Because it is good to harm by blaming one who is blameworthy for a morally wrong act, there is a reason that favors doing so.

D does not identify or give the meaning of a desert thesis for blame. This is because it does not in any way express the fitting relation that is supposed to hold, by virtue of desert, between the desert-base involving an agent's morally wrong act and the blaming that is itself that which is deserved. D only reports the kind of appraisal—deontological or axiological—a claim of desert is. So, it is best to think of D as *entailed by* a certain desert thesis rather than identifying it or giving its (complete) meaning. One way to construe the thesis, then, is that the goodness identified in D is *grounded* in desert.[6]

Note also that D is consistent both with a nondesert thesis and also with a desert thesis that is *not* basic. Recall our discussion from Chapter 2 (Section 2.6). There are two distinct theoretical alternatives to a basic desert thesis one might consider when seeking to provide the normative warrant for blame. One is to offer an account specifying the appropriateness of blame that makes no reference to desert at all. (Consider, for instance a view like Smart's [1963].) A different approach involves arguing that there are more basic normative principles providing the underlying rationale for claims of *what is deserved*, and hence for propositions such as

---

[6] In her excellent *The Problem of Blame* (2022), Kelly McCormick has recently criticized my earlier account of deserved blame (McKenna, 2012). She contends (2022: 47–51) that I ground basic desert in the noninstrumental goodness of (directed) blame and its attendant harms—so my proposal is not a basic desert thesis. Moreover, my proposal is subject to a wrong-kind-of-reasons objection; that it is good to blame someone is not the right kind of reason to blame, whereas desert is. This, however, reverses the grounding relation as I have specified it. My contention (2012, 2019a) is that the pertinent goodness is entailed *by* desert, not the other way around. The desert grounds the goodness. Hence, any reasons supplied by this goodness are themselves supported by all and only the reasons for an agent's deserving blame. McCormick proposes a fittingness account of deserved blame (2022: 50–1), a thesis I also defend (2022a and Chapter 6).

56 THE VIEW

D. This would amount to a *nonbasic* desert thesis. How so? The good mentioned in D could be construed as an instrumental good and then justified by reference to, for example, utilitarian or instead contractualist principles. On this approach, there would be important content to claims of desert that relate desert-bases to what is deserved in the proper sort of fitting manner. But the practices and underlying rationale for the claims of desert, and for a principle like D, would themselves be grounded on something that is more fundamental.[7]

Building upon D, here is a revised principle more carefully suited just for basically deserved blame:

> *Desert-Intrinsic (DI)*: Because it is intrinsically good to harm by blaming one who is blameworthy for a morally wrong act, there is a reason that favors doing so.

Some will object that harm to a person is never intrinsically good (e.g., see Scanlon, 2013: 102). But to appreciate what those wishing to endorse DI might have in mind, we can understand claims of intrinsic goodness in terms of cross-world differences. To illustrate, consider just for the moment not blame but instead punishment. Grant that it harms a person to sit in prison for five years; he is made to suffer in his isolation. Is this intrinsically bad? Yes. But now consider instead a person who sits in prison for five years *in response to* having brutally raped someone. Here is a way to appreciate the claim of intrinsic goodness in DI: All things being equal, it is a better world that this rapist sits in prison for five years for his act of rape than a world in which this same rapist causes the same

---

[7] This is roughly what Rawls has called "post-institutional desert" (1971: 103–4). James Lenman (2006), for instance, has explored an interesting nonbasic desert thesis for blame by appeal to contractualist considerations. In my estimation, this is how one should understand Wallace, who rests claims of desert on considerations of fairness (1994: 227). More recently, Manuel Vargas (2013) has advanced a nuanced consequentialist alternative.

BASICALLY DESERVED BLAME AND ITS VALUE   57

harm to his victim but undergoes no harm himself. That is fitting. Furthermore, in keeping with DI, because it is intrinsically good as a fitting response to the harm he caused, there is a reason that favors his being harmed.[8]

3.3 The Difference between Blame and Punishment

Before fitting the conversational theory of moral responsibility for a basic desert thesis for blame, consider the way in which blame differs from punishment according to the conversation theory. This is not a minor point. Some philosophers treat blame as informal punishment (e.g., Feinberg, 1970). In doing so they fix on the idea that blame is a species of sanction. But this gives added reasons for critics of desert-based theories of moral responsibility to damn claims of basically deserved blame by way of arguing against desert-based theories of punishment—especially full-blown retributivist theories. To the extent that blame differs from punishment, it might well be that the features of punishment that critics of retributivist theories find especially objectionable are lacking from blame's nature and, by extension, the norms governing its application.

Recall, as explained in Chapter 2 on the conversational theory, directed blame is a stage in a dynamic, unfolding conversation (conversational analog), and it plays a role in that exchange at an intermediary stage, the stage Moral Address. At a later stage, Moral Account, the blamed agent offers an account, a reply to the blame, in the form of an apology, an excuse, a defiant denial of guilt, and so

---

[8] Does this mean that it is not intrinsically bad that this criminal sits in prison for five years? No. It can be granted that incarceration is always an intrinsic bad. Still, that very thing, as a response to a crime, might be good as well along some other dimension. The appeal to a cross-world comparison between a world where the criminal is not punished and a world where he is helps to bring this out.

58   THE VIEW

on. At least in typical cases, punishment is yet a *further* stage in the unfolding conversation. Its conversational meaning is a response not just to the morally objectionable conduct that instigated the exchange, but also to the account offered wherein the blamed party replies to those blaming her. Punishment's meaning encompasses more than blame's does. (This is analogous to the way conviction and sentencing are treated in the law.)

Here, now, are two ways that blame differs from punishment. First, the harms to which a wrongdoer is exposed in our blaming practices are limited to the range of welfare interests delineated in Chapter 2:

- the capacity to engage normally in social intercourse and enjoy and maintain friendships;
- freedom from others' interference; and
- emotional stability.

While this range of harms is after all substantial and can "really hurt" as the saying goes, there is nevertheless an upper limit on such harms that is lacking in the case of punishment, which can include physical harms, confinement, monetary sanctions, obligations for community service, probationary periods, and formal means of banishment from organizations. Second, and perhaps more important, *by its very nature* punishment involves the intention to harm. But at least on the conversational model, blame need not. Blaming involves expressing and communicating one's regard for a blamed party's quality of will. It involves the conversational expectation and presumed burden of a reply from the blamed party. But its aim *need not* be to harm; its aim need only be to converse, to engage, to demand, and so on. Naturally, it is reasonable to think that competent moral agents engaged in blaming practices will understand that their blaming is liable to harm the one blamed. So, they are likely to harm knowingly. But what we do knowingly is much wider than what we do intentionally. Hence, punishment essentially involves the intention to harm as a means of sanction; blame does not.

3.4 Fitting the Conversational Theory for a Basic Desert Thesis

In fitting the conversational theory of moral responsibility for a basic desert thesis, I aim to avoid opposing charges from two different critics. There are those who would reject a basic desert thesis for moral responsibility because basically deserved blame involves a host of objectionable features that it shares with basically deserved punishment. Then there are those who would reject the conversational theory of moral responsibility if it fell shy of a theory that included basic desert for blame.

3.4.1 Resisting the Charge of Overcommitting

As for critics who are against a basic desert theory of moral responsibility because of its unsavory alliance with basically deserved punishment, what features of punishment might make it so objectionable? There are several potential candidates. One has to do with responding to a wrongful harm with a like harm: an eye for an eye. If, as the objection goes, justice is unpacked in terms of basic desert, and this is what desert comes to, justice commands acts of barbarism. There are, furthermore, worries about proportionality, of responding to a wrongful harm with a harm of the same degree. So those who torture and maim must somehow be caused harm proportionate to what they caused? Who is to shoulder this burden? Then there is the thought that justice would command intending to harm the one to be punished. Is this bloodlust? Vengeance? Even

60　THE VIEW

if neither, isn't it just cruel? An extreme view would have it that to account properly for true moral responsibility, one must be able to make sense of a blameworthy person's not just basically deserving blame, but, more drastically, as Galen Strawson would contend, the intelligibility of deserving eternal punishment in hell (1986).

If any of the above reasons are what motivate some to reject a basic desert thesis for punishment, none translates to the activity of directed blaming on the conversational model. If blaming functions on analogy with a conversational response to one who initiated a conversation, the proper metric is to be understood in terms of the intelligibility or meaningfulness of a reply that extends the conversation. It is not a matter of "saying" to the one who introduced the initial meaningful contribution just what she said back in reply. It is a matter of responding in a way that fits the salience of that contribution in a manner that gives expression to the blamer's demands, expectations, and so forth. Here also it is hard to see how this can be put in terms of proportionality *of harm*. It is better to think of any sort of proportionality in terms of the severity of the response being adequate to convey meaningfully the blamer's disapproval, her hurt feelings, and so forth. Also, worries about the extreme severity of deserved harm are out of place. As just noted, the range of harms the activity of blaming can cause according to the conversational model are limited to the range of welfare interests identified for directed blame. Moreover, unlike punishment, on the conversational model blaming does not *require* the intention to harm. Hence, charges of being essentially rooted in vengeance are unfounded. All of these considerations suggest that the pertinent harms in blaming should not be indicted with the harms that are (allegedly) taken to flow from basically deserved punishment.

One serious philosophical worry about the very nature of basically deserved blame arises from the idea that harm of any sort could ever amount to an intrinsic good. All harms, so the objection might go, only aggregate along the negative evaluative dimension of badness, negatively adding to any harm already done. Here

BASICALLY DESERVED BLAME AND ITS VALUE   61

reasonable minds can differ, and the best way to illustrate this is in terms of the claims of cross-world difference noted above (Section 3.2). But now we can do so, not in terms of a case of punishment, but in terms of a case of blame. Consider a case in which one performs a blameworthy act, say, making a hurtful, racist remark. Now consider two worlds, one in which the wrongdoer is in no way harmed in response to her remark. There is just the harm she causes and no harm accrues to her. Then consider another in which the wrongdoer is harmed in response to her wrongful harm in *only* the following ways, and only assuming that some sense of proportionality in the response is achieved: by others blaming her, her ability to engage in some spectrum of social intercourse is hampered, her freedom to live her personal life as she wishes is disrupted, and her emotional stability is unsettled.[9] Hold in mind, in imagining such a case, that the degree of these harms might also be fairly minimal and so would fall far shy of anything like extreme suffering. I fully acknowledge that some are likely to claim that, indeed, the first world is a better world. Adding one harm to another, they might argue, only increases the amount of intrinsic badness in the world; no intrinsic good can come from the addition. But I disagree. There is something fitting about a world in which a blameworthy wrongdoer is made worse off *in just the limited ways identified here.* That world is a better world than one where the wrongdoer is in no way harmed. Why? Well, one might say, because she deserves it.

3.4.2 Resisting the Charge of Normative Inadequacy

What of those who would reject the conversational theory because it falls shy of a basic desert thesis? There is a fair complaint about the

---

[9] Here we will have to stipulate that the harms do not result in good consequences, since then these could be justified by way of forward-looking considerations. Thanks to Derk Pereboom for raising this concern.

62 THE VIEW

bare bones of the theory as set out thus far—that is, when it is not explicitly fitted for a basic desert thesis. The conversational features of the theory unpack claims of appropriateness in a particular way. They aid in giving some content to the claim that blaming is an appropriate response to one who is blameworthy. Conversational meaningfulness or intelligibility is a thick, informative notion. Indeed, some who are foes of a desert thesis of any sort might point to the norm of intelligibility as a way to account for the fittingness of blame in the absence of any claim of desert. But the problem is that intelligibility or conversational meaningfulness is just not the right sort of normative warrant to engage in a practice whose nature involves harming those at whom it is directed. Some *further* normative warrant is needed, and so it seems the resources of the conversational theory cannot by themselves justify the harms in blaming, even if the harms that are identified are harms that flow from the conversational nature of the activities associated with directed blaming.

This seems right. The conversational theory of moral responsibility needs supplementing with normative resources that reach outside the conversational elements of the theory. My own view (2012) is that this can be done with resources that do not require commitment to basic desert. One can do so by appeal to exclusively nondesert-based resources (ala the work of a philosopher like Scanlon circa 1998), or, instead, one can do so by appeal to nonbasic desert resources (ala the work of someone like Lenman [2006]; Wallace [1994]; or Vargas [2013]). Nevertheless, as I shall now argue, one can also supplement the conversational theory by way of a basic desert thesis. The proposal is simple: Take the harms I have identified in directed blaming on the conversational theory. Now add the claim that one who is blameworthy deserves just this limited range of harms, in the basic sense of desert. I shall offer only two points to develop this proposal.

First, consider the norm of conversational intelligibility or meaningfulness as a fitting response to a meaningful contribution—wherein the contribution is the presumed agent meaning of the blameworthy agent's act. The conversational theory offers an illuminating way in which the elements of a desert-base can be said to fit in a case-specific manner the deserved response. In general, it is especially difficult to state the way in which a particular deserved blaming response could, in a case-specific fashion, be fitted for a particular desert base. In this respect, the conversational theory offers an elegant way to capture this. It's the sort of fittingness that uniquely pairs a particular conversational reply intelligibly with a prior particular meaningful contribution. In this way the current basic desert thesis for blame appears to avoid rather easily a (perhaps surmountable) problem for theories of punishment. How so? It is a truism to claim that, on a retributivist theory of punishment, the punishment should fit the crime. And this normative requirement of fit does seem to be motivated by the thought that this is a matter of what one who is to be punished really deserves. But with punishment, it is often hard to capture this. A person imprisoned for armed robbery might get five years, and so might a rapist or a corrupt banker. Where's the special fittingness between punishment and crime? Of course, this is not to say that properly justified forms of punishment could not be so tailored, but it stretches the imagination to think of how this could be so. (I attempt to do so in Chapter 4.) On the conversational theory of moral responsibility, there is an elegant way of conceiving of the special fittingness relation between an agent's blameworthy act and the blame she deserves.

Second, consider DI, which I offered as a way to understand a basic desert thesis for blame. It is easy to see how it might be altered to fit the conversational theory, as follows:

Desert-Intrinsic-Limited (DIL): Because it is intrinsically good to harm by blaming one who is blameworthy for a morally wrong act (where the harms in blaming are limited just to those identified on the conversational theory), there is a reason that favors doing so.

64   THE VIEW

I offer DIL as an initial formulation.

Elsewhere, I have offered (2012: 167–70) three observations to establish the claim of goodness as captured in thought experiments like those involved in the cross-world comparisons offered above (Section 3.4.1). These goods are meant to function as markers for or evidence of the good referenced in a principle like DIL. Here are three goods that can be cited when someone asks, "Why are the particular harms of blaming good?" First, it is good for the blame-worthy agent that she is harmed in the ways unique to directed blame on the conversational theory. This is because the potential harms to which she is exposed, such as the ability to engage in normal social relations with others, are harms to her only insofar as she is committed to membership in the moral community. Her liability to such harm is an *expression* of her being so committed. That is good. Second, it is good for the one blaming insofar as one's blaming is motivated by and an expression of one's commitment to morality. That, too, is good. Third, and finally, the relationship between blamer and blamed in the practice of blaming is itself part of an activity whose aim is to ameliorate and sustain the bonds of moral community.[10] That also is good. I defend these claims below.

3.5 A Challenge: Are the Goods at Issue Really Suited for Basic Desert?

Note that DIL is formulated in terms of intrinsic goodness. As such, it is not suited for the conversational theory. Consider the nature of the harm that, I contend, is good. On reflection, it is a distortion to describe its value as intrinsic. Why? The nature of the

---

[10] See Christopher Bennett's (2002) development of a basic desert thesis. Bennett makes the aim of our blaming practices moral reintegration, and he treats this as something that is good, and not merely for consequentialist reasons. Clarke (2013) draws upon a similar point as well.

BASICALLY DESERVED BLAME AND ITS VALUE   65

thing that is claimed to be good, the harm issuing from the conversational dimension of the blaming activity, gains its nature as a communicative and conversational response only by virtue of its relation to a collection of practices and norms against which the blaming activity can have a salience. Furthermore, insofar as its status is part of a stage in an unfolding conversation (or analog to one), it depends on what transpired prior to it as a meaningful contribution, and expectations about what might unfold after it, as felicitous as in contrast with infelicitous responses, for instance. So, it seems that its status as good is, after all, *extrinsic*, not intrinsic. Note, furthermore, that the goods I offered as evidence for the goodness of the harm in blaming were all in some way characterized in terms other than those internal, intrinsic features of the harm. All were in some way *extrinsic*. I drew attention to the agent's commitment to moral community, or the blamer's commitment to morality, or the way the interaction between blamed agent and blamer involves an activity aiming to sustain the bonds of moral community.

If what is required of a basic desert thesis for blame is that the good in the harm of blaming is intrinsically good in a strict sense, then I have fallen shy of a basic desert thesis. Derk Pereboom, for instance, often writes of a basic desert thesis for blame in such a way that if an agent is blameworthy for an act in the basic desert-entailing sense, then she deserves blame *just because* she so acted (e.g., Pereboom, 2013: 189). The "just because" invites the reading that the ground for the desert, found within the desert-base, and any claim of goodness entailed by what is deserved, cannot reach beyond the mere fact of the agent's so acting. Pereboom, it seems, requires that any good implicit in judgments of deserved blame has to be intrinsic.

In response, I propose a more liberal view of the value of blame. In her influential paper, "Two Distinctions in Goodness," Christine Korsgaard (1983), pointed out that the distinction between intrinsic and extrinsic goodness differs from the distinction between

66 THE VIEW

noninstrumental and instrumental goodness. Something might be noninstrumentally good since its goodness is not in the service of another thing, and yet its goodness might be dependent upon its extrinsic relation to other things. A simple example might be the beauty of a rare flower, whose beauty would not be so precious if flowers of that kind were commonplace. Another, I have suggested, is a musician's contribution to a musical piece, where the contribution gives meaning to but also acquires meaning from the accompanying instruments. My example (2012: 170) is the drum work by Joe "Philly" Jones on John Coltrane's album *Blue Train*.

Given this distinction, in earlier work I suggested, but did not develop, a basic desert thesis in terms of noninstrumental value (2012: 123–4, n. 18). Here is a revision to DIL designed to accommodate this more permissive conception of basically deserved blame:

> *Desert-Noninstrumental-Limited (DNL)*: Because it is noninstrumentally good to harm by blaming one who is blameworthy for a morally wrong act (where the harms in blaming are limited just to those identified on the conversational theory), there is a reason that favors doing so.

Does my concession that the pertinent good is merely extrinsic and not intrinsic weaken my thesis? Isn't DNL exposed to the indictment that the particular extrinsic facts that would ground a claim of goodness are also facts that show the good to be not merely extrinsic but, contrary to my contention, instrumental? In short, the charge might go: It's all well and good to distinguish between extrinsic and instrumental goodness. But drawing the distinction does not mean you can carry it off in this case. If the goodness of the harm you identify in blaming gains all of its value exclusively from serving the elements extrinsic to it, then it's not merely extrinsically good; if good at all, it's only instrumentally good.

I have two burdens here. One is to resist the thesis that anything shy of a strict claim of intrinsic goodness falls short of a proper basic-desert thesis. Recall, this arises from Pereboom's "just because" formulation, which seems to limit the thesis to intrinsic rather than any sort of extrinsic but noninstrumental good. On this view, while DIL might be a serious contender, DNL is not, and all the conversational theory offers is something like DNL. Another, assuming the first burden can be met, is to resist the worry that the goods I have identified as extrinsic but noninstrumental are, upon examination, merely instrumental goods and nothing more.

3.6 My Reply: Defending the Role of Extrinsic and Noninstrumental Goodness

Consider the first burden. Citing a good that is an extrinsic but noninstrumental good located in the harm of blaming would be enough to foreclose the worry that the good only gains its value by serving a consequentialist or contractualist end. Indeed, when Pereboom makes these claims about intrinsic goodness, he almost invariably clarifies by writing of the sense in which it differs from goods that could be justified by consequentialism or contractualism (e.g., 2013: 189). His most immediate worry seems to be that there is some more general moral theory or more general moral principles providing the justification for blaming, and any goodness in blaming gains its value from that theory or those principles. The extrinsic goodness figuring in the proposed conversational model is not meant to serve an instrumental purpose in relation to other general moral theories or principles.

Furthermore, consider use of the expression "just because" when Pereboom claims that, according to a basic desert thesis, an agent would deserve blame just because she so acted. It is not clear that we must understand the "just-because" relation so that it rules out

68   THE VIEW

the relevant value of the blame being extrinsically related to other things. It might function like an indexical, picking out what can be added, holding fixed other features of a system or set of relations that would then give something a certain value. Granting, for example, that there are so few flowers of a certain sort—and holding fixed other standards of beauty viewers might take to evaluating flowers—with all that in place, one might think a flower, growing alone in an open field is aesthetically valuable *just because* it is so beautiful. This might be so for the goodness found in the activity of blaming. Under the assumption that the practices and norms set context and salience for a blaming response, and they provide the constitutive resources to give the response meaning, one might say, adding the response of blaming is fitting—and deserved—just because the agent so acted.

Now consider the second burden. In assessing an earlier formulation of my proposal, Pereboom argued that the value in the communicative and conversational dimensions of the blaming activity, and the harms that attend it, are limited to instrumental goods (2013: 194–6). For instance, I cite the good in the blameworthy agent's commitment to membership in the moral community, claiming that it is noninstrumental. Pereboom replies:

> On the basic desert view, it is good that the blameworthy agent is harmed in the ways indicated just because he has knowingly done wrong, and in the context of the debate, this is just what it is for such a harm to be a noninstrumental good. Harm aimed at the good of membership in a moral community would, by contrast, be instrumental, since the harm is not envisaged as good in itself but instead as serving the good of such membership. (2013: 195)

Then, in response to my contention that the harm in blaming encompasses a range of noninstrumental goods whose status is

BASICALLY DESERVED BLAME AND ITS VALUE 69

dependent upon their relation to others and to sets of practices (and thus is good extrinsically), he writes:

> while it is plausible that certain kinds of obvious goods, such as mental and physical health, are partially constitutive of the noninstrumental good such as human flourishing, it is at least typically less credible that harms—as harms—are partially constitutive of noninstrumental goods, and for this reason count as noninstrumental goods themselves. Vaccination may be a prerequisite of physical health, and health constitutive of flourishing, but it is not plausible that the pain of vaccination is constitutive of flourishing, by contrast with being instrumentally required for it. (196)

Pereboom's criticism crystallizes the sort of objection I indicated above: granted, there are noninstrumental goods whose status is extrinsic, but the harms I have identified in the practice of blaming according to the conversational model are not among them.

I offer two points in reply. First, as I have noted previously (2012: 170), the goods that I contend are at issue might well be of a "mixed" variety, and so might thus serve some instrumental purposes. But they might *also* have noninstrumental value. Crucially, something can be of value because of the aim it takes on or its role in a practice with a certain telos—such as aiming at preserving the bonds of moral community—and have that value regardless of whether it actually helps to attain that end. Its value is in its commitment to that telos, and (not just) in its instrumental efficacy of achieving the desired end.

Second, recall the cross-world thought experiments I proposed to make sense of how one harm in response to another could constitute a good. Of course, I had originally put that in terms of capturing a sense of intrinsic value. But it can be employed to help establish similar claims about extrinsic, noninstrumental

70 THE VIEW

value. The cross-world comparisons just have to include in one world—and exclude in another—the extrinsic relations to the pertinent harmful activities that are alleged to issue in the good-making feature. To be clear, what is it that is a candidate for a noninstrumental good? It is the harm itself as it contributes to the blaming activity, an activity that is in response to, and so is extrinsically dependent upon, an antecedent blameworthy act. Bearing this in mind, Pereboom contends that it is less credible that harms can be partially constitutive of a noninstrumental good, as in comparison with certain benefits that can be partially constitutive of a noninstrumental good. As quoted above, he illustrates with a simple case of the pain of vaccination (a harm), which is only instrumentally good in the service of health and human flourishing. This is a powerful challenge, but note that it turns primarily on the force of the sort of example he enlists.

Here is different sort of case. Consider grief as response to the loss of the parents one loves, or in response to losing a sibling early in that sibling's life. Grief as part of the good of living a flourishing life might be seen as a noninstrumental good insofar as it is bound up with accepting the realities of our loving relations and our finitude. Grief is certainly a harm, but sometimes it is also a good, a noninstrumental good connected with accepting our humanity. Consequences aside, a life without grief in response to losing loved ones would be worse than one where, in the face of loss, one underwent an appropriate period of psychological pain and mourning. One who would not mourn the loss of his or her mother, for instance, is one whose life is in some way impoverished. Or at any rate, even if one disagrees, one can see the point of this sort of claim. The harm in blaming, a basic desert theorist might argue, *is like that*. It is intimately connected with commitments and modes of life within a moral community whose aim is itself good—and good not merely as an instrument for something else. Crucial to this test case for resisting Pereboom is the idea that grief might very well contain an element that is noninstrumentally or intrinsically bad while nevertheless contributing to a whole that is intrinsically or noninstrumentally good.

I take the preceding case of grief to be adequate to respond to Dana Nelkin's (2014, 2019b) challenge to my view. However, exploring how she might resist me will help sharpen my thesis. Like Pereboom, Nelkin also wishes to resist my claim that pertinent harms are good. Nelkin contends that the goods I identify in blaming, such as the care a blamed person might have for others' regard, can indeed be noninstrumentally good. And it might well be, she contends, that the harms that attend them come with these goods as manifestations of them, but it just does not follow from that that the goods I identify are good *in virtue* of these harms. Hence, it is, for instance, the caring about others that is, as she puts it, fundamentally good and not the harm that, she grants, may be noncontingently related to it. This is an excellent way to capture what is at stake. It poses a serious challenge to my contention that there are these goods-as-harms identified in the practices of blaming. In the case of grief, the challenge might go, what is fundamentally good is one's caring for family or friend and a life that involves the attendant intimacies that promote one's flourishing. The pain or harm of loss might be noncontingently related to this thing of fundamental value, given the fragilities of our human lives, but it simply does not follow that it is *itself* good.

Now why take grief to be the right sort of case to resist Nelkin's insightful challenge? Rather, doesn't she show precisely why my appeal to a case like grief falls short? I grant, on its face, it seems to Before offering a direct reply, note the following qualification: It is consistent with my view that it would even be a better world if it were the case that one could enjoy and celebrate the goods of family and friendship without the liability to grief. This might lead one to think that in a world where there is the good of friendship and familial love that *is* accompanied by the pain of loss, that the pain or loss itself could not be noninstrumentally good in any way as a mode of contributing to one's caring and loving. But this is just

72 THE VIEW

not true. Were we differently and, perhaps, better equipped beings, we might not be exposed to these vulnerabilities. But given that we are so exposed, there is the question of whether the harm attendant with grief due to caring can be a noninstrumental good. I contend that it can.

I turn now to my direct reply. Critics such as Nelkin appeal to an enticing analytic move by distinguishing the dimension of, say, grief that is appealing or seemingly good-making, which is the caring, and then separating that from the dimension that is unappealing and so seemingly bad-making, which is the distinctive pain of loss. This allows Nelkin to contend that any goodness in grieving—or blaming—is a goodness in virtue of just that dimension, the caring dimension, not the other dimension, the one to which we are averse, the painful dimension. But I reject this analytic move, this prying apart of the good-making feature as distinct from the alleged bad-making feature. Of course, it will not help merely to contend that, in certain cases, the alleged bad-making feature is necessary or noncontingently related to the good-making feature. Nelkin grants that. Instead, the burden here is to show that the relevant harm actually contributes to the goodness. In response, the harm, as *a distinct thing*—that is, merely as a harm—would not contribute to any goodness. But what a basic desert theorist can say in reply is that it is mistaken to infer from the fact that we can identify these different dimensions of grief or blaming that these can be understood as fully distinct ingredients—like separate necessary ingredients added together to bake a cake—rather than as a unity whose whole has a value that is not analytically decomposable in this way. They are not like separate parts that just "add up."

I suggested above that the liability to certain harms can be an expression of one's cares. Furthermore, the propensity of others to blame and in doing so harm is a way of registering the concern of the community of blamers. One way to understand this is that such expression is itself, accompanied by these distinctive harms, noninstrumentally good as an *organic unity*. It would not be good

BASICALLY DESERVED BLAME AND ITS VALUE 73

as that particular expression of one's cares absent its expression as a form of harm or suffering. When considering the nature of value as it bears upon the problem of evil, Marilyn Adams (1999: 55) usefully draws on a distinction introduced by G. E. Moore (1903) and Roderick Chisholm (1968). There is the evil that is balanced off by a greater good, but there is also evil that is *defeated* by what is good, and, in this defeating, one finds a kind of goodness. So, too, with grief. There is pain in grief on particular occasions, and so a kind of harm, even something that, it can be granted, is intrinsically bad, but as an expression of *this* way of caring for *this* person who suffered *this* loss, it is a "bad" or an evil that is not merely outweighed but defeated. The key distinction between merely outweighing and defeating is that, in outweighing, a good can be considered as making a positive contribution whose value is not dependent on the bad. The thing of disvalue could, so to speak, be subtracted and the good still stand (cf. Moore, 1903: 29). In defeating, the good gains its significance as a good *by* being a response to and finding goodness built from the thing of disvalue. So, for instance, in expressing one's affections, in expressing one's love when undergoing a period of grief, that pain in loss counts in the context of that set of extrinsic relations as something that is good given the good of the grieving response. So, too, I would say, for the harms I have identified in the activities of blaming according to the conversational model. Yes, it is a harm for the one blamed that she suffers the set back of others distancing themselves from her, but as this harm for her is also an expression of her concern for others, it likewise counts as a good that she is harmed in this way.

3.7 Conclusion

I offer the preceding as an account of basically deserved blame. On my proposal, what a blameworthy person deserves in a basic sense is a directed blaming response of a conversational nature, one

74   THE VIEW

that engages the blamed person in such a way that she registers the moral demands and concerns of those engaging her. This is a matter of holding her to account. Moreover, the harms that she is alleged to deserve—insofar as she deserves blame and not also something more like punishment—are *exhausted* in the activities of blaming her and of her registering them as such. These are social harms regarding the blamed person's relations with others. When expressed in a fitting fashion, say by pertinent conversational standards of intelligibility or meaningfulness, they engage the person as a moral agent and as a member of the moral community, or at least a potential member.

In developing this view, I have committed to the axiological thesis that, when deserved, the pertinent harms of blaming are noninstrumentally good. Many, I suspect, will reject this ingredient as a veiled form of barbarism justifying vengeance and inclinations toward brutality. Indeed, as noted above (Section 3.2), when considering a value-based conception of blame, Scanlon (1998) was emphatic in distancing himself from any such view about the goodness of causing the blameworthy to suffer. So, too, for Wallace (1994). Maybe, after all, this is the correct view, and so maybe one should, as Scanlon did in later work (2008), opt for an exclusively deontic version of a desert thesis for blame. But I note two considerations that need to be considered before rejecting an axiological view of the sort I have defended.

First, one should bear firmly in mind that the axiological claims of noninstrumental goodness involved in the desert thesis presented here are quite limited. What does a blameworthy person deserve on this view, and what would be noninstrumentally good for her to receive? No more than what is involved in that person having a proportionately pained response to others altering their interpersonal relations with her—and altering them as would befit their communicating to her their moral demands and concerns from a place of proportionate moral anger. *That is all.* No aim of writhing on the floor or the demand for the wearing of hair shirts is part of the mix.

Second, those favoring an exclusively deontic version face burdens of their own. As I argued above, if a strong version is ruled out for deserved blame, what is left is a weak version permitting but not requiring blaming the blameworthy. But merely permitting that the blameworthy be harmed by blaming supplies no reason why one blaming *should* harm them. So how do the exclusively deontic theorists avoid the charge that they are the ones who permit gratuitous harm under the banner of desert? They cannot really say it is not gratuitous *because* the person deserves it, since the deserving itself is—by hypothesis—no reason to favor treating the person in that way. So, there is some reason to worry that it is after all the exclusively deontic versions of a basic desert thesis that might just help to conceal barbarity and vengeance.

I close with one final point about whether anyone deserves blame in the basic sense specified here. In this chapter, I have only attempted to articulate a theory of what basically deserved blame is. I take it to be an open philosophical question whether anyone deserves it. I assume that if no one has free will, no one deserves to be blamed in this basic sense of desert. Nothing in the preceding discussion was intended to settle the free will question. As a free will realist, I do think that most people possess free will and that most of the time they act freely. However, I grant this is a contestable view. As result, so is the question of whether anyone deserves blame in a basic sense of desert. Nevertheless, one point I hope to have established has to do with *what* a blameworthy person would deserve if she did have free will, and what would be good about it. Some philosophers, such as Galen Strawson (1994), have argued that the freedom at issue in the free will debate is the type required to make intelligible deserved eternal suffering in hell. In my view, this sets the intuitive bar for the sort of freedom needed so high that it quickly becomes clear that nothing metaphysically possible

76 THE VIEW

for finite beings like us could hit that bar, which is exactly the conclusion Strawson himself draws (a thesis I will explore in some detail in Chapter 5). But if the theory of deserved blame offered above is anywhere within the vicinity of correct, then the freedom that would be needed to deserve blame would only help ground a culpable person's being subject to the limited interpersonal social harms identified here. That still might require a fairly robust freedom, but at least it seems to be within the reach of mere mortals like us.

4

Punishment and the Value
of Deserved Suffering

Is it good for a person guilty of criminal wrongdoing to suffer
by receiving the punishment that she deserves? More specifically is it good in a way that is not just about its instrumental role
in aiming at some other good. I this chapter, I develop the thesis
that it is. Inasmuch as retributive theories of punishment require
a commit to more than this, then what follows is not a defense of
retributivism but rather a defense of one familiar element in what
some philosophers take retributivism to be. In any event, whether
retributivist or not, I aim for a modest thesis built from the resources of the conversational theory of moral responsibility. Its
modesty is due to both the nature and the limited amount of suffering a culpable wrongdoer deserves for her crimes, according to
the conversational theory. What makes this emphasis on modesty
so important? The more modest a theory of deserved suffering is,
the harder it will be for free will skeptics to reject deserved punishment, and my aim is to resist these free will skeptics.

4.1 The Relevance of a Modest Theory of
Blame and Punishment

My strategy is similar to the one deployed in Chapter 3, where our
focus was justifications for blame. To explain, many understand the

---

An earlier draft of this chapter was originally published in 2020, as "Punishment and
the Value of Deserved Suffering," *Public Affairs Quarterly* 34: 97–123.

78 THE VIEW

free will debate in terms of basic desert-entailing moral responsibility. So construed, the free will debate is about freedom involved in the judgment that a person deserves blame for what she does just because she freely did something that she knew was morally objectionable. Free will skeptics argue that the freedom condition for basically deserved blame cannot be met, whereas free will realists, both libertarians and compatibilists, contend that it can. Given this way of framing the debate, I have argued that much turns on what deserved blame is. The more demanding desert is made out to be—the harsher the treatment involved and the greater the costs to the blamed—the heavier the justificatory burdens for the realist are. These heavier burdens, I contend, play out in more robust freedom requirements. Galen Strawson (1986; 1994), for instance, sets a bar for true moral responsibility in terms of making intelligible deserving the punishments of hell and the rewards of heaven. The upshot for Strawson is that no kind of freedom short of self-creation will suffice. Since this is metaphysically impossible for finite beings, a skeptical conclusion follows.

In previous work, I set aside the free will debate and so set aside directly taking issue with free will skeptics (McKenna, 2012). I left it as an open question whether anyone has free will and how we are to conceptualize it if we do (e.g., via compatibilism or libertarianism). Nevertheless, keeping the preceding considerations in mind, I explored just what an adequate basic desert theory of blame must come to in order to count as a bona fide desert thesis, the sort claimed to be at the heart of the free will debate (149–72). I sought a minimal and permissive thesis, one committed to as little as possible in terms of the harms implicated in deserved blame. My charge to the skeptic was that her rejection of the freedom required for basically deserved blame remained incomplete so long she only attended to conceptions of freedom and desert that justified extreme varieties of retaliatory suffering or other brutalities (146–8).

The free will skeptic might counter that the freedom requirement for deserved blame applies uniformly regardless of the sort or

PUNISHMENT AND VALUE OF DESERVED SUFFERING   79

severity of the blame that is basically deserved. If free will requires the ability to do otherwise, or ultimate sourcehood, or being an agent-cause, this will be so whether or not *what* it is a requirement for is an exceedingly demanding form of basically deserved blame, ala Galen Strawson, or a relatively gentle form, like the one I will propose here. I disagree. I think the two are linked—at the very least they are linked for purposes of fairly assessing intuitions among disputants in this debate. When it comes down to the nitty-gritty details of the arguments between the free will realists and the free will skeptics, testing for whether an agent retains freedom under the assumption of determinism (or lucky indeterminism) winds up being settled by asking whether an agent would deserve a certain response just because she so acted. Here, I say, our intuitions about the agent's freedom will be affected by both the nature and the severity of the putatively deserved response.[1]

For instance, consider the debate between Derk Pereboom and me over the soundness of his influential *four-case manipulation argument for incompatibilism*. Pereboom imagines an agent, Plum, who is manipulated directly into performing a morally wrong act but who nevertheless satisfies a rich set of compatibilist conditions for free agency.[2] Pereboom expects his audience to share his intuition that Plum does not act freely and is not morally responsible. Moreover, the manipulation is supposed to be no different in any relevant respect from a determined agent, and so an incompatibilist conclusion follows. In my hardline reply, I attempted to show that it remains an open question whether an agent so manipulated is not free and responsible when acting as she does. If she is free, then on my view, granting a requirement of basic desert, she would deserve

[1] My argument here, and in my earlier work (2012), is in certain respects similar to a strategy Christopher Bennett (2008) employs when theorizing about punishment rather than blame. According to Bennett, whether a broadly retributive response to wrongdoing will require highly demanding forms of free will depends in part on how damaging or severe that response is.
[2] See Pereboom (2001; 2014). This is his Case 1. I'll not give details here, as they are unnecessary to make the point at issue.

80 THE VIEW

blame and the harms attendant with it. To press the implausibility of my position—to show that our intuitions do not side with this hardline compatibilist strategy—Pereboom considers the views of the Calvinist preacher and theologian Nathaniel Emmons (1860/ 1987: 166–7). Emmons takes a hard stance toward Pharaoh, who is manipulated to do wrong by God and yet still deserves the sufferings of hell meted out by God. Emmons invites us to celebrate God's decree whereby sinners are "vessels of wrath" and "the smoke of their torments will be eternally ascending," and as witnesses to this suffering, the morally righteous ought not to be repelled but instead should say, "Amen, Alleluia, praise ye the Lord" (1860/1987: 402). Reflecting upon this case, Pereboom reports that he does not have the intuition that Pharaoh is morally responsible (2008: 167).

Like Pereboom, I, too, do not have the intuition that Pharaoh is morally responsible—not when his responsibility is cast in terms of deserving being a vessel of wrath who will suffer eternal hell fire. Indeed, I would go further: Not only do I lack that intuition, but I actually have the contrary intuition that he positively deserves *not* to receive *that*. This, however, does not threaten a compatibilist hardline reply to a manipulation argument like Pereboom's since I am not sure anything could be a justification for such a conception of deserved suffering. This is so regardless of what free will comes to. Or at any rate, this is so for mere fallible mortals like us who are less than pure gods or demons and so neither purely good nor purely evil.

Given these sorts of pressures, if the free will dispute is to be understood by reference to basic desert-entailing moral responsibility, we need to understand the nature and the severity of *what is deserved* in contexts of blameworthiness. Thus, before we adjudicate competing intuitions and responsibility-related judgments regarding Pereboom's Plum in his Case 1, we need some measure of what Plum's deserving blame would amount to.

So as not to mislead, let me be clear: I take it to be in dispute whether realism or skepticism about free will is true, and, for that

PUNISHMENT AND VALUE OF DESERVED SUFFERING   81

matter, assuming realism, whether compatibilism or libertarianism is true. My thesis is *not* that, if we ratchet down far enough the intensity and the nature of the deserved blame (or punishment), a compatibilist conclusion about free will follows. No. Even at the "gentler" end of the spectrum, it is an open question for which any position needs good arguments. No contender is entitled to claim that her adversaries are patently in the wrong. But I do contend that more excessive conceptions of what deserved blame or punishment comes to will favor extreme freedom requirements that are exceedingly metaphysically demanding. This will in turn illicitly tilt the dialectical scales in favor of the free will skeptic. If so, we need an independent purchase on what a bone fide basic desert thesis for blame comes to and, most importantly, how minimal a theory we can get away with while still counting it as an authentic desert thesis. The same applies to punishment, or so I will now argue.

4.2 Blame within the Conversational Theory

Consider blame as developed in the context of the conversational theory. Two distinct questions are pertinent to our goal of constructing a theory of punishment. First, what is blame's nature? Second, on what basis is one normatively warranted in blaming the blameworthy? We took up each of these questions in Chapters 2 and 3, respectively. So here we can be brief, noting only considerations especially salient to moving from a theory of deserved blame to a theory of deserved punishment.

4.2.1 Blame's Nature

Consider directed blame as characterized in Chapter 2. On the conversational theory, directed blaming can be understood on analogy

82 THE VIEW

with a reply to a conversation initiated by the alleged wrongdoer via the agent meaning of her act. When the blamed party then offers a reply to the blamer in the form of an excuse, a justification, an apology, a defiant embrace of her odious behavior, or whatever, she thereby extends the conversational-analog. This in turn opens up the possibility of extending the conversation in different ways, either by forgiving or further rebukes, but, also, crucially, in at least some cases, *by way of punishment*. The last point is important, since, as noted above, on the conversational model punishment is distinct from blame. It is a further move in an ongoing (analog to a) conversation. Interestingly, Antony Duff advances a communicative theory of retributive punishment rather than blame (2001). In various passages, he makes clear that he is thinking of the communicative enterprise to share the features distinctive not just of communication, but also of conversation. For instance, Duff writes that the relevant kind of communication "aims to engage [a] person as an active participant in the process who will receive and respond to the communication" (2001: 79). Hence, it is fair to interpret Duff as a conversation-based theorist as well. Although I will construct my theory of punishment from different resources, as it happens, it will share a good bit with Duff's proposal.

Crucially, blame differs from punishment in several respects. Punishment involves activities that allow for a wider array of potential harms than those identified for blame. These forms of hard treatment can include incarceration, perhaps physical suffering, financial sanctions, and other means of penalizing a person by depriving her of things she cares about, such as being sequestered from loved ones, other intimates, or for that matter, from the places one wishes to live. Key is the prospect of the use of force to ensure that a punishment is received. There is, moreover, a further difference. Unlike blame, punishment involves the intention to harm. *That is its aim.* Blame as characterized on the conversational model need not. One might directly blame knowing that it is likely, or even inevitable, that the blamed party will be harmed, and yet it might be that one does not intend to harm. Rather, it is consistent with blame that one only intends to communicate her hurt feelings, make more demands, express moral outrage, or protest how one or others have been treated or regarded. Not so for punishment. Returning to the themes of the prior section, it thus appears that the justificatory burdens for punishment are higher because the range of harms is more severe, there is the prospect of the use of force, and the harms are intended. Hence, the expectations for a more significant kind of freedom might be warranted.

4.2.2 Blame's Normative Warrant

Now consider matters of warrant. What norms govern blame? Before proceeding to more substantive matters, one minor qualification is in order. We can set aside questions of standing. Some considerations that bear on reasons to blame are not about the status of the person blamed: Does she deserve it, or would it be fair to her? Rather, they are about the status of the would-be blamer: Is she entitled or permitted to do the blaming? Although considerations of standing are important, for our purposes we can assume that, barring any general skeptical conclusions, at least some persons on some occasions do have standing to blame those who are blameworthy.[3]

Our goal here is to develop a communicative theory of punishment that, like blame, also builds in the constraints regarding conversational norms. One measure of a normatively warranted mode

---

[3] Perhaps I risk eliding an important detail in setting aside issues of standing. It could be that there are reasons why states do not have standing to punish, even if punishment can be normatively grounded in claims of basic desert, as I argue in this chapter. States' lack of standing to punish might be limited to certain contingent features of our actual world, or it might be due to more general reasons about the limits for justifying the authority of any state, even under ideal conditions. I leave all of this aside for the purposes of this chapter.

84 THE VIEW

of punishing a person who (let us grant) deserves punishment is that the mode of punishing engages the person in a way that is responsive to the meaning of her wrongdoing. A norm of conversational intelligibility will help to give some content or guidance to the familiar thought that the punishment should fit the crime. Clearly, on this proposal, familiar forms of punishment are woefully inadequate: A rapist and a white-collar criminal might both get thrown in the slammer for the same number of years. Nothing about this way of proceeding does anything to respond to either meaningfully in a way that engages the unique moral significance of their respective wrongs.[4]

As with our treatment of the normative warrant for blaming, I treat it as an open question whether some normative relation other than basic desert is a viable option in a theory of punishment. Regardless, we will just explore desert. Building on our results from Chapter 3, recall our axiological principle regarding deserved blame, DNL. Here we can work with a simpler principle entailed by DNL:

> *Deserved Noninstrumental Harm (DNH) for Blame*: When a person basically deserves blame, the harm in blaming her is noninstrumentally good.

In subsequent discussion, we will modify this principle to help account for deserved punishment.

Given DNH for Blame, the question becomes: When a blameworthy person is blamed, is it noninstrumentally good that she is harmed *just in the ways distinctive of our blaming practices*? Recall our case of Daphne and Leslie. Is it good if, in response to Leslie's racist remark, she is harmed just by way of her relationships with

---

[4] Duff is very much alive to this worry in developing his proposal for a communicative theory of punishment. He thus proposes a number of creative ways to modify punishments so as to facilitate a fitting communicative dimension to punishment meant to interact particularly with a wrongdoer's criminal activity (see Duff, 2001: 96–106).

others being impaired as fitting for her remark? Is it good if, as a result, her freedom is compromised just because she is put upon by others to acknowledge her wrong and perhaps make amends, apologize, and so forth? Is it good that she is made to feel emotionally taxed by these means of "conversing" with her?

Recall, to assess these questions, we can appeal to cross-world comparisons. Holding all else equal, and granting for the moment that Leslie acts freely, is it a better world in which Leslie freely and knowingly performs this morally wrong act, and only others are harmed by it? Or is it instead a better world in which, in response to Leslie's wrong and the harm she causes, she is harmed only in the ways identified above? Here, I grant that reasonable minds can differ, but setting aside the dispute regarding the reality of free will, I find it appealing to say that the second is the better of the two worlds. And this suggests that there is a distinctive kind of harm that could amount to a noninstrumental good located in basically deserved blame.

Return now to Plum's blameworthiness in Pereboom's example. If what is at issue in assessing Plum's freedom is to be understood in terms of deserving *blame* in light of (or despite) the causes determining his actions, then we need to attend not to whether he deserves some form of terrible suffering, but whether, in responding to him, he would deserve to undergo the harms involved in members of a moral community replying to him by way of conversational acts that express moral demands, expectations, and so forth. Given these relatively limited harms, I contend that it is easier to see how it might remain an open question whether either Plum or Pharaoh deserves blame. I grant, however, that when it comes to questions of deserved punishment, my hardline compatibilist proposal might be less compelling. After all, by my own admission, the harms in punishing can be much more taxing, and this is liable to elicit the expectation that a stronger sort of freedom is involved. Still, I say, we need first to consider what sort of punishment is at issue and how severe it is.

86 THE VIEW

4.3 Adding to the Conversational Theory

Before turning directly to punishment, I offer two amendments to the conversational theory as it applies to blame. Both are meant to help build a bridge from blame to punishment. Consider first Coleen Macnamara's (2015) account of reactive attitudes as communicative entities. Macnamara faces a puzzle for philosophers who agree with Gary Watson that the reactive attitudes are forms of communication (1987: 264). The problem is that episodes of reactive attitudes like resentment and indignation are themselves sometimes experienced privately or instead aimed at targets who cannot receive them, like the dead (Macnamara, 2015: 548). If so, how are they communicative? Macnamara develops an intriguing solution to this problem according to which any episode of a reactive attitude is communicative even if its message is "unsent." According to Macnamara, its communicative nature is due to its *nonintentional purposiveness*. Such attitudes, by their nature, have representational content designed to play the functional role of "evoking uptake" in pertinent recipients, in particular, those who are their target—that is, the blamed. This is true of these attitudes even when one who experiences them does not send any such message, just like when we write a letter and never send it. Its nature is to be intelligible as a message if sent. What uptake do these reactive attitudes seek in a blameworthy party? According to Macnamara, it is guilt in response to wrongdoing.

Here we can set aside Macnamara's argument that all instances of reactive attitudes like resentment *have* to be communicative. While this might be true, it is not necessary for advancing a communicative or conversational theory of responsibility. It is enough if a limited range of cases are communicated, in particular the episodes of reactive attitudes that also rely upon the social scaffolding of ordinary practices to do the work of conveying moral demands, expectations, and so forth. These are the ones implicated in directed blaming.

I am also not convinced that, of those instances of the negative reactive attitudes of resentment and indignation that are communicative, the uptake they seek is uniformly guilt and acceptance of wrongdoing. This is suggested by various theorists Macnamara cites, such as Darwall (2011: 331), and Smith (2013: 44). But it seems Macnamara and others are attending primarily to cases with relatively agreeable or welcome recipients of blame. Often, blame and the pertinent reactive emotions function well even when not received cooperatively but instead occasion a hostile, adversarial, or dismissive response. It is more plausible that what reactive attitudes seek insofar as they are communicative entities is some sort of acknowledgment or appreciation of a blamer's demands, disappointments or expectations (e.g., see McKenna, 2012; Shoemaker, 2015). The uptake, then, is more open-ended than Macnamara suggests. Or, at any rate, I cannot see how Macnamara can rule out this more permissive way of construing the functional role of these emotions. Nevertheless, Macnamara has identified something extremely important. For a blamer's resentment or indignation to be received via uptake that occasions guilt is certainly the blamer's *desired* response. At least it is in many paradigmatic cases; guilt in response to another's resentment or indignation is revelatory of a moral attitude fostering moral reconciliation. Except in unusual cases, it's what we want when we blame another, even if it is not all that we want. We want the culpable to receive our blame and experience guilt, and moreover extend the "conversation" in ways that meaningfully express that guilt—typically by way of apology, but also by other means of repairing damaged relationships, and so on.

Turning directly to the topic of guilt and desert, consider Randolph Clarke's (2013) development of an axiological version of a desert thesis. Clarke attends just to the self-directed moral emotion of guilt and considers a proposal on which what a guilty person deserves is to feel the distinctive mental pain of guilt. On an

88 THE VIEW

axiological view, this is a noninstrumental good. Here is his proposal, which is intended as a more precise development of the generic basic desert thesis that the guilty deserve to suffer:

(T6): It is noninstrumentally good that one who is guilty feel guilty.[5]

Note that Clarke's (T6) is compatible with my proposal set out in the previous section:

DNH for Blame: When a person basically deserves blame, the harm in blaming her is noninstrumentally good.

The harms identified in DNH for Blame, however, include the product of *others* blaming the blameworthy. Indeed, in developing the proposal, I made as central cases the second-personal ones while setting aside entirely the self-directed cases. Whereas the harms identified in Clarke's (T6) are only harms that are the product of a blameworthy person's own emotional response to her guilty conduct. These are, in a sense, harms she brings on herself. Of course, DNH for Blame is *consistent* with cases of an agent blaming herself and so harming herself by feeling guilty. Still, Clarke's more specific formulation, limited to intrapersonal cases, helps to capture something important that my focus on the interpersonal cases does not. Put simply, it identifies what is often, although of course not always, a more desirable way for the blameworthy to get what they deserve. Sometimes it is simply better if the noninstrumental harm they incur is the product of their own internal life. In this way, they "get" what others would wish to communicate when blaming them—and this links Clarke's proposal to my treatment of

---

[5] Clarke (2013: 155): Clarke improves on this proposal to restrict it to feeling the guilt at the right time and to the right degree. He is right to do this, and my prior proposal, DNH for Blame, also needs amending likewise. I set these details aside.

Macnamara. The desired result in another's resentment or indignation is achieved.[6]

This suggests yet a further point: The more fully a person experiences appropriate guilt for her blameworthy conduct, so long as the conduct is not too egregious, the less reason others have to blame her directly for it. In some cases, an agent's experiencing guilt for her poor conduct, when that is apparent to others, can constrain the reasons others have to blame her directly at all. Perhaps this is justified as follows: If she already gets it, there isn't any point in piling on. To invoke the analogy with conversation, if one speaker sees that her interlocutor already accepts a point she intends to convey, her conveying it is unnecessary. Moreover, there is a risk that by others adding further harms by their directed blame, a blameworthy person who already experiences an appropriate amount of guilt is at risk of being harmed *more* than she deserves. Naturally, this has a limit, and when an agent's wrongdoing is especially egregious, these considerations appear to be out of place. This will figure prominently in what follows, helping us to distinguish justifications of blame from justifications of punishment.

4.4 Introducing a Conversational Theory of Punishment

The preceding considerations suggest a way to theorize about punishment consistent with a modest variety of retributivism: Appropriate punishment should aim for criminals to experience a fitting kind and degree of guilt for their wrongdoing. I will now

---

[6] For a thoughtful argument against the contention that it is noninstrumentally good for wrongdoers to experience guilt, see Victor Tadros's discussion (2011: 44–51, and 75–8). Here I cannot take up Tadros's arguments against a thesis like Clarke's, but I would ask the reader to bear in mind that my goal here is simply to build up a theory of basically deserved punishment out of resources from my theory of responsibility. I do not mean here to offer a full-throated defense of it, but only to show what such a view might come to.

90 THE VIEW

develop a retributivist version of a conversational theory of punishment built from the resources of the conversational theory of moral responsibility. As noted above, my proposal will be similar to one developed by Antony Duff (2001), who writes in terms of aiming for the culpable to experience remorse. Although I will arrive at the view by different means, since I will build upon a more general theory of moral responsibility, and in particular on an understanding of the conversational nature of and norms for blame.

To begin, a few matters of clarification are in order. First, in what follows, I shall understand the term "crime" as a moral concept, not a legal one. It refers to moral wrongs that are sufficiently egregious that they justify the use of force either to cause others to refrain from such actions or to respond with force to those who have performed them. Second, I shall also understand "the guilty" to refer to morally responsible agents who have done morally wrong and have no excuse. In the context of punishment, "the guilty" picks out those who commit crimes and have no excuse. I intend these merely as terms of art and not as substantive contributions to the philosophy of law. Third, although I will write in terms of crime and draw upon examples of penal sanctions such as prison time, I do not mean to attend exclusively, or for that matter even primarily, to state-sanctioned forms of punishment. I mean to include informal modes of punishment not issued by the state. There might be further barriers to formal, state-sanctioned punishment, even under conditions far more agreeable to justice than under the current arrangement in, say, the United States.[7]

On the conversational theory, in certain respects punishment is like blame. It is, as Feinberg (1986) argued, a vehicle whereby

---

[7] Indeed, as Tadros points out, even if it can be established that it is noninstrumentally good for wrongdoers to suffer, it is a further matter whether *the state* would be justified in pursuing these goods (2011: 78–83). I have no interest in entering into this debate. Indeed, I have serious reservations about whether states could be so positioned, at least non-ideal states of the sort it is reasonable to expect from fallible creatures like ourselves.

PUNISHMENT AND VALUE OF DESERVED SUFFERING   91

members of the moral community, including victims of crimes, express moral concerns and communicate with the guilty. Like blame it goes beyond being expressive; it is also communicative (Duff, 2001) and, indeed, is conversational in nature. It provides a way of engaging with the guilty by means that communicate moral demands, expectations, outrage, protest, and the like *in response to* the meaning of—the quality of will manifested in— the guilty person's crime. However, punishment is *not* the same thing as blaming. It goes beyond blaming and is a further move in an exchange that presupposes both antecedent blame and the guilty person's response to the blame. A response to blame from a guilty party that involves apology and sorrow, for instance, rather than defiance, can be a relevant factor in deciding whether and how to extend the conversation further by then punishing. After all, forgiveness is sometimes an option. Also, as already noted, punishment is a mode of interacting that, unlike blaming, essentially involves an intention to harm, and it draws upon resources that go beyond the harms involved in blaming. In going beyond these harms, it also communicates something further that is not essentially a communicative ingredient in the content of what is expressed in blaming. I take this to be a key feature that distinguishes punishment from mere blame, a feature that involves content that is communicated in blaming. In particular, punishment communicates the view that the guilty person has gone beyond the limits of what will be morally tolerated without resort to some significant forms of sanction (Duff, 2001) In this way, it is distinctly expressive of a special class of moral demands registered by those who punish. In the case of state-sanctioned punishment, of course, it will be the special class of demands of the state. In this way, unlike blame, punishment is accompanied by the prospect of force deployed to achieve a sanctioning response.

But how are we to understand these sanctions? What are they designed to communicate? Recall that blame on the conversational

92   THE VIEW

model is designed to answer to norms of conversational intelligibility or meaningfulness. To blame a person for a racist remark rather than for neglecting to pick you up at the airport will involve modifications in one's relation to a person unique to her offense, and unique to what it reveals about her quality of will. Different blaming responses will be more or less fitting for what is revealed. Likewise for punishment on the conversational model. It will involve forms of treatment—means of delivering hard treatment—tailored to the meaning of the guilty person's crime. This is one way to make sense of the familiar idea that the punishment should fit the crime.

Have I said enough? No. How *exactly* can punishment achieve this conversational goal of speaking uniquely to a guilty person in light of her particular crime? How can it uniquely fit the crime?[8] Consider this. As noted above, often the *desired* uptake in blaming by way of reactive attitudes is for the blamed to experience guilt, which is a distinctive kind of mental pain in response to accepting that one is culpable for having done the particular wrong one has done. Indeed, in thinking about Clarke's proposal, for a range of moral wrongs, it seems preferable if a guilty person comes to guilt on her own rather than by our interventions in directly blaming her. However, there is a limit to this. *This limit marks a normative distinction between the justified role of punishment as compared to the justified role of blame.* Plausibly, some moral wrongs—crimes—are sufficiently egregious that it should not be left up to the guilty to accept what we would convey to them were we to blame them. We are prepared in this kind of case, so to speak, to force the point we intend to convey in our conversation with them. It's just not optional that "they get it." We are prepared to see to it that they do.

---

[8] Duff's work is especially helpful here (2001: 92–107). Rather than rely simply on generic forms of incarceration as the paradigm for punishment, Duff advocates such alternatives as criminal mediation, probation, and community service orders, along with incarceration. All are cast in ways that can be tailored uniquely to the communication needed to address a guilty person's particular criminal activities.

PUNISHMENT AND VALUE OF DESERVED SUFFERING   93

And we are prepared to "participate" with them in their accepting their guilt. Our goal is therefore to create conditions tailor-made to speak to their unique wrongdoing whereby they *do* get it, and, once having gotten it, to experience their guilt in an environment suitable for its expression. So it would be for rape, murder, violent assault, child molestation, and other significant forms of moral wrongdoing.

Punishment on the conversational model thus aims to provide conditions tailor-made for a guilty person to experience guilt for her crime. It *seeks* her experiencing guilt. However, its aim is not simply to *cause* the internal state of guilt itself. Why? No form of external treatment can itself ensure that another's internal affective response turn out a certain way. Nor should it. As Duff makes clear (2001: 82–4), the goal should not be to treat the guilty as an object to be manipulated, but as a person with dignity, to be engaged as an interlocutor of sorts. Thus, punishment functions in its communicative role as a form of persuasion to try to get one who is guilty of a crime to accept her culpability and experience guilt. To do so, it provides conditions that one with a guilty mind should regard as deserved, conditions that should befit her own internal response to registering the reality of the moral wrong she has done. As such, the proper modes of causing harm by punishing can be conceptualized as ways of enforcing external conditions that, if guilt were internalized by a guilty person, *should* count as fitting outward expressions of her deserved mental pain of guilt— and specifically deserved *as a response to her crime.* To make the point in a very simple way, punishment aims to get a virtuous person to see that she deserves her treatment.[9] It is fitted for what a person should feel about her crime were she to feel a proper degree of guilt for it. It is an outward expression of what those who

---

[9] Michael S. Moore understands guilt as the virtuous response that a culpable party should feel for her criminal act, although he denies that it should be used in a justification for punishment, as I propose here (see his 1987: 213–4).

94 THE VIEW

blame contend a virtuous person ought to feel as a response to her crime.[10]

Note five things about this proposal.

First, the punishment should not be conceived merely as a contingent or accidental arrangement that could be set aside if somehow the guilty could be brought to experience internal states of the mental pain of guilt while, say, whiling away one's days on the beach. Rather, the punishment creates external conditions that are designed to fit or provide fitting occasions for outwardly expressing one's internal life were one who is guilty to experience a fitting degree of guilt for her crime. These are conditions that one with a guilty mind would be prepared to accept as what she deserves since it would count as an outward expression of her guilt. Duff (2001), for instance, has advanced a view wherein the punishment takes on the secular role of *penance*. Naturally, there might be a variety of different ways to realize these external conditions.

Second, the justified modes of harming would not go beyond what would be required to provide reasonable conditions for a person to come to accept and experience guilt for her crime. Indeed, some forms of hard treatment would be ruled out as they would be more apt to cloud a person's perceptions and judgments rather than help clarify their own moral understanding of what they have done and its moral meaning. Incarceration that includes or requires reflections on one's crimes, probationary forms of punishment, forced modes of interaction with victims or others who could represent victims (so as to internalize the experience of their victims), sequestration from loved ones abused, and so on, are resources that can facilitate coming to experience a proper amount of guilt. But these can all be provided without further means of causing a person to live in miserable conditions or to experience other kinds of suffering.

---

[10] I am indebted to Gunnar Bjornsson and Ellie Mason for helping me with this formulation.

Third, it is likely that, for many who are guilty, providing conditions conducive to experiencing guilt will involve the affection and understanding of those who wish to help the guilty seek their moral reform and find suitable ways to express an apology. For many, it will be the possibility of love or friendship that will enable the guilty to appreciate the morally reprehensible ways they have come to treat others. The net result of this and the preceding point together is that, on the conversational model, the forms of punishment involved are consistent with both humane and even compassionate conditions for their application. The goal is to get the guilty to engage in a conversational exchange whereby they come to accept and internalize with suitable feelings of guilt that our moral demands and expectations should be embraced.

Fourth, a familiar element in formulations of retributivist theories of punishment is a requirement of proportionality: punishment should somehow cause the guilty to suffer proportionate in severity to the crime (e.g., Kant, 1797/2017: 142). This feature of retributivism is taken by many of its detractors to be one of its most unsavory elements, since it apparently supports forms of treatment that could involve exceedingly hard treatment. My own view is that, defining or not, this requirement should be abandoned from a theory of punishment. If that requires revisionism about retribution, then so be it. Indeed, if that requires giving up the term "retributivism," fine by me. In that case, treat this proposal as a theory of basically deserved punishment. There is, however, a kind of proportionality that my proposed theory can accommodate. The aim of punishment should be to provide conditions for a person with an appropriately guilty mind to appreciate that her being treated as such is fitted to the severity of her crime. It is so fitted because it provides external conditions that would be an intelligible expression of her own internal state of guilt were she to experience guilt. Punishment aiming for a guilty response that is too weak simply fails to reflect an authentic appreciation of the harm done in a criminal act. In addition, other forms of punishment will

96 THE VIEW

be too strong and instead suggest that a person who would experience guilt fitted for such punishment is being too hard on herself. The severity of any punishment, then, can be measured in terms of whether it would facilitate a suitably proportionate response of guilt by providing external conditions that would befit experiencing and accepting a proper degree of guilt for one's crime. It will be an open question whether the proper way to punish a guilty person is by means that are nearly as severe as the crime committed by the guilty party. Indeed, it is consistent with this proposal that one adopt an added guiding moral principle regarding humane treatment: Those punishing should seek a means for achieving external conditions for fitting guilt that involves the least amount of suffering possible while still communicating the moral community's regard for the agent and what she has done.

Fifth, the modesty of the current proposal turns on two points. One is that it seeks limited ways to dispense sanctions so that all that need be achieved are conditions that one who is guilty would take to be adequate expressions of their having internalized guilt. Much that goes under the name of punishment, even limited punishment falling far shy of the standards of *lex talionis*, involves imposition of sanctions just to extract a cost—say in the form of incarceration or even just financial penalties. The current proposal rules these out as ends worth delivering on the basis of desert absent their role in facilitating experiencing a suitable form of guilt. But, more crucially, the modesty of the current proposal is that it limits the aim of the *content* of what is expressed to whatever is involved in aiding the guilty party in a form of expressing suitable guilt for the meaning manifested in her particular acts of criminality. In that way, proportionality cannot be accounted for exclusively in terms of experiencing a suitable *degree* of harm or suffering in feeling guilty. It's not about mere amount. The differences are also qualitative, not just quantitative. Hence, if an inside trader and an assailant of physical assault feel, say, the same degree or amount of deserved pain for their respective wrongs, the proportionality of the degree or amount of deserved suffering settles nothing about the fittingness and so the deservingness of the response. The content of what is registered must be matched or fitted for the meaning of the wrongdoing. It is in these ways that the current proposal departs from other retributivist theses.

4.5 The Modest Retributivism in the Conversational Theory of Punishment

In light of the preceding discussion, consider this proposal for a simple retributivist theory of basically deserved punishment:

Simple Retributivism (SR): The guilty deserve punishment for their crimes.

And consider this as a natural extension of SR:

Deserved Noninstrumental Harm (DNH) for Punishment: When a guilty person deserves punishment for her crime, the harm in punishing her is noninstrumentally good.

To evaluate the credibility of both, take the mention of "punishment" to be limited just to the sort supported by the conversational theory. And take the harms to be limited just to those that would be required to create external conditions suitable for a person's accepting and experiencing guilt for her crimes, were she to have an appropriately guilty mind. Now, to assess DNH for Punishment, run the same cross-world thought experiment I previously used to assess the value of the harms in blaming. Consider a clear case of a criminal act—a violent and unprovoked assault that left a man permanently disabled. In one world, just the crime

98 THE VIEW

occurs and the victim is harmed while the guilty party does not suffer at all. The second is qualitatively just like the first, but the guilty person is caused to suffer by means designed to facilitate the wrongdoer's feeling an appropriate guilt, and in conditions that ensure an external means of expressing that guilt. Suppose, for instance, the guilty person is forced to spend a year in prison and made to interact with victims of brutal assaults and engage in therapy to understand how she has compromised another person's life. Is it a better world in which the moral community engages this criminal in this way, or is it not? If so, DNH for Punishment expresses an axiological version of a basic desert thesis for punishment.

I propose that we take SR and DNH for Punishment, when understood within the context of the conversational theory of moral responsibility, to constitute a modest retributivist theory of punishment. It is modest because the deserved harms that it identifies are, by comparison with other theories, mild and limited in kind. It is also modest because it rejects a strong requirement of proportionality, as clarified in the preceding section. It is, moreover, modest since its guiding aim is a kind of conversational understanding whereby the guilty come to accept and even in a sense participate in our moral perspective. This is central to Duff's (2001) proposal as well. It is *not* based on any sort of brute sense of justice where the infliction of suffering for the guilty counts as its own end.

Victor Tadros (2011: 44–51) has recently argued that, aside from instrumental considerations, it is not a good thing that one feel badly about wrongdoing. However, even granting this, it is, he explains, a further question whether punishing a person would *also* be a good thing. Tadros proceeds to argue that it would not be insofar as the kinds of suffering imposed by depriving the punished of various good and bad things cannot plausibly be thought to be (noninstrumentally) good (77–8). Here I cannot take up Tadros's argument that a wrongdoer's pain of guilt

PUNISHMENT AND VALUE OF DESERVED SUFFERING   99

cannot be a noninstrumental good. That's beyond the scope of my arguments in this chapter (see Chapter 7). My goal here has simply been to articulate what a modest retributivist account of punishment might come to. I have cast it in terms of aiming to elicit guilt in criminal wrongdoers. If guilt, as expressed in Clarke's (T6), is not after all noninstrumentally good, then the current proposal fails. On the other hand, if it is, then the proposal on offer presents a handy reply to Tadros's second point. The punishments on the conversational model I propose are structured solely to provide external conditions for the outward expression of one's experiencing an appropriate amount of guilt. They are not *simply* imposed as deprivations of the good or bad things the punished might otherwise enjoy. The noninstrumental goodness of the punishments that would be imposed would be good *because* of their role in aiming at the culpable wrongdoer experiencing and expressing an appropriate amount of guilt as a response to her crime.[11]

A critic might protest that the recommended forms of deserved punishment, and the value of them I have identified here, would be practically impossible to implement given the current state of the criminal law and the penal system in the United States. I assume that is true. My goal has just been to show that it is conceptually possible to develop a basic desert theory for punishment that, while modest and so shorn of the more excessive prescriptions of other retributive theories, nevertheless rises to the level of a bone fide retributivist theory, or at any rate, it defends a central desert thesis amenable to retributivism. Moreover, even if our current institutions are not equipped to realize it, it is possible under some idealized system of social arrangements to apply such a system of punishment to actual persons like us.

---

[11] In fairness to Tadros, he limited his argument to retributivists who believe that the kinds of punishments currently imposed, largely by incarceration, are not in need of revision (2011: 76). Clearly, I deny this.

4.6 Resisting Skepticism about Retribution

The desert theory under consideration is meant to apply only to agents who are free in some significant way—in a way that is central to the free will debate. Recall, I defined "the guilty" in terms of those morally responsible agents who have done morally wrong and have no excuse. If no one has free will, then everyone is excused. This bears on the impression one might have about whether and how my proposal should apply to the population of prisoners currently incarcerated in the United States. Here I would note that even if we sort out that small segment of the prison population that has actually performed a morally wrong act of a sort that *should* justify punishment by the state, there is the matter of who among them are free agents. Forget about global skepticism of the sort advanced by free will skeptics. To the extent that many in prison suffer from severe forms of mental illness, there is cause for concern that a good many are not free agents and were not free when they committed any egregious moral wrongs that landed them in prison. If so, they are not guilty; they have good excuses and do not deserve to be punished for their crimes.

This brings me, finally, to the free will skeptics who reject retributive theories because no one is free in the sense required for basically deserved punishment.[12] Here I can be brief. I do not take myself to have done anything to *refute* the skeptic. I assume that it is an open question whether anyone is free in the sense that would be required for them to basically deserve such punishment.

My own view is that most psychologically healthy people possess free will. I assume that they often act freely in the strongest

---

[12] I have no interest in other grounds for skepticism about retributivism. Perhaps there are good arguments for why state punishment is never morally justified because the state is never justified in using force to punish others. To the extent that such an argument does not depend on any claims about free will skepticism, nothing I have proposed is meant to engage such a view. I am only interested in skeptics about retributivism who base their skepticism exclusively on skepticism about free will.

PUNISHMENT AND VALUE OF DESERVED SUFFERING 101

sense required for moral responsibility. I take this kind of free action to include the prospect of being an apt target for basically deserving both blame and also punishment. In this respect, I am a free will realist. I am a compatibilist as well, about both free will and determinism and also about free will and the more inclusive thesis of naturalism (which includes indeterminism). Nothing in this chapter is intended to advance my views on any of these fronts. My only goal has been to establish a clear sense of what basically deserved punishment is—or put more accurately, what it comes to within the confines of the conversational theory as I have developed it. I have been especially interested in exploring how modest I can make it out to be while still preserving the sense that it is a bone fide desert thesis, the sort that free will realists and free will skeptics take to be in contention.

So in what sense am I resisting the skeptic at all? By playing defense. Reverting back to Section 4.1, I contend that it is incumbent on the free will skeptic to work within the range of conceptions of deserved blame and punishment that are plausible or realistic. These include formulations that do not have such dramatic commitments about what ways we humans can be justified in treating each other under the presuppositions of basic desert and retributivism. Thus, all I ask is that, in prosecuting her arguments, the free will skeptic not appeal to cases of outlandish or excessive punishments deserved by guilty wrongdoers. Doing so risks relying on what Daniel Dennett (1984) has called "intuition pumps" and other argumentative devices that are liable to cloud our assessment of what is in dispute rather than clarify it. Hence, if we are to assess Plum's freedom in Pereboom's Case 1, or instead Pharaoh's, by testing intuitions about what Plum 1 or Pharaoh deserves, let us set aside deserved punishments that include eternal hellfire or suffering of the sort Galen Strawson or Emmons invokes.

My work in this chapter is in a certain respect at odds with my prior strategy when treating blame. One strategy I deployed in accounting for basically deserved blame in the previous chapter

102 THE VIEW

included showing that deserved blame does not justify a range of severe forms of hard treatment precisely because it is more limited than punishment is. I also highlighted the fact that it does not require the intention to harm the way punishment does. To the extent that these are "selling points" for a theory of deserved blame and for the freedom required for it, they clearly will not help with the current proposed theory of punishment. They might even be regarded as, by comparison, reasons counting against it. After all, the harms in punishing are different in nature and also more severe than those involved in blaming. I myself argued above (Section 4.1) that more stringent burdens associated with desert theses are liable to give rise to more stringent freedom conditions. Hence, there is open conceptual space for one to adopt a form of realism with respect to the freedom required for basically deserved blame, but skepticism with respect to the freedom required for basically deserved punishment. That is not my view, but I grant that there is reason to think that we need a stronger kind of freedom to justify a kind of desert that involves the possibility of more extreme harms and harms that are intended by those who bring them about. Indeed, yet a further realist thesis would be that the freedom conditions for basically deserved blame are indeed met with compatibilist resources, but that the freedom conditions for basically deserved punishment are *also* met, but with stronger libertarian satisfaction conditions. I wish to remain committed to free will realism and compatibilism on both fronts, but I admit that I have never attempted to formulate the free will problem in terms of the conditions for deserved punishment.

PART II

CLARIFICATIONS AND FURTHER DEVELOPMENTS

5

The Free Will Debate and Basic Desert

Many contemporary philosophers working on the related topics of free will and moral responsibility contend that the proper way to understand the free will debate is in terms of basic desert-entailing moral responsibility. On their view, attempting to settle the free will problem by reference to any alternative normative grounds for holding moral responsibility fails to engage adequately with the traditional debate altogether. Why? Given these (allegedly) less metaphysically taxing normative bases for blame and punishment, there is no reason to think that determinism would be a threat; there's just no philosophical problem to solve.

This is how Derk Pereboom approaches the debate (e.g., 2001, xxi–xxii), and many others follow him on this point. Here, in commenting on Hilary Bok's (1998) compatibilist proposal, is an example of how Pereboom makes the point.

> But while this "legitimately being called to moral improvement" notion may be a bona fide sense of moral responsibility, it is not the one at issue in the free will debate. For incompatibilists would not find our being morally responsible in this sense to be

An earlier draft of this chapter was originally published in 2019, as "The Free Will Debate and Basic Desert," *Journal of Ethics* 23: 241–55. I have also drawn liberally from "Further Reflections on Free Will and Basic Desert: A Reply to Nelkin and Pereboom," *Journal of Ethics* 23: 277–90.

106 CLARIFICATIONS AND FURTHER DEVELOPMENTS

even *prima facie* incompatible with determinism. The notion that incompatibilists do claim to be at odds with determinism is rather the one defined in terms of basic desert. (2007: 86)

While I agree that it is useful to approach the traditional free will debate by reference to basic desert, I am skeptical of Pereboom's rejection of alternative approaches. *Must* the free will debate be understood in terms of basic desert-entailing moral responsibility? Does one who opts for an alternative normative basis for our responsibility responses do so on pain of the charge that she is changing the subject? Is she just side-stepping what's at issue in the free will debate?

5.1 Basic Desert and the Traditional Free Will Debate

Philosophers like T. M. Scanlon (1988, 1998) and R. Jay Wallace (1994) have adopted a different strategy, explicitly eschewing robust desert-based conceptions of moral responsibility and seeking to provide a justification for our blaming practices with resources that do not include basic desert. Consider, for example, this passage from Scanlon:

Let me call . . . the idea that when a person has done something morally wrong it is morally better that he or she should suffer some loss in consequence . . . the Desert Thesis. Notions of guilt, blame, and resentment that embody this thesis in the way just suggested, and the idea of responsibility that is necessary for their attributability, are what might be called desert-entailing notions. Since I regard the Desert Thesis as morally indefensible, my account of moral criticism and the notions of guilt, blame, and responsibility that it involves are not desert-entailing notions in this sense. (1998: 274)

THE FREE WILL DEBATE AND BASIC DESERT 107

Scanlon instead provides a justification for our blaming practices with contractualist resources that do not involve appeal to the notion of basic desert.[1]

Now consider Wallace. Wallace characterizes the thesis of retributivism as "the view that it is intrinsically good that wrongdoers should suffer harm, and that therefore we have a positive duty to inflict such harms on them" (1994: 60, n. 13). Here, I understand Wallace's formulation of retributivism to be an instance of a basic desert thesis (one that shares some similarities with Scanlon's formulation). About this desert thesis, Wallace writes,

> I think we should be careful not to take for granted an overly retributivist understanding of what we are doing when we hold people morally responsible. It certainly seems that I could blame someone for a wrong, and even engage in sanctioning behavior toward the person (avoidance and censure, say), without believing it to be an intrinsically good thing that the person should suffer harm. While our practices of holding responsible may tolerate a retributivist interpretation, it would be a mistake to suppose that such an interpretation is necessarily embedded in the self-understanding of ordinary participants in the practice. (60)

Like Scanlon, Wallace offers a justification of our blaming practices that is not grounded in basic desert. Instead, Wallace appeals to considerations of fairness.

Indeed, Wallace is emphatic about his rejection of a desert thesis as the basis for justifying our blaming practices.

> It is true that I have not provided a basis for the strong conclusion that wrongdoers positively deserve to suffer the harms of moral

---

[1] I restrict my attention to Scanlon's view of responsibility set out in *What We Owe to Each Other* (1998). More recently, Scanlon has developed an intriguing desert thesis that differs from his earlier view (2008: 188–9). Nevertheless, the Scanlon of 1998 clearly counts as someone who, according to Pereboom, would be changing the subject in applying his account of responsibility to the free will problem.

108 CLARIFICATIONS AND FURTHER DEVELOPMENTS

> sanction in this way. I have repeatedly urged against building such a retributivist interpretation into the very stance of holding morally responsible. . . . Furthermore, the principles of fairness I have articulated provide no support for these retributivist conclusions. (1994: 227)

Admittedly, Wallace does endorse a *negative* principle of desert that he takes to be an ingredient of the pertinent conception of fairness: People do *not* deserve to be blamed if they have not done anything morally wrong (1994: 135). But he rejects the thesis, as indicated in the passage just quoted, that in a basic sense, a person could deserve to be blamed, and deserve the harms attendant with blaming, just because she so acted. And it is this thesis that Pereboom and others take to be crucial to the free will debate.

Reading the work of Scanlon and Wallace, as well as others operating in a similar manner, I believe we can understand them in way that does after all directly engage incompatibilists like Pereboom, and not just about the justification for our responsibility practices but about free will, too (e.g., Scanlon, 1988, 1998; Wallace, 1994: 93–109). This is so even if they themselves (seem to) eschew the free will problem, as Wallace himself announces in the opening paragraph of this book.

> This book is about moral responsibility. . . . The approach I advocate gives central place to distinctively rational powers among the conditions of responsibility. Being a responsible agent, I believe is not really a matter of having freedom of the will. Rather it primarily involves a form of normative competence: the ability to grasp and apply moral reasons, and to govern one's behavior by the light of such reasons. (1994: 1)

No matter. I say Wallace and Scanlon offer views that *do* after all bear on the traditional debate. It is worth noting here, in response to this passage by Wallace, that one way to unpack an ability to grasp

THE FREE WILL DEBATE AND BASIC DESERT   109

and apply moral reasons is in terms of reasons-responsiveness, and there is a rich literature devoted to explaining free will in just such terms.[2] Perhaps there is a mildly revisionist aspect to their proposals, but, as I see it, their contributions can handily apply to the traditional free will debate.

In this chapter, I argue that it is wrong to insist upon basic desert-entailing moral responsibility as inescapably tied to the free will debate. It will be useful to begin by reflecting on what the presumed role of free will is as it bears upon this notion of basic desert-entailing moral responsibility. I will restrict attention to the dimension of moral responsibility concerning blameworthiness.

5.2 Free Will and Grounding Blameworthiness

A curious detail of the free will debate is that, with few exceptions, there is little in the way of support *for* the thesis that basic desert-entailing moral responsibility is crucial. It is typically just asserted. So far as I know, no one has argued for the point. So, I begin with a simple question: What is it about basic desert that seems so fundamental to the free will debate that other normative notions (allegedly) fail to capture it? What might a philosopher have in mind by insisting that we theorize about free will in terms of basic desert?

Here is my proposal. An appealing picture of the relationship between free will and moral responsibility can be framed in terms

---

[2] For example, see Fischer (1994), Fischer and Ravizza (1998), Haji (1998), McKenna (2013b), and Sartorio (2016). I suspect that Wallace's remark is best understood in terms of a way of thinking about free will cast exclusively in terms of the ability to do otherwise, and absent any specification of free will in terms of the control required for moral responsibility. But the philosophers referenced here all understand the metaphysical debate by reference to the control presuppositions required for appraisals of moral responsibility. And it is highly plausible to interpret Wallace in his book (1994) as committed to a control requirement for moral responsibility for what one does. So, it seems to me, despite how he opens his book, Wallace *is* committed to engaging in the metaphysics of the free will debate—when that debate is understood in the terms that I and numerous others understand it.

110 CLARIFICATIONS AND FURTHER DEVELOPMENTS

of *grounding*. Consider a morally wrong act for which an agent is blameworthy. Suppose that her being blameworthy renders it appropriate that she is blamed. Assuming other agent-involving conditions are in place, her exercising of her free will ability in so acting is what grounds her being blameworthy and so an apt target of blame. This is because her free will affords her direct control over the most basic actions she is able to perform.

Perhaps putting it this way overstates free will's role; this makes it sound as if free will is doing *all* of the grounding work. Blameworthiness also presupposes other significant conditions. Free will is better thought of as one essential ingredient among others that work together to ground blameworthiness and the aptness of blame. For instance, further nontrivial requirements for blameworthy action might also involve an agent's either knowingly doing morally wrong or doing so from culpable ignorance. And I have argued that a further condition is acting from a morally objectionable quality of will. Some might also require further that a blameworthy agent is one who has and is able to act from values and principles that she acquired in an authentic manner (e.g., Mele, 1995; Haji, 1998). These ingredients might also be thought of as part of what grounds blameworthiness and the aptness of blame. There are, as well, the actual facts regarding what counts as morally right and wrong, and so the basis for the evaluative character of her act as morally impermissible. But, however these further details are ironed out, exercising the free will ability is at least an essential part of the grounding "cocktail" for an agent's being blameworthy and for it to be appropriate to blame her. Most significantly, exercising the free will ability can be thought of as the element of the complete ground that is within the agent's direct control, so that, in a literal sense, when an agent is blameworthy, by an exercise of free will, *it is she* who makes it so that she is blameworthy.

In light of free will's proposed grounding role, we can begin to see why philosophers might be exercised by the requirement that the desert at issue in the free will debate is basic. At a minimum, what is

THE FREE WILL DEBATE AND BASIC DESERT   111

required for deserved blame to be basic is that the normative status of the desert at issue is not itself justified in terms of other more fundamental normative principles. What might an alternative look like? On a consequentialist rendering, for instance, one might justify blame by arguing that what makes blame appropriate is that it makes society better off. On a contractualist rendering, instead, one might justify blame by arguing that it would be the product of a reasonable agreement rational agents ought to accept or, instead, could not reasonably reject. Perhaps the reason that, as some might see it, these proposals don't measure up to what is offered by way of basic desert is that the normative warrant for blaming is, at least to some extent, taken out of the control of the free agent. If the aptness of blaming an agent depends on what benefits others, or if it depends on what it would be reasonable for others to agree upon generally as part of a contract, *then she is not in control*. Or, put more cautiously, she is not in as much control over the grounds for her being to blame. Other agents, their interests and rational commitments, also play a role. By contrast, when the desert is basic, so long as other features of the world cooperate (e.g., so long as the agent does not drop dead, no birds fly in front of the bullets she fires, and so on) in acting freely, it is up to her—and *just* up to her—whether she deserves blame.

To be clear, I have only offered the preceding rationale in an effort to understand why some take it that the free will problem is essentially linked to a basic desert-entailing conception of moral responsibility. I do not endorse this rationale. I only intend to give voice to it.

5.3 Clarifying Basic Desert as Applied to Blame

Perhaps one might understand blame and its expression so that it is conceptually possible to decouple it from any propensity to harm. If so, it would make sense to decouple questions of deserved blame

112 CLARIFICATIONS AND FURTHER DEVELOPMENTS

from questions of deserved harm. One could then explore a basic desert thesis for blame that was in no way about the harm a blameworthy agent deserves. But, at least within the context of the free will debate, I assume that the sense of blame that is in dispute is a kind that, when overtly directed at a culpable wrongdoer, is liable to harm or cause the wrongdoer to suffer some loss, as specified in Chapter 3 (see also Pereboom, 2021: 11–12). Hence, I also assume that the argumentative burden for advancing a basic desert thesis for blame includes an account of the normative warrant for a culpable agent's being harmed by being blamed.

As regards deserved blame so understood, the desert-base for a blameworthy act involves only salient features of *the agent* and *her act*, features that make the agent blameworthy for it. On the proposal I offered in the previous section, it is the freedom component identified within the desert base that does the work of placing squarely within the scope of the agent's direct control whether a blaming response is fitted for her manner of acting.

What animates contestants to the free will debate is the prospect that some harmful treatment or consequence delivered to a blameworthy agent could be normatively warranted as a response to her culpable conduct. For this reason, it is best to attend primarily to directed episodes of the reactive attitudes and instances of blaming. Tending just to these cases, we can ask what they involve and then think about whether the normative warrant for them and the freedom presuppositions bearing on them are or should be limited to basic desert.

5.4 Is Basically Deserved Blame Essential to Our Moral Responsibility Practices?

As noted, on my view, philosophers like Scanlon and Wallace operate within a shared domain of dispute between them and others regarding issues of *both* freedom and responsibility. But then the

THE FREE WILL DEBATE AND BASIC DESERT   113

question is, What is that shared domain? Does it provide the proper ties to the traditional free will debate? Freedoms, after all, comes in degrees, and some pose no metaphysical puzzles at all. I propose that the shared domain is the set of practices bearing upon our application of the concept of moral responsibility and, more directly to the point, our application of the concepts of blameworthiness and blame when we hold each other to account by means that are potentially harmful. If a theorist could offer an adequate competitor account of the norms governing our blaming practices, one that did not rely upon basic desert, and if the account on offer did not presuppose anything more than minor revisions to the practices themselves *while all the same relying upon robust freedom presuppositions*, then, it seems that they would after all be joining issue on a substantive philosophical matter regarding the metaphysics of agency and action.

As Pereboom sees it, a considerable range of our blaming practices presupposes the notion of basic desert. He writes,

> The free will skeptic will call into question any blaming practices that presuppose that the agent being blamed is morally responsible in the basic desert sense. Since much actual human behavior has this presupposition, any skeptical account of blame will be revisionary. (2013: 190)

Pereboom contends that our responsibility practices presuppose a normative warrant grounded in considerations of basic desert.[3] One way Pereboom *might* attempt to discard my proposal is to say that when we look to the practices themselves, they have built into them a presupposition of basic desert in such a way that we cannot identify the practices and then ask if there is some alternative

---

[3] Other philosophers, like G. Strawson (1986), also operate under the assumption that we can discern from our moral responsibility practices a commitment to the notion of something like basic desert.

114 CLARIFICATIONS AND FURTHER DEVELOPMENTS

normative warrant absent basic desert that could be used to underwrite them.

Were Pereboom to make this move, then on his proposal those like Scanlon and Wallace could not be offering a competitor account of those very same practices absent basic desert. Right out of the gates, they would be changing the subject. This, however, would be to assume not only that the pertinent practices have a presupposition of basic desert built into them, but that this presupposition also is *essential* to our understanding of those practices, and to, as Wallace might put it, ordinary participants' self-understanding. But this seems an implausible way to defend Pereboom's thesis. Do any of our moral practices have normative presuppositions essential to them so that *in principle* there cannot be alternative means of justifying those very practices?

A more promising rendering is as follows: Our moral responsibility practices are relatively plastic and do presume a notion of basic desert. Still, there are resources as part of the practice, and as part of the folk participants' self-understanding, for alternative norms which could also be brought to bear in a justification *for these very same practices*. Hence, all Pereboom targets in his skeptical assault on blame, and all he presumes to be essential to the free will debate, is one sort of normative warrant, one involving basic desert, for a set of practices; the practices themselves might remain, perhaps with some mild revisions, by alternative means of providing a normative warrant for them.

Manuel Vargas resists the very idea that we can discern in the practices themselves a presumption of basic desert built right in.

> Consider an ordinary case of judging that someone deserves blame. Suppose we judge that Fitzgerald deserves Jackie's blame for having an affair with Marilyn. On Pereboom's account, we are purportedly committed to (A) the "basic"-ness of Fitzgerald's deserving Jackie's blame—i.e., the desert base—is settled by features of Fitzgerald and the moral qualities of his action, and

THE FREE WILL DEBATE AND BASIC DESERT   115

(B) a desert base that cannot appeal to consequences, even indirectly.

But why think all of that? I find it more plausible to think that when we judge that Fitzgerald deserves Jackie's blame what we are mainly committing ourselves to is the idea that Fitzgerald has done something wrong, and that in light of that violation, blaming is called for. In making this judgment, we need not have any view one way or another about the particular details of why that blaming is called for. We must, of course, think that the blaming is in some way sanctioned or justified. However, it seems strange to suppose that we have worked out views about just how that sanctioning or justification would go. For ordinary practical purposes, all we need to know is that the agent has done something wrong and that something about that wrongdoing licenses blame. What that something comes to is, I think, not anything about which we have formed thoughts or strong convictions. Indeed, from the standpoint of our ordinary discourse and practical life, what is important is confidence that we are correct and justified in our first-order judgments. The justifiers and their precise nature are ordinarily of secondary and considerably lesser importance. (Vargas, 2013: 252–3)

Vargas has a point. Basic desert, rather than mere desert *simpliciter*, is after all an esoteric notion. Maybe the folk are not operating with anything that fancy. On the other hand, Pereboom might reasonably reply that many ordinary folk notions, like lying, involve complex concepts for which the folk would not be able to offer clear, theoretically lucid explanations or justifications. This is in no way evidence that the concepts are not operative in ordinary folk practices.[4] Given this difference between Vargas and Pereboom, it seems best just to grant this to Pereboom, even if Vargas is right to raise the worry. Let's assume for argument's sake that, as esoteric as

---

[4] In correspondence he suggested just this reply.

the concept of basic desert is, there is reason to think that the folk apply it in their ordinary moral responsibility practices, but that it is not essential to those practices.

Pereboom (2019) rejects my contention that we can find alternative justifications embedded in our practices that still presuppose a robust freedom condition. Moreover, he argues that we cannot treat our practices as the shared domain of dispute as I have proposed here. According to him, it as an open question whether there is some justification available to free will skeptics that could be used to support our practices as they are. If, for instance, the forward-looking best consequences for moral improvement of the sort Pereboom supports are achieved by our actual practices, then his skeptical position would be compatible with our actual practices.

> My position, accordingly, is that it's open that our actual practice of holding responsible, including our practice of justifying penalties, is in turn morally justifiable on the basis of consequentialist or contractualist considerations. I also think that this does not conflict with my incompatibilism. . . . Thus, I disagree with the claim that the shared domain of practices can play the key role in providing the substantive division between compatibilists and incompatibilists. (2019: 263)

Of course, in one clear sense Pereboom is right. This is an open question. Whether our actual practices, consistent with a free will skeptical thesis, have overall better consequences for moral improvement than any viable set that involves significant departure from these practices is an empirical question. (Although this is highly unlikely.) So, what's left to my contention that the shared domain of dispute is our actual practices?

Note that there are two ways to understand what is meant by "our actual practices." One leaves some flexibility for variation on the reasons or justifications we supply for forms of treatment, including the forms of treatment understood as directed blame.

THE FREE WILL DEBATE AND BASIC DESERT   117

Another treats the justificatory reasons offered as part of that mix. This, I take it, is what Pereboom has in mind by qualifying his claim to include "our practices of justifying penalties." In other words, if people make noises about (basic) desert when they blame or punish, or if somehow these considerations implicitly play a role in their deliberations, then that, too, is part of the practice. Understood in this way, a free will skeptic like Pereboom has to go fictionalist or plump for an error theory to preserve a justification for our practices as they are. Pereboom (2019: 262) quotes his early formulation of such an approach:

> One might propose that even if hard incompatibilism were true, it would still be best to behave as if people were morally responsible [in the basic desert sense]. Even if the claim that we are morally responsible cannot be justified, there may be a practical argument for nevertheless treating ourselves and others *as if it were true*. Dennett suggests a position of this kind:
>
>> Instead of investigating, endlessly, in an attempt to discover whether or not a particular trait is of someone's making—instead of trying to assay exactly to what degree a particular self is self-made—we simply hold people morally responsible for their conduct (within limits we take care not to examine too closely). And we are rewarded for adopting this strategy by the higher proportion of "responsible" behavior we thereby inculcate. (1984: 66)
>
> In the final analysis, whether Dennett is right would have to be decided by careful empirical investigation. (Pereboom, 2001: 156, emphasis added)

The cost of doing business this way is that our practices themselves will be misguided at the level of the first-order reasons people have for justifying their blaming and punishing practices.

118 CLARIFICATIONS AND FURTHER DEVELOPMENTS

I propose that in holding fixed our actual practices we allow variability in the justificatory reasons ordinary participants supply for those practices. These reasons should not be regarded as misguided or illusory bases for the practices, but as substantive normative grounds for our practices as they are. Do some of those competitor justifications—ones appealing to normative considerations that do not involve basic desert—occasion worries about free will?

5.5 Preserving the Free Will Debate in the Absence of Basic Desert

The question immediately before us is whether we can make sense of the traditional free will dispute without basic desert as the normative warrant *for these same practices* as just specified above. As a starting point, I offer a simple observation. If one attends just to the practices characteristic of directed blaming, there is no special reason to think that the freedom presuppositions are ineliminably tied to a normative requirement of basic desert. Implicit in the practices of blaming is, for instance, the presumption that a person under extreme duress does not act freely, nor does a person who is thoroughly deceived into acting contrary to what she would judge best. Similarly, a person is not free if she acts from a severe compulsion or some forms of extreme delusion. Her freedom seems compromised if she suffers from various motivational deficiencies, such as severe depression, and so forth. Likewise, it seems that she is not free if she has no other option than to act in just one way. (Of course, there is much dispute over whether this is true.) Our practices bear out these presuppositions. And when then we *do* blame and take it that we are justified in doing so (by whatever means), what seems implicit in our activity of blaming is that an agent who is blameworthy acted freely.

Can't we find pertinent alternative normative grounds for blaming other than basic desert? To be more precise, can't we find

THE FREE WILL DEBATE AND BASIC DESERT 119

alternative norms that preserve the sense that a requirement for justified directed blaming or punishment is that an agent is free, and free in such a way that can give rise to the problems traditionally associated with the freedom of the will? Is basic desert really essential here? Must we have, for instance, a judgment that it is intrinsically or noninstrumentally good that a blameworthy person be harmed by being blamed? Absent this, can we not link blameworthiness properly to a rich freedom requirement? Reflect upon the preceding treatment of blame in Chapter 2, and then our formulation of basic in contrast with nonbasic desert as cast in Chapter 3. There does not seem to be anything about desert's being *basic* that gives it a monopoly on a strong freedom requirement on practices that involve our blaming each other. Or, at any rate, this is my challenge to those who would resist. The burden is on them to state precisely why basic desert has this feature that other justifications for blame cannot provide.

While Pereboom and other likeminded theorists want to partition off from relevance to the traditional free will debate any theory of normativity pertaining to moral responsibility that attempts to make do without the notion of basic desert, I propose a case-by-case approach. Whether any candidate theory ought to be taken seriously in the context of the traditional free will debate needs to be assessed in terms of the details of that theory in relation to the freedom offered along with it. What is required to join issue with those incompatibilists like Pereboom is simply a matter of whether the freedom up for consideration is a sort about which one can render intelligible the metaphysical worries that have been at the heart of the free will debate.

Clearly, there are proposals regarding the justification of our blaming practices that are so easy to satisfy that there is no reason to think there are any puzzling metaphysical worries to address. Smart's (1963) straight utilitarian proposal was one, which was a proposal in the fashion of others like Schlick's (1939). These were cast in terms of simple influenceability for the aim of social benefit.

120 CLARIFICATIONS AND FURTHER DEVELOPMENTS

Pereboom also seems correct about Bok's (1998) proposal. Bok cast hers in terms of a practical standpoint in which we are able to assess our choices in terms of our own moral improvement. But there are other theoretical options that track more delicately the freedom presuppositions of our actual moral practices. Let's consider three.

5.5.1 Lenman's Contractualist Account of Nonbasic Desert

James Lenman (2006) has argued on contractualist grounds that we have reason to agree to treat others as accountable for their conduct insofar as it affords us a social environment for being treated as creatures with dignity. This exposes us to risks, including the potential pain of others' blame. Here, the risk and the harms are not justified in terms of basic desert. However the details are ironed out, Lenman treats this justification as one that, roughly speaking, supports our moral responsibility practices *as they are*. Hence, they should also give rise to the presuppositions about free agency that in turn can give rise to worries about whether anyone is free in the requisite way if they are unable to do otherwise, or are not the ultimate originators of our acts, and so forth.

Dana Nelkin (2019a) rightly worries that certain appeals to contractualist considerations might be too revisionary to do the work I seek here. She cites T. M. Scanlon's (2008) contractualist proposal as unabashedly revisionary, and so inconsistent with my own contention that contractualist resources could be used to justify our actual moral responsibility practices and not some revisionary variation on them. I'll grant that she is right about Scanlon (of 2008). But she also includes Lenman's contractualist proposal. About his proposal, she writes,

while there are structural similarities in the kinds of sanctioning responses licensed by contractualist views such as Lenman's that

THE FREE WILL DEBATE AND BASIC DESERT   121

have parallels to excuse and justification when it comes to moral responsibility practices, it is less clear that such pictures include *blaming* in a sense that is closely related to responses like the reactive attitudes as seems an important part of our practice. . . . The reactive attitudes arguably commit us to ideas of desert, and the case for this is, at the least, more plausible than that they can be licensed by, or are otherwise essentially connected with, a contractualist understanding. (2019a: 270)

In a footnote (270, n. 5), Nelkin further comments on Lenman's proposal, whereby contractors would adopt principles "very much like" ours in terms of excuses and exemptions. But Nelkin then expresses skepticism that these principles would be able to account for our actual practices with "all of their current content" in a way that avoids the notion of desert.

In reply, Lenman *is* committed to a desert thesis. It is just that it is not basic. So, one way to appreciate what he is up to is that he provides normative resources of a contractualist sort to help justify our persistence in drawing upon the reactive attitudes we have, and so also on thoughts about what agents deserve.[5] For instance, about the reactive attitudes, Lenman writes,

The difference between those Human Beings who are preeminently worthy of love and respect and those Human Beings who are preeminently unworthy of love and respect are too central and important a governing feature of human life and human relationships for the reactive attitudes involved in recognition of such worthiness and unworthiness to be, either ideally or in fact, open to abandonment. (2006: 19–20)

Lenman considers Scanlon's (1998: 294) reasons for rejecting a desert thesis, which include the consideration that, as Lenman puts

---

[5] This would amount to what Rawls (1971) might call "post-institutional desert."

122 CLARIFICATIONS AND FURTHER DEVELOPMENTS

it, "when people morally screw up" one might think, "there but for the grace of God go I" (2006: 23). About such a thought, Lenman contends that, on the account of autonomy he endorses and given his contractualist proposal, for Human Beings, "it is plausibly reasonable to think this gamble is a worthwhile and reasonable one for them to make" (23). In short, our commitment to desert is justified on contractualist grounds despite the risk of unwelcome costs that we are exposed to by embracing it.

To be fair, I take Nelkin's point to be that, even if this is so, the contractualist anchor used to justify the role of our reactive attitudes is likely not to preserve in full our intuitions and practices that are *directly* about what culpable wrongdoers deserve. Hence, her remark about "all of their current content." Fair enough. But this leads to a second point. What I contend, and what Nelkin rightly interprets me as contending, is that our actual practices can remain our actual practices while at the same time undergoing some minor alterations. This is needed to avoid the charge, as I have just argued, that any variation amounts to changing the subject in the fashion of a revisionist proposal. If so, these very practices might be plastic enough to remain *those very same practices* even if some of the actual aspects of them could be shed or treated as ancillary. With contractualist resources we might be able to find a justification for our actual blaming practices, including some notion of what agents deserve, where this justification requires a strong freedom condition but does not invoke the notion of *basic* desert.

5.5.2 Scanlon's Non–Desert-Based Contractualist Proposal

Now consider Scanlon's earlier (1998) view as it bears on what he called *substantive responsibility*. Substantive responsibility as Scanlon understands it concerns judgments about what people

THE FREE WILL DEBATE AND BASIC DESERT   123

are (and are not) required to do for each other, as these flow from his proposed contractualist resources (248). On his view, these judgments are best justified in light of the value of choice, since we have reason to want outcomes for responsible agents to depend on the way they respond to alternatives (257). Note that Scanlon commits to a requirement of avoidability for substantive responsibility. The relevant sense of avoidability, he argues, is to be understood in terms of agents being offered reasonable options in light of the expectations of the moral community. An example Scanlon offers is of a reckless woman who is harmed by ignoring adequate warnings and thus being exposed to toxic chemicals at a clean-up site. According to Scanlon, she bears the burdens of the harms done to her and so is responsible for them because she cannot reasonably issue complaints against the community. Conditions were created for her to be able to avoid the bad outcome. Scanlon then argues that incompatibilist worries are misplaced because the relevant sense of avoidability is settled by the community's conditions for offering alternative means of acting (262).

Admittedly, it appears that Scanlon's view *supports* Pereboom's contention. The thin sense of freedom operative in Scanlon's account of substantive responsibility is far too weak to have any relevance to the traditional free will debate—a point Scanlon himself seems keen to make. I agree. But I agree only insofar as we simply accept Scanlon's own reasoning about the case and about the conditions for substantive responsibility. Do they involve no measure of condemnation or censure of a sort that involves pertinent harms of blaming (as set out in Chapter 3)? If so, we can grant Scanlon his dismissal of the relevance of any robust freedom constraint. But if we are in the arena of a kind of responsibility that involves accountability proper—complete with harmful condemnatory responses to wrongdoers—then his proposal is far less convincing. I advise resisting Scanlon here while still preserving his overall non–desert-based contractualist rationale. One might do so

124 CLARIFICATIONS AND FURTHER DEVELOPMENTS

by arguing that offering citizens options to avoid a toxic site by voluntary means is regarded as reasonable because it is *also* assumed that these individuals are able to exercise their own freedom to comply with or defy the posted warnings. Hence, a pertinent ability to do otherwise *is* a part of the mix in a contractualist and non–desert-based justification for this notion of substantive responsibility. If so, it is an open question what sort of metaphysical requirements are presupposed by this sense of freedom.

5.5.3 Wallace's Appeal to Fairness Rather Than Desert

What of Wallace's proposal? In developing his view, Wallace explicitly rejects an alternative proposal, the economy of threats strategy of the Smart or Schlick variety, because

> in making deterministic worlds so obviously safe for responsibility, the strategy deprives itself of the resources for explaining the attraction of alternative, incompatibilist views. One might say that the economy of threats approach renders compatibilism so plausible that it cannot be correct as an account of what we are actually doing when we hold people morally responsible. (1994: 58)

So, by his own lights, Wallace intends to advance a view, unlike the economy of threats view, meant to speak *directly* to the considerations of free agency of concern to incompatibilists. According to him, the normative warrant for blaming is a matter of whether it is fair to blame a wrongdoer. Given this, an incompatibilist might argue that it is not fair unless an agent who acted wrongly was able to avoid doing what she did, and so a proper understanding of this condition shows it to be incompatible with determinism. Of course, Wallace resists this incompatibilist move (103–9). But the point is that his proposed normative warrant, a

THE FREE WILL DEBATE AND BASIC DESERT   125

non–desert-based warrant, still leaves it as *an open question* what sort of freedom is required and whether it is compatible with determinism.

Some might protest, arguing that fairness entails desert. Indeed, Wallace considers the possibility that incompatibilists conceive of the free will debate by "relying upon a notion of fairness as *desert*" (1994: 106). However, he rejects this approach in favor of one that he contends is distinct from it. He writes,

> But desert does not seem to be the only concept of fairness that the incompatibilist could be relying upon. A second candidate is the concept of fairness as *reasonableness*. Consider an example: A young child does something morally wrong—lies to her parents, say, about whether she should clean her room. There may well be good reasons to scold or punish the child in this situation, but I take it we would think it unfair to hold the child fully responsible for her deed, in the way we would ordinarily hold morally responsible an adult who lies for personal advantage. It would not be unfair to the child in the sense that we would be failing to play by the rules of some practice from which we ourselves had gained, nor in the sense that the child does not deserve to be punished or blamed. Rather, it would be fair roughly in the sense that it would be unreasonable to treat the child fully account in the first place. Similarly, the incompatibilist might try to show that it would be unfair to hold people responsible if determinism is true, roughly in the sense that it would be unreasonable for us to hold people morally accountable if they lack strong freedom of the will. (108)[6]

Naturally, this does not settle matters. Wallace might be wrong. His appeal to reasonableness might after all entail desert. Or fairness so understood might so closely track desert in all the judgments

---

[6] Wallace cites Morton White (1979) as one who explicitly appeals to reasonableness "as the moral basis of the incompatibilist position" (Wallace, 1994: 108, n. 33).

126 CLARIFICATIONS AND FURTHER DEVELOPMENTS

that it issues that it will yield an extensional equivalence. It could then be protested that, even if it is distinct, the difference is trivial. Momentarily I'll return to considerations of fairness and explore these possibilities.

5.5.4 Desiderata for Preserving Free Will Absent Basic Desert

Reflecting on the range of proposals from Smart, Schlick, Bok, Lenman, Wallace, and Scanlon, here are three desiderata for an alternative to a basic desert-based theory of moral responsibility, one that could fill the bill in resisting Pereboom and his allies regarding the relevance of free will:

First, any candidate theory must be able to explain our *actual* moral responsibility practices in the current complexity. These will include our blaming and praising practices; our practices of offering excuses, justifications, and exemptions, as well as mitigating considerations; and our practices of apologizing, forgiving, atoning, and so on.

Second, any conditions of freedom specified in a theory of responsibility must be true to the best descriptions of the complexity of our own agency as we know it to be—at least when we are operating at considerably better than merely a minimal level. We know that agents have powers of reflective self-control, that they have the ability to adopt higher-order attitudes to and evaluations of their own actions and motives, are responsive to a complex range of reasons, are able to draw on resources in the face of temptation to act contrary to better judgment, are able to do otherwise at least in some sense of the expression, and so on. Any theory that would find an "adequate" freedom to justify some species of blaming practices, and in which the freedom fell far shy of capturing these features of our agency, would just be too impoverished to have any bearing on the traditional free will debate.

THE FREE WILL DEBATE AND BASIC DESERT   127

Third, recall the earlier discussion of grounding (Section 2). I proposed that those committed to a basic desert thesis make basic desert essential to the free will problem because they assume this gives rise to a strong grounding role for exercises of free will. In deference to this rationale, the third desideratum might be put this way: The freedom on offer by any competitor theory of the normative basis for our moral responsibility practice must afford the agent, by an exercising of her own free agency, a significant role to play in grounding her being blameworthy and an apt target of blame, where this blame involves a liability to harm. In some manner, that freedom must make it so that, at least to some nontrivial degree, it *is* up to her, by exercising her free agency, whether she is blameworthy and to blame for how she acts. Admittedly, when the normative warrant for an agent's blameworthiness depends on considerations that include others' interests, or principles others rationally ought to adopt, she is in *less* control of her status as blameworthy as in comparison with how she would be were the grounds for her blameworthiness rooted in basic desert. On these competitor proposals, more of the grounding would be distributed in ways that are out of her control. That's undeniable. She would therefore indeed have more control over her status as blameworthy were the normative warrant limited to basic desert. This might after all show why some find basic desert a more palatable theoretical option. But so long as the control required of her on a competitor proposal is not *expunged*, so that at least some element of the grounding of her being blameworthy is up to her, it remains credible to treat the freedom at issue as bearing on the traditional free will debate.

5.6 Further Reflections on Fairness

Both Nelkin (2019a) and Pereboom (2019) have raised concerns about my contention that we can draw upon fairness as a

128 CLARIFICATIONS AND FURTHER DEVELOPMENTS

substantive competitor notion to desert in this dialectical context, in the fashion of Wallace (1994). Because their challenges are especially insightful, I return to the topic to consider the matter more carefully.

5.6.1 Nelkin on Fairness

Nelkin rightly points out that, in the context of questions of just distributions, some distributions might count as fair that would not count as deserved. The unlucky lorry driver whose negligence results in killing a dog might fairly receive a sanction even when the lucky lorry driver would not. Yet if both acted in the same negligent ways and the difference in outcome was only due to luck, both might deserve equally unwelcome treatment (Nelkin, 2019a: 270–1). However, when considering fairness understood as reasonableness, she writes,

> Wallace (1994) appeals to a notion of fairness as "reasonableness," or as what it is reasonable to hold people to account for (108). This notion does not obviously sort cases differently from desert, and so appears to track blameworthiness. At this point, however, important questions arise: Does reasonableness itself depend on desert? Can we say more about what reasonableness comes to so that it offers a distinctive content? (271)

Nelkin takes it as a virtue of the proposal that an appeal to fairness-as-reasonableness would track our evaluations of blameworthiness as desert does. Her question, however, is whether it depends on it. And her perfectly understandable challenge to those like Wallace or me is to say more about reasonableness to help show how it really is a normative resource that does not tacitly invoke desert. If it can be shown that it does not, then it seems she would grant that we have an interesting substantive normative thesis that is a competitor to

THE FREE WILL DEBATE AND BASIC DESERT   129

basic desert, one that does after all presuppose a robust freedom requirement.

In reply to Nelkin, return to the passage from Wallace quoted above.[7] Wallace's most basic insight is that it is unfair to make demands of someone if it is unreasonable to expect that they comply with the demands. One way such a demand might be unreasonable is that the demand is not the sort that can be justified. It'd be great if every time a good friend showed up at my house they hand-washed and waxed my car. But this is not reasonable to demand, and, insofar as such demands are unjustifiable, one could not be expected to comply with them. That is a kind of reasonability, and it might very well entail that such a demand would be objectionable on grounds of desert. But Wallace's case is that of a child whom, we might think, simply lacks the capacities to comply with pertinent moral demands. In this case, it is not just that it is unreasonable to expect that she complies; it is unreasonable to expect that she is *able* to comply. She's just not psychically equipped as of yet to execute such tasks reliably. Wallace contends, and I agree, that this might be a constraint on fair treatment that does not invoke considerations about desert. Admittedly, when dealing with basic normative concepts like these, some will protest. I am not confident much more can be said to dissuade someone who would consider the case and insist that the basis for unreasonableness in this case does after all rely upon or entail some judgment of desert, as Nelkin is worried that it might.

It may also be that whether it is easy to pry these notions apart turns on substantive normative commitments that I have not thus far invoked in this context. In particular, if desert entails noninstrumental goodness (as I argued in Chapter 3), it might be easier to see how the case of the child appeals to a notion of reasonableness that is distinct from desert. The claim of reasonableness

---

[7] My reply to Nelkin here departs from my earlier effort (2019b). I depart because, well, I was wrong about how I was thinking of fairness, desert, and justice.

130 CLARIFICATIONS AND FURTHER DEVELOPMENTS

here is not at all about the absence of a noninstrumental good in punishing that would be present if the child would be able to comply. It is just that if she were able to comply, it would be fair to make these moral demands of her and to dole out reprimands or punishments for failures to comply. If then desert in these contexts does, but fairness does not, entail noninstrumental goodness, we might have a way to support my reply to Nelkin. But in fairness to Nelkin, it bears noting that there are two ways my current proposal could go wrong. First, one might hold, in opposition to my prior arguments, that desert as it pertains to blame and punishment does not entail any noninstrumental good. If so, then desert and fairness would be on equal footing, at least in this respect. Another option suggested by Pereboom (2019: 261) is instead to argue that fairness in a basic form, like desert, *does* entail noninstrumental goods.

I leave the matter unsettled and grant that this remains an open question. Nevertheless, I hope to have responded to Nelkin's challenge to say more to help us understand how it might be that fairness as reasonableness does not after all presuppose desert.

5.6.2 Pereboom on Fairness

Pereboom's challenge is interestingly different from Nelkin's. Nelkin treats it as a virtue of my proposal that fairness would track our evaluation of blameworthiness just as desert does; she just asks for some explanation of why the one does not actually entail the other. But Pereboom instead treats it as a vice. Even if distinct, Pereboom suggests, fairness in a particular domain and desert come to the same thing in terms of their extension. If so, he argues, it is a hollow victory to contend that fairness supplies an alternative normative basis to desert for blameworthiness. Reflecting on basic desert and basic fairness, he writes,

THE FREE WILL DEBATE AND BASIC DESERT   131

These notions are indeed distinct. Suppose all the people God creates are initially granted the same level of talent and material goods. That distribution seems, *ceteris paribus*, basically fair, yet not basically deserved. However, suppose we set aside fairness of distribution, and restrict our attention to what might be fair or deserved in the domain of moral responsibility: blame and praise, penalties and rewards. In this domain, the central cases of what is deserved are instances of what it is appropriate to impose due to wrongdoing, and to bestow due to doing what's right. Deserved penalties are appropriately imposed due to wrongdoing; deserved rewards are appropriately bestowed due to doing what's right. But similarly, in the domain of moral responsibility, fair penalties are appropriately imposed, and fair rewards are appropriately bestowed. Accordingly, I propose that, in this domain, what's basically deserved and basically fair coincide.

This proposal would be falsified if there are impositions of penalties that are intuitively basically fair but not basically deserved. No such cases come to mind....

Thus, I propose that, in the domain of moral responsibility, what's basically fair to impose or bestow coincides with what's basically deserved, and furthermore, in this domain, justifications that invoke basic fairness are not distinct from those that invoke basic desert. On this picture, the sense of moral responsibility as the control required for basic fairness does not qualify as distinct way to ground the debate between compatibilists and incompatibilists; that is, a way distinct from its basic desert counterpart. Moreover, even if a nuanced way of distinguishing basic fairness and basic desert in the domain of moral responsibility turns out to be plausible, the two notions are so similar that I could take on board the claim that the debate can be made substantive by either of these notions without this constituting a significant change to my view. (2019: 261)

132   CLARIFICATIONS AND FURTHER DEVELOPMENTS

Pereboom offers two challenges in this passage. First, in the domain of moral responsibility, what's basically fair and what's basically deserved coincide, so the result I defend on Wallace's behalf is trivial. Second, even if there is *some* difference, there is no threat to Pereboom's free will skeptical thesis. I'll take each in turn.

Pereboom considers beings created by God wherein claims of fair distribution come apart from claims of desert. But when it comes to appropriately imposing penalties for this same population, there are no differences between evaluations in terms of fairness or desert. Pereboom then recognizes that his proposal would be falsified if there would be penalties that would be fair but not deserved. I'll not offer such a case here. But note that his proposal would also be falsified if there were cases wherein a penalty is deserved but not fair. Here is a case that, I contend, meets Pereboom's challenge. Consider another sort of case involving God's creation, but not with several individuals. Instead, make it just one. God creates a world with only one agent, Frank Zappa, imbued with talents and abilities and motives to do various things, some of which would please God and some that would defy him. Suppose Zappa does various things, some of them pleasing to God, some of them offensive. They include great works of art and, say, defiling some of God's natural beauty. It is plausible to think that if God were to praise him and blame him, reward and punish him, it would be deserved. But would it be fair to Zappa? Perhaps intuitions differ here, but it seems to me that without a comparative class of agents who might or might not be treated likewise for similar conduct, judgments of fairness are misplaced.

But now, isn't this just the sort of nuanced effort to distinguish different normative bases for justified blame and punishment that Pereboom grants he can take on board? Suppose both, though distinct, generate metaphysical worries about the freedom presuppositions implicit in them. My reply to Pereboom's contention here is to insist that this is no challenge to my thesis. Here he grants my point. If Pereboom's skeptical diagnosis applies to

THE FREE WILL DEBATE AND BASIC DESERT   133

the freedom presuppositions implicit in basic desert, I contend that there is no reason to think it would not apply equally well to similar presuppositions of freedom implicit in fairness as I have attempted to understand it here. What's key is just that there are indeed alternatives to basic desert that can play the relevant normative role in helping to formulate the metaphysical problem of the freedom of the will. Naturally, as a compatibilist, I am not prepared to grant Pereboom's free will skeptical diagnosis framed in terms of basic desert. And so likewise I am not prepared to grant this when framed in terms of fairness. All I contend is that *if* we treat a resolution to the free will problem as an open question, then we can nevertheless frame it in ways that set basic desert aside. An appeal to fairness is one way to do so.

5.7 Conclusion

A familiar divide among philosophers working on the topic of free will is between those who explain free will in terms of the freedom or control condition for moral responsibility and those who reject this way of theorizing. Some argue that we should understand free will in a way that is independent of considerations of moral responsibility (e.g., Clarke, 2003; Ginet, 1990; van Inwagen, 2008; Vihvelin, 2013). Others, however, explain free will in terms of the control or freedom condition for moral responsibility (e.g., Fischer and Ravizza, 1998; Haji, 1998; McKenna, 2013b, Mele, 2006; Pereboom, 2001, 2014; Sartorio, 2016). I have no interest in entering this debate here. My concern in this chapter is exclusively with philosophers who account for free will in terms of the conditions for moral responsibility.

I have argued that, for those philosophers who theorize about free will in terms of moral responsibility, they are wrong to limit their view only to accounts of moral responsibility that involve basic desert. This is not a trivial result. To restrict the free will

134 CLARIFICATIONS AND FURTHER DEVELOPMENTS

debate to one particular normative ground for justifying blame and punishment risks rendering the free will debate irrelevant. Why? It might be that basic desert is a benighted notion regardless of the freedom requirements for it, at least when it comes to deserving any of the harms that come with blame or punishment. Maybe, for instance, no person for any reason could ever deserve to be harmed unless it is in the service of some other good—in which case the desert would not be basic. Or maybe basic desert does entail the noninstrumental goodness of a culpable person receiving harmful treatment. But maybe it is after all an unacceptable entailment that it could ever be noninstrumentally good that a person be harmed. So, these philosophers should modify how they formulate their accounts of free will. They should not account for free will in such a way that it is limited *just* to the type of moral responsibility that is basic-desert-entailing. Instead, they should identify free will with the sort of freedom that as it happens *is* implicated in basic desert. But they should allow that that sort of freedom is not limited just to notions of moral responsibility that involve basic desert.

These results bear significantly on the overall project of this book. While my goal is to explain the role of desert in our theory of moral responsibility, I do not necessarily mean to endorse basic desert unequivocally. I only mean to understand it and offer the best case for it. There are viable normative bases for our full suite of moral responsibility practices besides those limited to basic desert. These include bases that bring with them robust freedom conditions of the sort at issue in metaphysical disputes about the freedom of the will.

6

Fittingness as a Pitiful Intellectualist Trinket?

In diagnosing the alleged failure of his libertarian adversaries, P. F. Strawson (1962) once remarked that they sought to fill a gap in their proposal with an intuition of fittingness, which he characterized as a pitiful intellectualist trinket. Really? Pitiful? Despite my great admiration for Strawson's essay, I've always found that particular remark to be a cheap shot, an especially ungracious dismissal of what instead should have been charitably explored. Indeed, I regard it as the worst thing about that otherwise inspiring essay. In this chapter, my primary goal is to resist Strawson's caricature of fittingness and show that, at least in the domain with which he was most directly concerned—moral responsibility—fittingness plays an important role. This will prove useful, since thus far I have invoked the notion of fittingness at various junctures but have not paused to clarify it.

I will proceed in three steps. First, I will offer a general characterization of fittingness, one that applies to a range of domains, such as the credible, desirable, and humorous, though my interest will be limited to moral responsibility. Second, I will scrutinize Strawson's disparaging assessment of fittingness and consider what specifically about the debate among his contemporaries might have led him to be so harsh about appealing to that relation. It is illuminating that at roughly the same time Strawson published "Freedom and

An earlier draft of this chapter was originally published as "Fittingness as a Pitiful Intellectualist Trinket," in C. Howard and R. Rowland, eds., *Fittingness* (Oxford University Press, 2022: 329–55).

Responsibility and Desert. Michael McKenna, Oxford University Press. © Oxford University Press 2024.
DOI: 10.1093/9780197679999.003.0006

136 CLARIFICATIONS AND FURTHER DEVELOPMENTS

Resentment" (1962), in "Justice and Personal Desert" (1963) Joel Feinberg instead explored the intimate link between fittingness and desert, including the arena of desert that was of central concern to Strawson, rewards and punishments as well as praise and blame. Why such different responses? Third, building on what we can learn from Strawson and Feinberg, I will turn to contemporary debates about free will and moral responsibility, showing what role fittingness currently plays in this domain. In doing so, I will argue that desert as it bears on blame and punishment is best construed as a species of fittingness, but also, if no one deserves blame or punishment because no one has free will, certain responses to wrongdoers will remain fitting. In this way, fittingness is a more basic and encompassing relation.

6.1 Fittingness

Consider first appropriateness, or aptness, as featured in the following principle proposed by R. Jay Wallace in *Responsibility and the Moral Sentiments*:

> (N) S is morally responsible (for an action x) if and only if it would be appropriate to hold s morally responsible (for action x). (1994: 91)

Wallace argues that the burden of a theory of responsibility is to "specify the norms by reference to which the appropriateness of that stance [of holding morally responsible] is to be gauged" (92). Treating correctness in similar fashion, Wallace remarks,

> The terms "appropriate" and "correct" are bland and noncommittal terms of general appraisal. To render the normative interpretation [(N)] more determinate, it will be necessary to specify particular substantive norms by reference to which the question

FITTINGNESS   137

of the appropriateness of holding people responsible might be answered. (92)

I understand the terms "apt," "appropriate," and "correct" as Wallace does. And I will treat "fittingness" and "fit" as terms that name a distinct, substantive normative specification of appropriateness.[1] So, where Wallace himself unpacks appropriateness as it figured in (N) in terms of fairness (1994), we might consider fittingness as a competitor proposal in a theory of moral responsibility, as David Shoemaker (2015, 2017b) has recently argued. For those who would balk at this proposal, note that some think of desert as a species of fittingness (Feinberg, 1963; McKenna, 2019a, 2022a), and while it might on its face seem unsatisfying to account for the normative basis for holding morally responsible exclusively in terms of fittingness, it is regarded by many as canonical do so in terms of desert (e.g., Carlsson, 2017; Clarke, 2013, 2016; Feinberg, 1963; McCormick, 2022; McKenna, 2012, 2019a, 2020; Nelkin, 2013; Pereboom, 2001, 2014; Scanlon, 2008, 2013).

So, what is fittingness? Fittingness identifies a distinctive—*sui generis*—rational relation that fits a response to a particular object in such a way that the response accurately represents its object. Hence, desire is a fitting response to the desirable just in case the object is desirable—and, moreover, the desire accurately represents that aspects of the object in virtue of which it is desirable.[2] A similar gloss applies when we say that humor is a fitting response to the humorous, belief is a fitting response to the believable, fear a fitting

---

[1] See Feinberg (1970: 56–7), who also clearly is thinking of appropriateness as Wallace does. Others (e.g., Howard, 2018) treat "apt" and "appropriate" as synonyms for "fit" and "fittingness." As these are terms of art, I do not think there is a substantive dispute here. However, because in philosophical discussions "appropriateness" is used so liberally, it seems wise to reserve "fit" and "fittingness" as naming a more precise normative relation.

[2] Desiring a good piece of cheesecake or a good shag are quite different, and the desires best be suited for their objects. Desiring a good piece of cheesecake by modes suited for a good shag is ample reason to seek therapy.

138 CLARIFICATIONS AND FURTHER DEVELOPMENTS

response to the fearsome, and so on. So, too, on such a proposal, and more directly to the issue of moral responsibility, blame is a fitting response to the blameworthy, praise is a fitting response to the praiseworthy, and an emotion such as guilt is a fitting response to the fact that one is guilty.

Fittingness also supplies a distinctive sort of normative force, varying across different domains. It assesses its object by reference to standards of evaluation internal to its domain (cf. Feinberg, on desert 1970: 61). In doing so, it supplies reasons for distinctive responses expressive of the appraisals it features. Thus, a morally offensive joke can be positively evaluated for being humorous insofar as it is fitting to be amused by it—because it really is funny—even if a moral assessment is negative (e.g., see D'Arms and Jacobson, 2000). Likewise, my belief that my son thinks his father is a tool is fitting in light of my credible evidence. This is so despite my desiring that he does not think this. Any reasons supplied by my desire that he not think of me in this way have no bearing on it being fitting that I believe this, what with all his eye-rolling and so on.

Reasons supplied by considerations of fittingness are *pro tanto* and cannot assure all-things-considered reasons to respond as fittingness counsels (cf. Feinberg on desert, 1970: 60). So, for instance, the morally offensive features of a joke could outweigh the *pro tanto* reasons for fittingly finding it funny. Of course, that cuts both ways. Maybe sometimes the reasons of funniness outweigh the moral reasons not to do so. After all, maybe the joke was very funny and the moral considerations were not that weighty.

This accounts for what are often referred to as *wrong kinds of reasons* (cf. Feinberg on desert, 1970: 59). The morally offensive nature of a joke is a wrong kind of reason to conclude that the joke is not funny, and the undesirability of my belief that my son thinks I am a tool is the wrong kind of reason for me not to believe this. Wrong kinds of reasons, then, are unfitting. Yet such reasons can bear *either positively or negatively* on the all-things-considered reasons to respond or refrain from responding in accord with fitting reasons. That wrong kinds of reasons can play a supporting role in relation to fitting reasons often goes unnoticed. While there can be moral reasons not to respond to a humorous joke with laughter, there can also be moral reasons *to* so respond. It might signal a much-needed expression of solidarity, for instance.

The preceding point has special significance for those working on moral responsibility who are impressed by Strawson's (1962) own reference to wrong kinds of reasons. Strawson scolded his compatibilist contemporaries who favored utilitarian theories more generally for justifying our costly practices of blaming and punishing exclusively in terms of social utility. These sorts of consequentialist considerations were, Strawson complained, the wrong kinds of reasons for our practices of blaming and punishing. This was key to Strawson's own efforts to do better. But of course, reasons of utility—at least in central cases—often *favor* our persisting in blaming and punishing those whom it is, by the standards Strawson endorsed, *appropriate* to blame or punish. Strawson even went out of his way to emphasize that there was no reason to dispute that utility has some important justificatory role: "It is far from wrong to emphasize the efficacy of all those practices which express or manifest our moral attitudes, in regulating behaviour in ways considered desirable" (1962, as reprinted in Watson (2003: 93).

Here, I propose one further feature of fittingness. Fittingness fits a response to its objects in a case-specific way. It tailors proper responses to instances in a manner that defies appeal to general principles or algorithms. For instance, as I have already noted (in Chapters 3 and 4), a conversational reply to an interlocutor can be fitting or unfitting. That evaluation can only be settled by the particular meaning of an interlocutor's conversational contribution within the context of the assumptions shared in *that* conversation. This is also borne out by considering belief. If p is believable or credible, then believing that p is fitting. Note just how case-specific that relation of fit is. The accurate representation involves believing that p is manifested in the myriad particular sentences a believer

140 CLARIFICATIONS AND FURTHER DEVELOPMENTS

would be willing to assent to in virtue of her belief that p, and in the inferences a rational believer would take to be licensed by the content of p rather than some other equally believable proposition q. Indeed, we can get even more case-specific than that. Two believers, S and R with nonoverlapping sets of beliefs, might both come to believe p, but given S's other beliefs where they differ from R's, S might be licensed in making inferences unavailable to R. So, too, for R: R might be licensed in making inferences unavailable to S. The particular way S's or R's belief that p is fitting will thus vary. To the best of my knowledge, this case-specific feature highlighted here is not explicitly recognized among philosophers who make use of fittingness. Nevertheless, my strong suspicion is that this further feature is often implicit in the way fittingness is used (e.g., see Feinberg, 1963).[3]

This completes my presentation of fittingness. I offer one preliminary remark regarding its application in the arena of moral responsibility. Clearly, one way to unpack Wallace's principle (N) is in terms of desert. Below we will explore the relationship between fittingness and desert. At this point, all I note is that every point identified so far regarding a feature of fittingness *also applies to desert*, at least as it is used by philosophers like Joel Feinberg (1963). This is key, and will figure crucially in subsequent discussion.

6.2 Feinberg and Strawson on Fittingness and Our Moral Responsibility Responses

Now consider first Feinberg's and then Strawson's mention of fittingness in those two prominent papers from the early 1960s. Bear in mind that Feinberg's focus was importantly different. He was interested in an analysis of desert itself and in its application to a range of domains, including awards and prizes, assignments of grades, and reparation, as well as issues bearing directly on moral

---

[3] On this point, I am indebted to conversations with Mark Timmons.

FITTINGNESS 141

responsibility—praise and blame, and reward and punishment. He didn't mess with the metaphysics of free will. Strawson made specific mention of fittingness only as it bore on a particular metaphysical solution to the free will problem, one supporting a libertarian diagnosis. Thus, any putative relation between fittingness and moral responsibility for Strawson was only by way of his philosophical adversaries' linking moral responsibility to a particular solution to the free will problem. What I now want to show is that, in contrast with Strawson's disparaging reference, Feinberg's edifying appeal to fittingness to help understand desert was available to Strawson. Indeed, appreciating this helps us with an interpretive problem in understanding Strawson. Charitably construed, Strawson was, in all but name, *embracing* a relation of fittingness—even if suggesting the label might have driven him to a state of apoplexy.

6.2.1 Feinberg on Fittingness

In arguing that utility is not a desert basis for deserved treatment,[4] Feinberg noted that reasonable people "naturally entertain certain responsive attitudes toward various actions, qualities, and achievements" (1970: 81), and he treated these as the proper candidates for deserved responses. Included in his list of responsive attitudes were two that were central to Strawson's focus, gratitude and resentment. Each kind of response, Feinberg contended, has its own appropriate target, and these can be assessed by standards internal to a domain. Comparing these judgments to aesthetic judgments, he wrote,

> If this is so, then the kind of propriety characteristic of personal desert is not only to be contrasted . . . with qualification under a

[4] Just as Strawson argued that utility was not a proper basis for our blame-and-praise-constituting reactive attitudes.

142   CLARIFICATIONS AND FURTHER DEVELOPMENTS

rule or regulation; it is also to be likened to, or even identified with, a kind of "fittingness" between one person's actions or qualities and another person's responsive attitudes. This suggests in turn that responsive attitudes are the basic things persons deserve and the "modes of treatment" are deserved only in a derivative way, insofar perhaps as they are the natural or convenient means of expressing the morally fitting attitudes. That punishment, for example, might be deserved by the criminal only because it is the customary way of expressing the resentment or reprobation he "has coming." (Feinberg, 1963, as appearing in 1970: 82)

Note two things about this passage, each of which is crucial for what is to follow. First, Feinberg entertains but does not commit to the thesis that desert is a species of fittingness. Instead, maybe desert should only be compared with fittingness. He says nothing else to settle the matter. Moving forward, I will take the liberty of assuming that, for Feinberg, desert *is* a species of fittingness, and in Section 6.3 I will shore up this position. Second, Feinberg endorses a thesis that I will eventually reject: What a deserving agent most basically deserves are responsive attitudes (what Strawson would call "reactive attitudes") rather than various modes of treatment.

Focus for now on Feinberg's contention that desert is a species of fittingness. Recall that, as noted in Section 6.1, all of the properties identified for fittingness are featured in Feinberg's formulation of desert. I'll not rehearse each point of comparison here. One, however, bears highlighting before we press on, the case-specific feature of fittingness. Feinberg contends that when a response is deserved, it is so just in virtue of a relation between a response and its target object's *desert base* (1970: 58–61), where the desert base features reasons bearing only on features *internal to the domain of evaluation*. He calls these *basal reasons* (59). A person deserves to win a prize, for instance, exclusively in virtue of basal reasons regarding

FITTINGNESS 143

a winner's "preeminent possession of the skill singled out" (64). As an upshot, any particular prize for any specific exercise of any particular skill will be deserved or not in virtue of the reasons supplied by the particular skillful performance. Hold this thought, and now let us turn to Strawson.

6.2.2 Strawson's Disparaging Dismissal of Fittingness

Strawson called the compatibilists he criticized "optimists." What they were optimistic about, as he framed it, was the prospects for retaining the legitimacy of our moral responsibility practices were we to discover that determinism is true. Of particular concern was the justification for potentially harmful practices of blaming and punishing. Strawson's compatibilist contemporaries argued that the social utility of blaming and punishing was justified exclusively in virtue of regulating behavior for moral improvement, and this sort of justification was compatible with determinism (e.g., Schlick, 1939; Smart, 1963). They then reverse-engineered, so to speak, the freedom conditions for moral responsibility so that freedom simply amounted to whatever features of agency are such than an agent is susceptible to being influenced by blame and punishment, as well as praise and reward. Talk about buying compatibilism on the cheap!

Strawson's criticism of his compatibilist contemporaries just was a wrong-kind-of-reason objection. When considering the reasons bearing on the efficacy of our practices of regulating behavior in socially desirable ways, Strawson wrote, "But this is not a sufficient basis, it is not even the right sort of basis, for these practices as we understand them" (1962, as appearing in Watson, ed.; 2003: 74).[5] Well, then, what will supply us with the *right* sort of basis?

---

[5] Here Strawson was giving voice to libertarians and other incompatibilists who objected to the compatibilists' proposal. But he clearly agreed with this objection.

144 CLARIFICATIONS AND FURTHER DEVELOPMENTS

Strawson contended that if we focus upon the reactive attitudes we will exhaust all that is needed for a justification when we blame or punish a person whom we take to be blameworthy.[6] Attention to the attitudes themselves, he argued, fills in the explanatory and the justificatory gap left by these optimistic utilitarian compatibilists. Unfortunately, Strawson protested, his libertarian contemporaries were blind to this insight. Strawson called these libertarians "pessimists." What they were pessimistic about were the prospects for retaining the legitimacy of our moral responsibility practices were we to discover that determinism is true. Failing to register the salience of the reactive attitudes themselves, Strawson explained, they argued that more was needed to supply the justification lacking in the optimists' account, something that requires heavy-duty metaphysics—not cheapo reverse-engineering. Here, in light of this dialectical context, is the crucial passage:

> The pessimist does not lose sight of these attitudes, but is unable to accept the fact that it is just these attitudes themselves which fill the gap in the optimist's account. Because of this, he thinks the gap can be filled only if some general metaphysical proposition is repeatedly verified, verified in all instances where it is appropriate to attribute moral responsibility. This proposition he finds it difficult to state coherently and with intelligible relevance as its deterministic contradictory. Even when a formula has been found ("contra-causal freedom" or something of the kind) there still seems to be a gap between its applicability in particular cases and its supposed moral consequences. Sometimes he plugs this gap with an intuition of fittingness—a pitiful intellectualist trinket for a philosopher to wear as a charm against his own humanity. (Strawson, 1962, as appearing in Watson, 2003: 92)

---

[6] Strawson foreswore (certain sorts of) justifications, but he embraced justifications *internal* to our practices.

FITTINGNESS   145

Now why *exactly* did Strawson describe any libertarian appeal to an intuition of fittingness as a pitiful intellectualist trinket? It is difficult to say. The passage is cryptic. Strawson specifies no concrete proposal by any of his contemporaries. There are no quotations or references to any actual libertarian philosophers' views. Instead he describes their efforts, whatever they might come to, derisively, and parenthetically alludes to the expression "contra-causal freedom."

Here is my assessment of what Strawson must have meant. Let's begin with some historical context. In roughly the fifty years leading up to Strawson's essay, the viable options for libertarian freedom were either by appeal to *agent causation* of the sort developed by C.A. Campbell (1951)[7], and later Roderick Chisholm (1964) and Richard Taylor (1966), or instead a *noncausal* theory of freedom espoused most notably by Henri Bergson (1889/1910), and Jean-Paul Sartre (1948), but also found in Wittgensteinian approaches to action theory more generally, not just free will, such as A. I. Meldon (1961). One of these strategies featured a distinctive kind of causal relation between agent-as-irreducible-substance and action. The other featured a noncausal relation between agent and action. Either way, what both libertarian proposals required as a condition for an exercise of free will is the falsity of the proposition that, antecedent to any basically free act, conditions obtained (states, events, or processes) that casually necessitated the act itself. Both strategies accepted that the mere absence of a deterministic cause is not enough for the act to be free. That negative condition alone affords the agent no control over the act whereby she initiates it rather than it merely be something that just happened. This, I assume, is the metaphysical proposition that, Strawson complained, the libertarians of his time had difficulty stating coherently. It involved some positive account—with noncausal or agent-causal resources—of the agent's bringing about a free act in the absence

---

[7] Campbell makes liberal use of the expression 'contra-causal' in his formulation—an ugly and misleading term for a view that features centrally causation by agents.

146   CLARIFICATIONS AND FURTHER DEVELOPMENTS

of garden-variety event causal production by necessitating prior events.

We are not yet at the target of the "pitiful trinket" dig. Suppose, somehow, these libertarians were able to offer a coherent and intelligible story about the nondeterministic freedom-conferring relation between every agent and every basically free action that amounts to an exercise of free will. Strawson grudgingly entertained the possibility that some libertarian thesis might succeed. This is the stage Strawson envisages when in the passage quoted above he writes, "Even when a formula has been found." The worry now is this: Who cares? Why does this matter? Recall, the requirement for a justification involves a normative consideration, not just a metaphysical explanation. What do we need to be able to *justify* harmful blaming and punishing practices if as it turns out appeal to utilitarian considerations only generate the wrong kinds of reasons? This, I take it, is what Strawson meant by complaining that "there still seems to be a gap between its applicability in particular cases and its supposed moral consequences."

Now we can begin to see what Strawson had in mind by objecting to the idea that right here the libertarian can invoke an intuition of fittingness. As Strawson presents it, the libertarian contends that when we get the metaphysics coherently stated, we can have a direct intuition of fittingness supplying a normative justification for blame and punishment. Such a justification was pitiful, Strawson thought. But why precisely? We still don't have a full accounting of Strawson's remark. Strawson characterized this libertarian's appeal to an intuition of fittingness as a pitiful *intellectualist* trinket to wear as a charm *against his own humanity*. Why intellectualist? And why against his own humanity? Why not as an expression of it? This, I take it, was what Strawson found especially pitiful.

As indicated in the passage quoted above, Strawson's indictment of these libertarians was that they failed to appreciate the crucial facts about the relevance of the reactive attitudes. They did not lose sight of them, he told us, but they did fail to appreciate their

FITTINGNESS **147**

significance. Strawson argued that these attitudes *could* supply the resources to fill the gap left by the failure of the utilitarian-compatibilist justification. This sort of libertarian, as Strawson put it, "rushes beyond these facts" (89) to excessive metaphysics. Here, I propose, is the specific focus of Strawson's searing indictment. Suppose, as Strawson did, that the reactive attitudes and our expression of them in our adult interpersonal lives are *manifestations* of our humanity. Our angry responses toward those who culpably harm us and others express our nature. The fittingness called forth by these libertarian metaphysicians, Strawson suggested, cast the freedom they identified as a justification for blaming *despite* these natural human responses. Their appeal to an intuition of fittingness is a charm *against* our humanity; it is by no means an expression of it, much less a commit to it. It is in this sense that Strawson as a naturalist protests to an "intellectualist" libertarian metaphysics that he saw as in some way nonnatural.[8] His complaint, then, in this biting remark, was that the libertarians' appeal to an intuition of fittingness as they used it *in this specific dialectical context* was normatively unhelpful. It would not answer any more effectively the moral question that the utilitarian compatibilists of his day were unable to answer. If this is correct, we do not have much reason to think Strawson was opposed to fittingness per se, but rather just to the way that, as he saw it, the libertarians of his day made use of it.

6.2.3 Why Strawson Needs Fittingness

So, how does Strawson fill the gap? How does his attention to the reactive attitudes *alone* do the work that both his compatibilist and

---

[8] Some might even say supernatural. Recall the libertarian Chisholm's (1964) remark that if persons have free will they must have a power normally only attributed to God, to be a prime mover unmoved.

148 CLARIFICATIONS AND FURTHER DEVELOPMENTS

libertarian peers failed to do by looking beyond them? His reasoning here is not at all transparent. It has led philosophers to go in one of two different directions in interpreting him.

Strawson carved out the extension in which reactive attitudes of moral anger (resentment and indignation) were rendered appropriate by attending to the scope of our excuses, justification, and exemptions, wherein such anger is *not* appropriate. If we extrapolate away from such cases, we are left with the cases where there is *not* a defeater to the proper application of our moral anger. This moral anger for Strawson is the medium by which we hold to account when we blame and punish. So, this means there is a not a defeater to blame or punishment.

But we need more. Strawson's contemporaries were trying to show what *positive* justification we might identify when we blame and punish. With the resources he provided, he showed us when, according to our practices, we should not blame or punish. But what is the positive normative glue that justifies our doing so when no excuse, justification, or exemption applies? What licenses us being angry with and harming others with these potentially costly practices? Here is one interpretation of Strawson that, if correct, is rightly damning:

> When an agent does act with ill will or an insufficient degree of good will, and when a potential blamer perceives this, by a brute bit of nature, she is just disposed, causally, to have a reactive emotional response. There is no more normativity to be found. There are just psychological causes.

This is a dispositionalist interpretation of the proper extension of being blameworthy and the conditions for blaming and punishing. This is just how we are built. End of story.

Various critics have entertained the prospect that this dispositionalist interpretation was Strawson's view, a crude form of naturalism, built with no more than primitive psychological facts

FITTINGNESS 149

(e.g., Fischer and Ravizza, 1993: 18–19).[9] Interpreting him in this way, they have proposed that what is needed is an upgrade by instead advancing a normative interpretation, one that departed from what Strawson intended. Indeed, this is Wallace's (N) quoted above. But the textual evidence to support the dispositional interpretation of Strawson over the normative one is thin. Strawson is to be faulted for remaining silent where he should have said more. He needed to offer some positive account of the normativity that relates an angry blaming response to perceived ill will in a wrongdoer. Nevertheless, Strawson's commitment to some positive basis is implicit in his remark that his compatibilist contemporaries supplied the wrong kinds of reasons for blaming and punishing by attending to considerations of social utility. If there are wrong kinds of reasons, aren't there right ones? These reasons would offer the requisite normative justification. Moreover, when criticizing the libertarians, he claimed that they sought to fill a justificatory gap left by the utilitarian-compatibilists (optimists), and his claim was not that there was no gap, but that attention to the reactive attitudes was sufficient to fill it. So, as I read Strawson—and admittedly I am offering a highly charitable interpretation—he was implicitly operating with a normative understanding and took calling attention to the reactive attitudes as responses to good and ill will as providing those normative resources; he was not saying we don't need any justification.

Many Strawsonians will strenuously protest at this point. Strawson was insistent that all his contemporaries who were participants to the debate overintellectualized the facts by seeking some external justification. Perhaps this is why Wallace (1994) should be read as departing radically from Strawson's naturalism. It might be argued that Wallace *did* offer an external *normative* (rather than metaphysical) justification for our harmful blaming

---

[9] I'll not bother to rehearse here the litany of well-founded criticisms one might heap on the dispositionalist reading.

150 CLARIFICATIONS AND FURTHER DEVELOPMENTS

and punishing practices; they are justified by reference to principles of fairness. Maybe so. Maybe we should understand Wallace as standing opposed to Strawson in terms of providing an external justification for the appropriateness of our reactive attitudes and their attendant responsibility practices. I myself am doubtful.[10] Regardless, there is no reason to think that the normative interpretation of Strawson I am suggesting runs afoul of his prescription that we not seek an external justification. Denial of an external justification does not change the fact that when we do become morally angry with someone who treats us or others with ill will, in treating them poorly in response, we ought to be able to supply some justification of the propriety of our doing so. Strawson was cool with justifications internal to our practices.[11] *This is just what fittingness of the sort Feinberg identified would do for Strawson.* It would supply a justification internal to our standards for moral anger as a response to ill will. And it would do so in just the case-specific way I highlighted in my presentation of Feinberg's proposal.

Here is what Strawson should have said in order offer a complete answer to his contemporaries regarding the justificatory gap between blameworthy wrongdoers and blaming and punishing responses. When we react with anger to the ill will or lack of sufficient good will perceived in the wrongdoing of another, our anger and our outward expressions of it by blaming or punishing are not just brute automatic reactions. They are *appraisals* of the wrongdoer's regard for us or others.[12] When no justification, excuse, or exemption applies, they are accurate appraisals.

---

[10] Why? Because the considerations of fairness Wallace appeals to are supported by judgments internal to our practices.

[11] See Watson's discussion of Strawson wherein he treats the reactive sentiments as modes of valuing that susceptibility to which provides a normative ground for our responsibility practices (2014: 21–2).

[12] For a striking comparison, see Feinberg when discussing gratitude and resentment. He writes, "These attitudes are not mere automatic responses to stimuli, but self-conscious responses to desert bases, not mere 'reactions to' but 'requitals for'" (1970: 70).

FITTINGNESS   151

By standards of appraisal internal to the domain of their kind—the domain regarding expectations of good will—they supply us with reasons to fit our angry response to the particular objectionable nature of the offender's will. This just is fittingness as I have specified it above.[13] What I would say here, boldly and with woefully inadequate textual evidence, is that this is what Strawson had in mind. Insofar as he did, far from eschewing the role of fittingness in philosophical theorizing, in all but name he was relying upon it.

6.2.4 Comparing Strawson and Feinberg on Fittingness and Desert

Feinberg did not specify fittingness as the normative relation bearing on blame and punishment. He relied upon desert. Shouldn't we interpret Strawson likewise? Shouldn't the preceding section be rewritten in terms of it being the desert that Strawson needed? That depends on just what distinguishes fittingness from desert. As I have read him, Feinberg's thesis is that desert is a species of fittingness. On his view, what more is there to desert than there is to mere fittingness? Feinberg does not say. All of the logical properties he assigned to desert in his essay apply to fittingness as I characterized it above (Section 6.1). If there is no more to desert than fittingness, this question amounts to no more than a choice of nomenclature. Desert is just another name for fittingness, and Feinberg was wrong to contend that one was a species of the other; one just is the other. But if there is more to the relation of desert than there is to fittingness, it's an open question how best to understand *both* Feinberg and Strawson. For all Feinberg said, maybe he was right to think of desert as a species of fittingness but wrong to identify the relation he described in his essay in terms of desert.

---

[13] This chain of reasoning is so close to Feinberg's that I encourage readers to see his own expression of it (1970: 80–2).

152 CLARIFICATIONS AND FURTHER DEVELOPMENTS

Maybe he should have just relied on the more generic notion of fittingness.

As I argue below, there is a substantive issue here, a crucial point at which desert involves more than mere fittingness. Granting this, it is in dispute how to chart a path forward for Strawsonians in our own time. A modest strategy would attempt to make do with just fittingness, whereas an ambitious approach would take on desert as a more robust normative relation.

6.2.5 Diagnosing an Alleged Mistake and the Current State of the Debate

Before wrapping up our assessment of both Feinberg and Strawson on fittingness, it is worth reflecting on why Strawson's harsh criticism of his libertarian contemporaries seemed so compelling. If he was correct, they were making a bad mistake. Well, were they? Our question is not just academic. I intend to use it as a lesson for our time.

I have argued that Strawson's dismissal of fittingness was limited to a particular application of it to supply the normative basis for blame and punishment, linking exercises of free will directly to appropriate blame and punishment. Grant to Strawson that these libertarians made this appeal to an intuition of fittingness in a way that extracted it from the context of the relevant moral emotions. As he saw it, they ignored the salience of these attitudes for their justificatory enterprise. These metaphysicians thereby applied this normative relation of fittingness *outside the context of any domain that could help guide an application of the relation.* Recall, as set out above, fittingness identifies a relation *within* a domain that contains its own standards of evaluation. These moral emotions provide that domain. They supply resources that make sense of appraisals of ill will by expressing moral anger in ways that could be fitting, and so justified. Without

FITTINGNESS 153

such a context, fittingness has no anchor, no substance to inform applications of it.

Now *if* Strawson's description of his libertarian contemporaries were accurate—*if* indeed they had looked past the crucial relevance of these morally reactive emotions—he would have been dead right to protest that their appeal to fittingness was a pitiful intellectualist trinket, one divorced from their own humanity. But I am doubtful. Here I am not interested in a historical exploration of his contemporaries. Instead we can use this as an occasion to transition to the contemporary debate. Regardless of what the libertarians of his day actually thought, it was open to a thoughtful critic to resist Strawson then, as it clearly is in our time, by pointing out that, on a normative interpretation of his proposal, it is unsettled what sort of basal reasons pertain to fitting expressions of moral anger. Mightn't there after all be ingredients *internal* to standards of appraisal for our anger that raise questions about an agent's freedom? If so, libertarians and other incompatibilists might find a basis for their metaphysical conditions on freedom that is *internal* to our pertinent interpersonal norms regarding expression of these emotions.[14]

With this, we can leap forward a good half century. Derk Pereboom (2001; 2014: esp. 128–9) contends, and many others agree, that a presupposition of moral anger and angry blame, at least in many familiar cases, is that the target of one's anger deserves be a recipient of unwelcome treatment, issuing in harm or pain. A further presupposition of deserving such treatment is that its target acted freely or of her own free will, where the freedom at issue is metaphysically demanding. In short, angry blame presupposes the freedom of those at whom it is directed. Others deny that the anger pertinent to theorizing about moral

---

[14] Perhaps at least one of Strawson's critics did see this path for resisting Strawson, even though he did not endorse it. See Jonathan Bennett's (1980) discussion of a Spinozistic element in our folk understanding implicit in our reactive attitudes. This was in a critical piece assessing Strawson's (1962) proposal.

154 CLARIFICATIONS AND FURTHER DEVELOPMENTS

blame and blameworthiness has such a strong desert presupposition built into it (e.g., Shoemaker, 2015; Vargas, 2013). In light of our contemporary understanding of the debate, Strawson's easy dismissal of his libertarian adversaries was far too quick. We can embrace along with him the centrality of the reactive attitudes in theorizing about moral responsibility while nevertheless seriously entertaining the possibility that the satisfaction conditions for fitting anger involve freedom of the sort specified by libertarians and other incompatibilists. It's an open question.

6.3 Desert as a Species of Fittingness: Two Paths Forward for Strawsonians

I will now argue that desert is a species of fittingness.[15] With this in place, I'll turn to the options for contemporary Strawsonians regarding how best to theorize about moral responsibility.

6.3.1 Desert Is a Species of Fittingness

When we assert that the guilty deserve to feel guilt, the culpable deserve punishment, the blameworthy deserve blame, and that the praiseworthy deserve praise, we can assert with confidence that it is fitting for the guilty to feel guilt, fitting to punish the culpable, fitting to blame the blameworthy, and fitting to praise the praiseworthy. This is not limited to the responsibility concepts that are our focus here. If Jane deserves to have won the race, then it is fitting that she won it. Indeed, whenever there is a true sentence of the form *x deserves y*, there is a true sentence of the form *it is fitting for*

---

[15] Note that Kelly McCormick (2022) has recently developed an intriguing fittingness account of deserved blame.

x to *y*, or instead, *y is a fitting response to x*. But not so in reverse.[16] Consider above the examples of belief and desire. It is fitting to believe the believable, and fitting to desire the desirable. Yet there are many instances of belief wherein it is fitting to believe a credible proposition while no consideration of desert is salient. The same for the desirable. Peanut butter and jelly sandwiches are obviously desirable (duh!). Surely then it is fitting to desire them. But they do not deserve to be desired.

Moreover, if we think of desert as a form of appraisal falling within the domain of justice, as I am now proposing we should, following Feinberg (1970: 55), the preceding point is even clearer. We do no injustice to peanut butter and jelly sandwiches in failing to desire them. Nor do our undergraduates do an injustice to *modus ponens* when they fail to believe its validity. Not so for failing to praise the praiseworthy or punish the culpable. In such cases, questions of potential injustice are at least intelligible, even if sometimes there are reasons to deny an injustice has been done in not giving a person what she deserves. Why the hedge? An example from Feinberg illustrates the point (1970: 64). A runner who is clearly fleetest of foot might deserve to win the race and receive the medal, but because she pulls a muscle and turns up lame someone else crosses the finish line first. In that case, no injustice is done in giving the less-deserving runner the first-place prize.[17]

The preceding point needs to be handled with some care. Some deserved responses, like blame, are optional in such a way that there is no question of injustice if one fails to blame a person who deserves it. Still, other questions of justice bear on these sorts of responses that don't for mere fitting responses like belief or desire.

---

[16] Howard renders this crystal clear (2018: 7). My argument here builds on his insights regarding the relationship between desert and fittingness.

[17] Feinberg (1970: 57) explains this in terms of qualifying conditions or rules used to help set the stage for assessing questions of desert. The rule says that the first to cross the finish line wins the medal. But the aim of the rule is to thereby award the medal to the most deserving. Sometimes procedures for achieving this aim fall short.

156 CLARIFICATIONS AND FURTHER DEVELOPMENTS

An injustice is done when one is blamed who does *not* deserve it, whereas no injustice is done when one unfittingly believes that it is possible to square the circle or that no human has walked on the moon.

Have we arrived at a substantive basis for distinguishing desert as a species of fittingness? No, and for two reasons. First, for all that has been said, maybe the distinction rests on no more than linguistic convention. Maybe we just call fittingness within the domain of justice "desert," but there's no more to it than that. Second, maybe there is partial overlap in the extension of two distinct relations, so that they do not stand to each other as species to genus. Desert is one thing; fittingness is another. Maybe instead, as Randolph Clarke and Piers Rawling (2022) suggest, they just share the same grounds in certain domains.

Taking the latter challenge first, one reason to think desert is a species of fittingness is that when one of the properties of fittingness fails to apply to a case, rendering it unfitting, it provides grounds for the judgment that it is not deserved, and it helps explain or illuminate assessments of desert. If my blaming Mati for Njeri's poor conduct is unfitting because my blame does not accurately represent the wrong as properly attributed to Njeri and not Mati, that is as well the same reason to judge that blaming Mati is not deserved.

Consider instead the case-specific feature of fittingness I have highlighted and reflect on the familiar claim that the punishment should fit the crime. Here are two cases. Geraldine embezzles a modest amount of money from a homeless shelter, and Leslie gets drunk and throws trash about the streets in his home town. Both being culpable, suppose both deserve a mild punishment that causes only two units of harm.[18] A judge considers two punishments, each of which, as it happens, would be received by both Geraldine and Leslie as equally unwelcome to the tune of those two units. One

---

[18] I don't endorse this sort of hedonistic calculus. I use it as a toy model just to make a simple point.

punishment involves spending three Saturdays cleaning the local streets. The other involves three Saturdays preparing food in the kitchen at the local homeless shelter. Were the judge to dole out as punishment kitchen work at the homeless shelter to Leslie, who trashed the streets of his hometown, and the street cleaning to Geraldine who embezzled money from the homeless, his allocation would in some manner be unfitting. It would also not optimally supply either with what each deserved. The key point here is that fittingness helps to inform us about the content of what is deserved, and this in turn is a reason to think that we do not just have distinct relations that overlap or share the same grounds.

Now consider the former concern, that there is no real substance to the distinction. Desert just is fittingness, and in the sphere of justice we use the more limited term. It's just linguistic convention. How might we resist this charge? One possibility builds on the contention that evaluations of desert entail judgments of noninstrumental goodness (as I argued in Chapter 3), whereas evaluations of fittingness do not. It is noninstrumentally good that the praiseworthy are praised, and noninstrumentally good that the culpable receive punishment and the pain or harm accompanying it (a central assumption for some versions of retributivism). Suppose this controversial thesis is true; desert entails noninstrumental goodness; the world is rendered better when the deserving get what they deserve. Regrettably, this won't help distinguish desert from mere fittingness. There are cases of mere fittingness that plausibly entail noninstrumental goodness. For instance, it is fitting to respond with grief to the loss of a loved one, and, while this response and the pain accompanying it might be noninstrumentally good (see Chapter 3), the pain of grief is not deserved (Carlsson, 2017; Nelkin, 2013, 2019b).

What is needed is some principled way to show that reasons of desert are stronger than reasons of fit, or have more demanding logical properties in relation to other reasons, so that we get a natural parsing wherein one is a species of the other. Consider, for

158 CLARIFICATIONS AND FURTHER DEVELOPMENTS

instance, the debate over the role of the reasons supplied by promising, what some have characterized as *exclusionary reasons*, as in contrast with other reasons (e.g., Raz, 1977; Wallace, 2019). One who has promised now has reasons that do not just outweigh reasons for other courses of action, but rather discount or exclude them.[19] If I have promised you we'd share dinner Saturday night, then a later chance to see a good movie with another friend is not just outweighed by my reasons for having dinner with you. They don't count at all; they're to be excluded from my deliberations. I'm committed by virtue of my promise. Perhaps we can make use of a similar distinction.

Here is a first pass at such a strategy. Focus on negative evaluations of desert, when what is deserved is unwelcome or harmful, as in the cases of directed blame and punishment. Desert supplies reasons to *discount* or *silence*—and not merely outweigh— moral considerations that otherwise apply. Grant that morality demands of us that when interacting with the moral community we do not, as Strawson himself expressed it, "acquiesce in the infliction of suffering" (1962, as appearing in Watson, 2003: 90), at least not unless it can be justified for instrumental reasons. Reasons of desert supply reasons to discount or silence that sort of moral reason and thus support forms of treatment otherwise opposed to morality's counsel. Mere reasons of fit do not work that way. When reasons of humor outweigh moral reasons not find to amusement

[19] As Derk Pereboom has keenly noted in correspondence, "discount" might be construed as the same as outweighing. That is not what I intend. The clearest cases are those wherein some reasons are excluded altogether, but I wish to leave it as an open possibility that a reason might be weakened by the presence of another reason while not being totally excluded. This is still a more powerful effect than *mere* outweighing. To illustrate, suppose reason R1 has a force of 10 and is just outweighed by reason R2 that has a force of 15, yielding a force of 5. But now, consider R3, with a force of 15 that excludes R1 such that R1 has no effect all, yielding a force of 15. Finally, consider R4, with a force of 15 that discounts R1's force by half (from 10 to 5), yielding a force of 10. Of course, I do not mean to commit to such a crude view of the force of reasons. This is just a toy model. I only mean to leave open the possibility that reasons of desert need not completely annihilate the force of certain other reasons for reasons of desert to have a more powerful role than merely weighing in the mix against other reasons.

in the funny joke, they do not silence reasons of morality. They just outweigh them. Not so for desert—or so I contend. *That*, on the proposal I am exploring here, is the distinguishing feature of desert that sets it apart from mere fittingness.

Will this do? Perhaps, but there are details that need to be worked out. For instance, blame differs from punishment in that in the case of blame there is no pertinent strict requirement or duty not to cause harm to others of the sort involved in punishment. Granted, overt blame directed at the blameworthy often involves some harm or the risk of it. But in a wide range of cases there is no moral *requirement* bearing on these sorts of harms that we can clearly identify as the reason silenced by considerations of deserved blame. Why? Suppose blame is, at least in some cases, a partial withdrawal of good will toward those at whom we direct any variety of angry blame; it involves withdrawal of a degree of good will that is otherwise expected of those who are in good standing within the moral community (they are not blameworthy). Arguably, we do not *owe* our good will or, say, our friendly relations to others.[20] There is no requirement here. So, what is the moral reason discounted or silenced in cases of justified blame where there are not clear moral requirements upon us? In reply, distinguish between *requiring reasons* and *favoring reasons*. Morality broadly construed can supply both. There are favoring reasons for us to show others some reasonable degree of good will in our interactions with them, even if we are not morally bound to do so. Desert can supply reasons to discount or silence these as well.

Yet another challenge concerns *positive* deserved responses, such as praise and reward. Reasons of desert in positive cases do not discount moral reasons for not treating people with more good will than might be expected or heaping a prize or reward

---

[20] Scanlon, for instance, focuses on this point about our interpersonal relations (2008). When, motivated by blame, we withdraw our previously friendly relations with others, our doing so (at least often) violates nothing that we owe to one whom we might blame. Morality allows us leeway here.

160 CLARIFICATIONS AND FURTHER DEVELOPMENTS

on them. In the absence of a consideration of desert, no harm or wrong would be done to one who is praised or rewarded even if it is not deserved. True. But there are other reasons in the offing. It is commonly thought that gratitude is owed toward those who have acted in praiseworthy ways and so benefited us, and that rewards are owed to those meritorious persons who have acted in morally heroic ways. Were we not to praise or reward them, we would fail to do something that morality requires or at least favors. In the case of positive desert, then, we do *not* owe it to others to treat them as we do those who deserve our gratitude or our reward. The reasons silenced, then, are reasons about the moral neutrality or optionality of the sort of treatment involved in showing gratitude and giving awards. There are now requiring or favoring reasons for treating the deserving in positive ways.

The distinction proposed here between the normative force of desert and the normative force of mere fit helps correct a mistake in Feinberg's proposal. Feinberg contends that it is attitudes such as resentment or gratitude that are basically deserved, and various modes of treatment, construed as conventional means of expressing the attitudes, are only derivatively deserved. That can't be right. If Jones deserve punishment and gets only clues of our resentment or indignation—genuine boiling moral anger—but receives no punishment, there is little sense to thinking, "Boy oh boy did she get what she deserved!" Contrary to what Feinberg contends, I propose that a further difference between mere fittingness and desert is that in cases of the mere fittingness of pertinent attitudes, what is basically fitting *is* some attitude. Modes of treatment as expressions of those attitudes are a derivative matter. In the case of desert, *what is basically deserved is a mode of treatment that expresses the pertinent attitude.* Of course, the attitude might still play a crucial role. If two people are locked in a room for three days, one accidentally because she shut the door and the handle broke so she could not leave, and the other is locked in a room as an expression of moral anger via retributive punishment, both might be guilty and deserve

FITTINGNESS   161

three days in the pokey, but only one gets what she deserved. The other is just unlucky; karma got the better of her.

This difference regarding basicness is supported by the difference identified in the normative force of reasons as between fittingness and desert. When fittingness gives us reasons to express our amusement, it does seem that what is most basically fitting is the attitude, the finding humorous. Outward expressions of humor are then only derivatively fitting. But note that the reasons supplied by the fittingness of humor do not discount moral reasons not to express amusement even if the reasons of humor outweigh the moral reasons. The moral reasons in these cases are hardly silenced. On the other hand, supposing reasons of desert do operate by discounting or silencing other sorts of moral reasons, these reasons of desert, so to speak, "reach outside" their domain of applicability and can defeat other normative evaluations. In this way, they recommend not just attitudes we might have, but ways we might act as an expression of these attitudes despite what would otherwise be reasons against doing so. Thus, reasons of desert supply stronger reasons for *acting* than the sort offered by mere fittingness, and this helps explain why, for desert but not for mere fittingness, what is basic is a mode of expressing an attitude in action.[21]

To avoid any confusion, the point here is not that desert supplies all-things-considered reasons. Granting all that has been said, a person might deserve punishment, and not merely the angry attitudes of others, and still the reasons to punish her are only *pro tanto*. If some great tragedy would unfold by punishing her, like the destruction of the world, then, for consequentialist reasons, all-things-considered she ought not be punished. The point is only that reasons of desert discount or silence some other range of reasons that otherwise would supply *pro tanto* reasons to act in opposition to pertinent reasons of desert.

---

[21] See Pereboom (2021: 50–1) and Andreas Carlsson (2017), who make a similar point about desert.

162 CLARIFICATIONS AND FURTHER DEVELOPMENTS

Admittedly, the preceding proposal is just a sketch. It is an effort to find a way to argue for the contention that reasons of desert are in some particular respect more forceful than reasons of fit. It is also an attempt to show how and why it is that, in the case of desert, the most basic forms of response are forms of treatment and not mere attitudes, as in contrast with mere fittingness for a range of attitudes. Suppose careful inspection proves the preceding sketch inadequate. Another option is to treat the thesis I defend here as a brute fact. Reasons of desert just are more normatively forceful than reasons of fit, and one of their distinguishing features is just that the basic responses that are deserved are forms of treatment and not mere attitudes. I leave the matter unsettled and press on.

6.3.2 Desert in the Domain of Moral Responsibility

My proposal can be distinguished from the view that desert is a species of fittingness pertaining *only* to matters of responsibility (e.g., Miller, 1999; Pojman, 1997). The problem with this view is that it excludes too much (cf. Feinberg, 1970: 56). Suppose no one is morally responsible for anything because, for instance, no one has free will, so no one deserves praise or blame, reward or punishment (e.g., Pereboom, 2001, 2014). Still desert remains. The swiftest runner still deserves to win the race and the slowest lose it, the good and bad students each deserve their good and bad grades, and so forth. In short, it is not plausible that desert is limited just to the domain of moral responsibility.

So how should we situate moral responsibility in relation to desert? Just as fittingness applies differentially to the differing domains of the desirable, the credible, the humorous, or the disgusting, so, too, desert applies differentially to different domains. Moral responsibility is but one domain among others. As noted above, fittingness evaluates different objects by standards internal to different domains. So does desert. As Feinberg noted,

FITTINGNESS 163

the desert base for these different domains varies, and the basal reasons applying to them vary. Hence, just as reasons of fit that bear on something's being desirable differ from those bearing on something's being believable, so, too, do reasons of desert bearing on considerations of responsibility differ from reasons of desert bearing on grading or awarding prizes in a competition. Feinberg mentions five different varieties of desert: awards and prizes; assignment of grades; rewards and punishments; praise, blame, and other informal responses; reparation, liability, and other modes of compensation (1970: 62). In doing so he made "no claim to taxonomic precision or completeness" (62).

To dial in on the desert distinctly bearing on the domain of moral responsibility, and to return to our reflections of Strawson's relevance to our own time, we need to focus upon the desert base for deserved blame and punishment.[22] This in turn needs to be settled in terms of the basal reasons in virtue of which assessments of deserved blame or punishment are settled.

We can begin where Strawson (1962) began, and others before him, for example, Austin (1956–1957), in "A Plea for Excuses," with pleas meant to *defeat* judgments of blameworthiness. *Exemptions* show that a person is not a competent candidate for being able to comply with moral demands at all. *Justifications* show no wrong has been done. *Excuses* naturally divide into those that show a person was nonculpably ignorant of wrongdoing and those that show that she did not act freely when she did wrong. From these clues, we can construct a credible desert base consisting of a collection of basal reasons. When no plea applies—that is, when a person *is* morally responsible in the sense of being blameworthy for something or other—all of the following considerations bear on her deserving some sort of blame or punishment. First, she is a competent person

---

[22] Praise and reward, too, but we'll not attend to these here. A further issue as well is the desert bearing on a person's status as a morally responsible agent. The young man or woman who is no longer a child might speak plain truth to his father or mother by demanding that he or she deserves to be treated like a responsible adult.

164   CLARIFICATIONS AND FURTHER DEVELOPMENTS

capable of guiding her intentional conduct by reasons, grasping moral demands, and suffering from no major impairments of agency of the sort involved in severe mental illness. Second, she actually performed an act (or omission) that was morally wrong or in some manner morally objectionable. Third, she did so either knowingly or from culpable ignorance. Fourth and finally, she did it freely. Something like this set of basal reasons figures in capturing the desert base in virtue of which an agent might deserve blame or punishment.[23]

6.3.3   Robust Freedom in the Distinctive Desert Base for Moral Responsibility

Now focus just on the freedom condition. It is but one condition figuring in the total set of basal reasons in virtue of which an agent might deserve harmful blame or punishment. On the current proposal, the desert base provided by the full set of basal reasons for deserved blame or punishment must provide reasons strong enough to discount or silence, and not merely outweigh, some (but of course not all) reasons not to cause persons harm or suffering. Given this, it is plausible to suppose that the freedom condition offered as part of the desert base should involve a relatively industrial-strength degree of agential control over one's conduct. Freedom and control come in degrees, and lesser freedoms seem inadequate. Dogs and lesser evolved creatures have some control over and so some freedom with respect to their behavior. Notably, they can be influenced with the aim of improvement by rewards and punishments in the manner highlighted by

---

[23] I will work with this, although in accord with arguments I have made elsewhere (Chapter 3), a further Strawson-inspired condition would also seem to be required— that an agent acted with a morally objectionable quality of will. My commitments here don't bear on the arguments to follow, so I set them aside.

FITTINGNESS 165

the utilitarian-compatibilists of Strawson's time—cheapo freedom. Clearly, a more substantial sort of freedom is called for. What might it be?

I propose the following as a robust freedom condition to help *ground* deserved blame or punishment when either involves expressions of our moral anger. Suppose all of the other essential basal reasons are in place for an agent's deserving harmful blame or punishment but for the freedom condition. Grant that, absent the agent's freedom, she does not deserve harmful blame or punishment for any untoward conduct. Now add the following. When an agent exercises freedom of the sort at issue here—call it freedom of the will—she acts in such a way that she *settles* whether she deserves hard treatment. What such freedom supplies are the resources that make it true that when she acts, *it is up to her* whether she deserves this sort of treatment. When she does, she thereby *brings on herself* this unwelcome treatment. These three features of an industrial-strength freedom—up to one, settling, and bringing on oneself— do the grounding work to help justify deserved harmful blame and punishment: By agential resources that are up to her, an agent who acts of her own free will settles whether she deserves harmful blame or punishment, and, in doing, so she thereby brings upon herself any forms of unwelcome treatment as expressions of the moral anger had by those who would hold her to account.[24]

Far from offering no more than a pitiful trinket—something irrelevant to the justificatory role involved in harmful blame or punishment as an expression of our moral anger—the preceding proposal for a robust freedom condition captures something rooted deep in our commonsense understanding of moral responsibility. Indeed, when reflecting on free will so understood, I confess to having...wait for it...*an intuition of fittingness.* For what it's worth, I might add that, in response to Strawson's derisive remark,

---

[24] See Chapter 5, where these ingredients are first introduced.

166 CLARIFICATIONS AND FURTHER DEVELOPMENTS

in surveying my own psychic state I cannot find any evidence of feeling even the least bit panicky.

6.3.4 Desert versus Mere Fittingness: Two Paths Forward

We now have before us, first, an argument for the thesis that desert is a species of fittingness; second, an account of the desert base unique to the domain of moral responsibility; and third, the specification of a robust freedom condition figuring in that desert base. Given these resources, return to our assessment of Feinberg and Strawson. As explained above (Section 6.2.4), it is unclear how we should develop their conceptions of the normativity bearing on responsibility responses. One path forward involves fittingness; another involves desert. Moreover, on a normative interpretation of Strawson's view, I argued (Section 6.2.5) that it is an open question whether there is a robust freedom condition *internal* to our normative standards for moral anger. If so, Strawson was just wrong to think he could handily dispense with libertarian metaphysical presuppositions. Bearing in mind these two issues, we can now size up two options for contemporary Strawsonians.

Here is the more ambitious way forward. The normative resources deployed to justify the gap Strawson sought to fill between morally objectionable behavior and our reactive anger is a matter of desert. When our moral anger is a deserved response to the moral wrongdoing of another, we are at least *pro tanto* justified in expressing our anger through modes of unwelcome treatment via blame or punishment. In these cases, what is most basically fitting—because deserved—is the *treatment* and not just the reactive emotion of anger which that treatment expresses. In being so justified, moral reasons against inflicting pertinent forms of harm or suffering on others are silenced or defeated. Indeed, on some accounts of desert, bringing upon the deserving the harm attendant with blame or punishment is noninstrumentally good, and this goodness provides reasons to favor, even if not require, causing such harms (see Chapter 3). However, the desert base for such a normatively weighty relation involves basal reasons featuring a robust sort of freedom—freedom of the will. Equipped with this freedom, a person who deserves blame or punishment *settles* whether such treatment of her is justified, because it is *up to her* whether she acts in morally objectionable ways, and, when she does, she *brings it on herself* that she is the deserving recipient of such unwelcome treatment.

Of course, this more ambitious path is philosophically riskier because it brings with it taxing metaphysical burdens. Doesn't libertarian freedom just fall right out of the proposal? No. That is an open question, too. The compatibilists' burden on this approach is more demanding, but many contemporary compatibilists take on precisely the project of offering an account of free will that can accommodate the requirements of basic-desert-entailing moral responsibility.[25] If some contemporary Strawsonians wishing to retain their commitment to compatibilism reject this more ambitious path only because they assume that in taking it on they simply must accept libertarianism, they are mistaken. The metaphysics can be industrial-strength *sans* libertarianism.

The more cautious way forward for Strawsonians might after all be the wiser. Committing only to mere fittingness, a Strawsonian might argue that she can avoid the weighty burdens of any commitment to a robust freedom condition. When one's anger is a justified response to the morally objectionable conduct of another, it is simply fitting. In being fitting, reactive anger still accurately represents conduct as, for example, issuing from ill will. In doing so, it appraises the conduct negatively by standards internal to its domain, and so on. But any reasons it supplies for expressing fitting moral anger in outward modes of treatment do not silence or

---

[25] For example, Fischer and Ravizza (1998), McKenna (2013b), Nelkin (2011), and Sartorio (2016).

168 CLARIFICATIONS AND FURTHER DEVELOPMENTS

defeat competing moral reasons against inflicting harm on others. Of course, it still might override those reasons, just like, as I noted earlier, fitting reasons for expressing amusement might outweigh moral reasons not to laugh at a mildly morally offensive joke. But it is consistent with the mere fittingness of reactive moral anger that the weight of any reasons of fit to treat harshly a blameworthy person *are never strong enough on their own to outweigh the moral reasons not to inflict such harm.* This is key.

On this more cautious proposal, there will still remain basal reasons for fitting anger. These will figure in what might be called a *fittingness base*, rather than what Feinberg called a desert base. And these basal reasons will track roughly the kinds of reasons also bearing on a desert-based approach, as I set it out above. It will remain unfitting to respond with an attitude of moral anger to one who is not a competent person, who did nothing morally wrong, who was nonculpably ignorant of any wrongdoing, or who didn't act freely. But the freedom condition here can be downgraded considerably. It will be enough if the agent did what she wanted to do, was not coerced, was not acting from a powerful compulsion, and so on. Key to this less robust freedom condition is that the basal reasons for fittingness only directly provide reasons for a reactive *attitude*—moral anger. On this view, that is all that will be basically fitting. Any modes of treatment as an expression of that anger will only be derivatively justified, if justified at all.

Although several philosophers working in the Strawsonian tradition seem to opt for this more cautious strategy,[26] with one exception, none has made explicit their commitment to it. David Shoemaker, however, clearly has, arguing that, in a theory of moral responsibility, our aim should be to account for the fittingness and not the desert of our reactive moral emotions (Shoemaker, 2015: 221–3). He even points out that questions about harsh treatment ought to be treated as a moral concern extrinsic to both the

---

[26] For example, see Graham (2014), Hieronymi (2004), and Smith (2007).

fittingness of a sentimental response and to theorizing about moral responsibility.

> I want to insist on the crucial distinction . . . between the fittingness of various sentimental responses and the appropriateness of harsh treatment of offenders. The latter is a distinctively moral response and it simply does not bear at all on whether we have reasons of fit for the former. The latter does of course bear on whether we have all-things-considered reasons to respond to certain people in certain ways, where these are a weighted function of reasons of fit and moral reasons. . . . The real question, then, is whether the practices of harsh treatment to offenders are also necessarily and essentially responsibility responses, alongside the sentiments I have discussed. But I cannot see that they are, once this distinction has been highlighted. (2015: 223)

Shoemaker's admirably executed proposal is clearly more cautious than one that opts for an appeal to desert. It is easy to appreciate how one could handily skirt any taxing metaphysical freedom requirements. All that is at issue is the mere fittingness of an emotional response to a wrongdoer when nothing further is involved in justified forms of harsh treatment. Nevertheless, the appeal to mere fittingness also has a considerable cost. *It risks changing the subject.* Strawson (1962) originally proposed that we focus upon the reactive attitudes as a way to fill the lacuna he claimed to find in the justification offered by his contemporaries for our moral responsibility *practices*, including our practices of blaming and punishing.[27]

---

[27] One perfectly fair way to resist my charge here is just to note that maybe the subject needs to be changed. Not all philosophical traditions and topics are venerable, after all. Maybe this preoccupation with (noninstrumental) justifications for harm and related obsessions about control is simply misguided. There are, one might protest, more edifying ways to revise and upgrade our practices and our justifications for holding others to account, ones that promote more constructive ways of shaping human agency. Perhaps this is what, for instance, Manuel Vargas (2013) might say, along with Victoria McGeer (2015, 2019), and Anneli Jefferson (2019). I'll not engage these revisionist

170 CLARIFICATIONS AND FURTHER DEVELOPMENTS

My own view, which I cannot defend here, is that the proper way forward for Strawsonians is to take the more ambitious path: Appeal to desert as the species of fittingness pertaining to the appropriateness of our morally reactive attitudes. Admittedly, we cannot achieve what Strawson thought we could by taking this path, which is an effortless end-run around the thorny metaphysical problems that the libertarians of his day attempted to face head on. But in paying this price, we afford ourselves a theory of responsibility that treats as a central burden the justification of our interpersonal practices of blaming and punishing the blameworthy.[28]

It must, however, be granted that fittingness is a more basic and encompassing relation. In this respect it has a virtue that desert lacks in that it is more stable. How so? If it turns out that no one does deserve blame or punishment because no one has free will, as skeptics like Derk Pereboom (2001, 2014) and Galen Strawson (1986) argue, there appears to be no reason why the Strawsonian could not retreat to the more cautious position and so retain the highly plausible, Strawson-inspired naturalistic contention that, come what may, there remains some reasonable sense of the appropriateness of responding with at the very least an attitude of moral anger to the morally objectionable behavior of fellow members of the moral community. In the spirit of Strawson's "Freedom and Resentment," this truly is an inescapable part of our nature, isn't it?

theses here, but do wish to note that I have offered nothing to speak to the force of their concerns.

[28] The proposal I offer here differs from Kelly McCormick's leaner and, admittedly, more elegant fittingness account of desert (2022: 84–90). She contends that we can get desert as applied to angry blame from (mere) fittingness and, in particular, the fittingness of reactive emotions such as resentment and indignation. As an upshot, she remains ecumenical on the control requirements as part of the desert pertaining to angry blame (2022: 86). Contra McCormick, my contention is that mere fittingness will not do. It has to be a species fittingness that supplies more forceful reasons that bear on whether an emotion accurately appraises its object—in this case that an agent acted from ill will. The right kinds of reasons in cases where the fittingness involves desert, I contend, involve more robust freedom requirements than it seems McCormick is willing to commit to.

6.4 Conclusion

My main goal in this chapter has been to explore with great care the relevance of fittingness to theorizing about moral responsibility, especially as a tonic to Strawson's derisive and ungenerous name-calling. I have argued here that we can make good sense of fittingness as a distinctive and informative normative relation in developing a theory of moral responsibility. In the form of desert, it might after all give rise to metaphysical questions about free will that Strawson would have rather avoided. But there is nothing opaque or incoherent or unintelligible here. There are just hard philosophical problems that merit serious answers. Were the ghost of Strawson to appear before me now and, with not so much as a single argument focused on any concrete proposal, accuse me of panicky metaphysics, incoherence, or whatnot, I have an intuition that the following would be a perfectly fitting reply to such name-calling: I'm rubber; you're glue; whatever you say bounces off me and sticks to you.

7

Guilt and Self-Blame

What is self-blame, and what role should it play in a theory of moral responsibility? Moreover, what of the emotional response of guilt? Some philosophers have recently placed guilt and self-blame at the heart of moral responsibility's nature. They have also made the deservingness of both the most fundamental normative consideration in justifying the harms of blaming (e.g., Carlsson, 2017; Duggan, 2018; Nelkin, 2013, 2019b). Doing so appears to threaten conversational (McKenna, 2012) and other communicative theories of moral responsibility (e.g., Hieronymi, 2004; Macnamara, 2015; Watson, 1987). This is because the central cases of blame according to these communicative theories involve others overtly and directly blaming the one who is blameworthy and so communicating in some way to the culpable party. But if one blames oneself, and if one feels guilt for her culpable wrongdoing, nothing needs to be communicated. And if guilt and self-blame are most fundamental, providing the grounds for the other responsibility-related phenomena, then considerations about the communicative or conversational features of our moral responsibility practices seem to be of secondary importance.

An earlier draft of this chapter was published as "Guilt and Self-Blame within a Conversational Theory of Moral Responsibility," in A. Carlsson, ed., *Self-Blame and Moral Responsibility* (New York: Cambridge University Press, 2021).

7.1 Self-Blame and Guilt: My Proposal

Communicative and other conversational theories of moral responsibility take instances of directed blame to be paradigmatic cases of holding morally responsible. In these cases, it is natural to understand blame as communicating some content to another who is the target of blame and who can come to grasp the meaning in what is communicated. By contrast, when one blames oneself, she does not need to be the recipient of a meaning that is communicated by her to herself.

The same remarks apply to the other-directed reactive emotions that many philosophers take to be essential to blaming—resentment and indignation, which we can think of as distinctive forms of anger. These stand in contrast with the self-directed reactive attitude of guilt. Plausibly, these other-directed emotions are the central ones figuring in a communication-based theory. Indeed, communicative theories of responsibility were originally inspired by Gary Watson's insightful remark that these reactive attitudes are "incipiently forms of communication" (1987: 264). Hence, just as self-blame is not treated as paradigmatic of the central cases of holding responsible that need explaining in a communicative theory, so, too, is guilt not treated as paradigmatic. The focus is understandably on the other-directed emotions.

Given these reasons to favor the other-directed forms of blaming and the other-directed emotions, in earlier work (2012) I mistakenly treated self-blame and guilt on the model of other-directed blame. That is, I built an account of these self-referential elements out of and treated them as parasitic on my proposed communicative and conversational account of other-directed blame. Self-blame and guilt, I previously argued (2012: 72–4), should be accounted on the same model as one agent morally addressing another. On this proposal, we are to understand self-blame on analogy with talking with oneself. And we then treat guilt as a reactive response to one's presumed culpability, as if one is directing moral anger

174 CLARIFICATIONS AND FURTHER DEVELOPMENTS

toward oneself in the same manner that we direct our moral anger at another when we directly blame her. But on its face this proposal is implausible. It's phenomenologically inaccurate to think that, in paradigmatic cases of self-blame, when we hold ourselves to account, we conceive of our culpable conduct as something that we need to take up with our own selves. Of course, this does happen, perhaps in moments of uncertainty and struggle, or when we engage in self-remonstration for some shortcoming or failure. One thinks to oneself, "My God! You fool! You ass! How could you have done that? And after all she has done to support you." But often, without any need to address ourselves, as it were, we seamlessly register and hold ourselves to account. When we do, we experience an episode of guilt. As for guilt, it is inaccurate to conceive of guilt as a form of self-directed anger, as I had in earlier work (2012: 66; see also Greenspan, 1995: 130; Shoemaker, 2015: 111). Admittedly, like anger, guilt involves a pained response, but it is a pained response to registering one's own blameworthiness or culpability rather than as a response to a threat or harm (Morris, 1976: 104; Clarke, 2016: 124). Also, guilt's action tendency, unlike anger, is not to retaliate, strike back, seek revenge, or even just confront. It is, rather, to self-correct. One seeks reconciliation or reparation with those whom one has wronged (e.g., see Baumeister, Stillwell, and Heatherton, 1994; Prinz and Nichols, 2010).

To do better, reflect on the target phenomena a communicative theory of moral responsibility is meant to explain: a practice of holding one another to account via our praising and blaming responses for our morally significant conduct. Such a practice, as P. F. Strawson (1962) claimed, was poorly justified by theorizing exclusively in terms of social utility as a basis for forcing others to pay costs for wrongdoing. What is needed is an explanation of our responsibility practices wherein we presume that we are morally licensed to hold each other to account in ways that, as Strawson put it, *express* our nature rather than merely exploit it. This involves accommodating the sorts of reasons that actually matter to and motivate us. So it is that in holding each other to account, we are liable to and often assume we are justified in doing blamey things to one another *for* certain reasons, and with certain emotional proclivities. In these ways, communicative theories of responsibility are supposed to treat our practices of holding responsible, including the directed expression of our emotional responses, as having certain aims supported by these reasons. These aims can be justified or unjustified, and so subject to critical assessment. Crucially, according to communication-based theorists, they can be illuminated by reflecting on their communicative features. So, what roles *do* self-blame and guilt play in accounting for these aims involved in holding each other to account?

In light of these consideration, I propose that self-blame should be accounted for as the desired or preferred response at which we aim, expect, or demand by way of our other-regarding blame when we hold others to account. The same applies to guilt.

Consider self-blame first. To explain self-blame within the context of a communicative theory, we need not understand it as if an agent is addressing herself. Rather, it is the attitude or stance an agent ought to adopt as a fitting response to our blaming her were we to do so. This is consistent with self-blame in contexts in which, as a matter of fact, no one else blames the self-blamer. In conversation, we aim for our audiences' understanding and agreement, anticipating further responses should we be successful in our audience both *understanding* and *endorsing* what we mean to communicate. So, too, in blaming another, at least in many familiar cases, we seek our target's appreciating and endorsing what we convey in morally engaging with them. Thus, if self-blame involves any communicative properties, in paradigmatic cases it should not be thought of as the self-blamer's conveying to herself that she is blameworthy. Instead it should be understood in terms of two features that work together. First, self-blame can be understood in terms of a proper received response from others who would be warranted in expressing their blame were they to do so. Second,

176 CLARIFICATIONS AND FURTHER DEVELOPMENTS

self-blame provides reasons and motivation for further sorts of communicative—and, on my view, conversational—engagement with others in the form of apology, contrition, reconciliation, reparation, acceptance of punishment, or penance.

Now consider guilt. If guilt is characteristically the expression of self-blame, we can treat it in a like manner. Guilt should not be thought of as angrily blaming oneself, as if one is then motivated to confront or retaliate against oneself. It is, rather, the *preferred or desired* response at which other-regarding blaming emotions aim. My proposal here is inspired by and is close to Coleen Macnamara's (2015), as discussed in Chapter 4. I propose to treat guilt as the preferred response from those toward whom we direct our moral anger when they are in fact blameworthy, at least in prototypical cases.[1] In such cases, a blamed agent would express an *endorsement* of the moral demand attendant with others' resentment or indignation. Hence, on my proposal, guilt is the response a blameworthy agent ought to have were others to blame her via their moral anger. Its appropriateness is in part a function of it being a fitting response to the fitting blame of others *when one is in fact blameworthy*.

7.2 Appropriateness, Fittingness, and Desert

Thus far, I have considered the nature of self-blame and guilt rather than ask about their norms. Of course, implicit in the discussion so far is that there are normative standards in play. If self-blame is or can be a meaningful response to the blame of others, as with guilt, and if meaningfulness includes a communicative or conversational dimension, then one normative constraint will be

---

[1] In various degenerate cases, this is not true. One senator might angrily blame an adversary not with the aim of seeking guilt but to provoke. In general, all of our responsibility practices can be weaponized for objectionable means. A full discussion of the ethics of blame would take up such topics, something I'll not pursue here.

GUILT AND SELF-BLAME 177

a function of intelligibility. Just as in actual conversations, some replies to a speaker will be intelligible and so felicitous rather than unintelligible and so infelicitous, so, too, some forms of self-blame and some guilty responses can be evaluated as meaningful or intelligible responses to the blame of others and to the wrongdoing that is a basis for it. This as in contrast with other responses that are not. Still, as I have argued (Chapter 3), norms of meaningfulness or intelligibility are not sufficient to capture the sort of ethical or moral foundation required for *directed* blaming responses to the blameworthy, at least when what we are interested in is moral blameworthiness. This is because, like punishment, even if less so, blame involves exposing its targets to forms of unwelcome treatment, treatment we have moral reasons to avoid in the absence of an adequate justification. To proceed, I will assume that when an agent is blameworthy for something, the salient justification of her self-blame and guilt is a matter of desert; she deserves to blame herself, and she deserves to feel guilty.

Here we can rely upon the work done in Chapter 3. Recall *appropriateness* as it figures in Wallace's biconditional.

(N) S is morally responsible (for an action x) if and only if it would be appropriate to hold s morally responsible (for action x) (1994: 91).

(N) simply specifies that there exists some normative warrant of one sort or another for blaming one who is blameworthy. Various candidates such as fairness, on Wallace's (1994) account, might be considered, but the two that will concern us here are *fittingness* and *desert*. In the previous chapter, I argued that we can think of desert as a species of fittingness. This is contrary to how several others theorize about it (e.g., Carlsson, 2017; Clarke and Rawling, 2022; Nelkin, 2016, 2019b; Shoemaker, 2015). They treat appraisals of the fittingness at issue to be distinct from desert. Are they correct? Tending to the norms for both self-blame and guilt, we can put

178 CLARIFICATIONS AND FURTHER DEVELOPMENTS

pressure on my opposing view. But first we need clarity on the relation between them.

7.3 Blame and the Reactive Attitudes

Set aside for the moment normative considerations regarding fittingness and desert. How should we understand the relation between blame and negative reactive attitudes? Thus far, I have discussed self-blame and the reactive attitude of guilt separately. Above I characterized guilt as the affective complement or expression of self-blame. Some will balk. Why treat them separately? Following P. F. Strawson (1962), many treat blame exclusively in terms of the negative reactive attitudes of resentment, indignation, and guilt. On views of this sort, blame is simply *identified* with the pertinent reactive attitudes (e.g., Russell, 2004, 2017; Wallace, 1994). For instance, as Andreas Carlsson has recently argued, to self-blame just is to feel guilty (2022). According to these philosophers, one blames just in case one experiences an episode of a negative reactive attitude of resentment, indignation, or guilt. I assume that many who defend this claim think of it as a necessary truth. Getting clear on these issues bears on the above normative considerations regarding desert and fittingness. If after all guilt and self-blame are distinct, then perhaps we would do better to assess one in terms of desert—blame—and another in terms of fittingness—the reactive emotions.

So, should we *identify* blame with the negative reactive attitudes, and so self-blame with guilt? If so, should we take this identification to express a necessary truth? In response to both questions: No. Consider first the claim of necessity. Even if it is true of human beings that one blames just in case one experiences an episode of a negative reactive attitude, this is not a necessary truth. My argument is simple. Grant that directed blaming is of a piece with a set of responsibility practices that involve holding members of a moral

GUILT AND SELF-BLAME 179

community to account relative to standards set by the moral community. These practices involve making demands that members act with a reasonable degree of good will toward one another. Community members respond negatively when other members do not act with sufficient good will, and they do so by means that communicate moral demands and indicate expectations for apology, restitution, and modifications to objectionable behavior. In holding to account by blaming, they signal sanction-like policies toward the culpable in terms of the sorts of relations the blamed person might expect from others. And so on. But, as noted in Chapter 2, it is possible that there are beings who do not have emotions, or at least do not have emotions like ours, but hold each other to account in just the ways discussed here. This is intelligible. If so, it is not a *necessary* truth that to blame one must experience an episode of a negative reactive attitude. Nor is it a necessary truth that to self-blame one must feel guilty.

Some will be unimpressed by the preceding argument, countering that our theory of moral responsibility *should* be anthropocentric. We don't care about Martian self-blame. We care about us. Fair enough. Indeed, I agree (2012: 110–2). So what if it is a contingent truth that one blames just in case one experiences a negative reactive attitude. It is still true of us, isn't it? Some might argue that it is a necessary truth *about us*, a proposal we considered in Chapter 2. But I do not think it is true, even as a contingent truth restricted to critters like us. There are plausible cases where it seems a person self-blames and yet does not feel guilty, and there are also plausible cases where a person feels guilty but does not self-blame.

Let's start with cases where a person can credibly be said to self-blame but yet does not feel guilty. Maria is severely depressed. Prior to her depressive episode she treated Martin horribly at a party and went home thinking nothing of it. As her illness set in, and after a friend reminded her of the event in a conversation, it dawned on her that she wronged Martin. As her affect is so flattened by her current state, she simply does not have any distinguishable pained

180 CLARIFICATIONS AND FURTHER DEVELOPMENTS

response at all to her poor conduct. All the same, she recognizes that she has wronged Martin. Indeed, she is self-aware enough to know that were she not depressed she would feel terrible. Still, as it happens, she doesn't. Yet she accepts that she was blameworthy for doing so, and somehow despite her illness she resolves to take steps to hold herself to account for treating Martin so poorly. She recognizes Martin's recent cool treatment of her as his way of blaming her, and she accepts it as fitting. She calls Martin and apologizes, makes various mental notes to herself to correct her behavior in future interactions, and takes steps to signal to Martin in future interactions that she'll take more care with how she treats him in social settings. I say Maria blames herself, but she feels no guilt.

Here is one more case. Double M has dropped acid with a group of friends.[2] In hysterics, he makes a wise crack about a fellow traveler, Crispin, and it cuts deep. It's a terribly cruel joke, even though by all accounts from those around it's hysterical. Except to Crispin. Poor Crispin is visibly wounded. With tears of laughter running down his face, Double M apologizes to Crispin profusely, "I am so sorry man! I should never have said that. Really, I mean it." He does everything he can in his drug-addled state to hold himself to account for what he clearly registers as a blameworthy remark on his part. Still, *he feels no guilt at all*. He can't. His ability to do so is finked by the acid. He even goes on to laugh about his current psychic state, reporting to his fellow trippers that he knows he should feel terrible, but he just can't. It's all too hilarious. Here, too, I say Double M blames himself, but he feels no guilt.

Now consider cases where a person feels guilty and yet she does not blame herself. I offer two sorts of cases. The first involves recalcitrant emotions. The second involves a failure of commitment. The first sort is familiar enough. Fernando has just had sex with

---

[2] For the uncool, "dropping acid" means ingesting LSD, a hallucinogenic drug that can induce extreme euphoria.

GUILT AND SELF-BLAME 181

Manuel, and though he fully believes there is nothing wrong with doing so, he feels terribly guilt. All of this he realizes is the upshot of his Catholic upbringing, wherein homosexual sex is regarded as a sin. But Fernando rejects all of it. In no way does he hold himself to account. He takes no steps to correct his behavior; rather, he redoubles his efforts to enjoy his sexual life as a gay man. He has no commitment at all to apologize to anyone for what he has done, and he is strongly disposed to resist rather than embrace the blaming behavior from anyone who would be inclined to blame him for doing something that they would regard as immoral (cf. Pereboom, 2021: 34; Roberts, 2003: 89). In this case, Fernando's recalcitrant emotion of guilt does not rise to the level of self-blame, so long as we understand self-blame as a means of holding oneself to account for conduct taken to be blameworthy.

The second sort of case involves a failure of commitment in the face of appropriate guilt. Both Buster and Manny join in with a bigoted crew who harass and berate a local Jewish family whose financial success in their community is interpreted through the lens of stereotypical Jewish caricature. Their piling on contributes to the local community shunning the family. As a result, the family moves out of town to protect their children from derision and isolation. Later, both Buster and Manny confess to each other that they feel guilty about joining in with that crew. They confess to each other that they now see it almost exclusively in terms of a tribal inclination to fit in. Indeed, they both agree that they are blameworthy. However, Buster and Manny respond to their guilt differently. Buster holds himself to account. He resolves not to treat members of groups such as Jewish people poorly and to resist those from the prejudicial group he previously went along with. He decides to apologize in person to the father and mother of the Jewish family if ever he has a chance to see them, and he accepts that any blaming treatment from the family or others in his community is fully legitimate. He'll not resist, and he'll be contrite if and when confronted. As for Manny, none of this is true. He feels guilt, but he does not commit at all to holding himself to account in light of the ethical considerations in virtue of which he is blameworthy. In this respect, he is morally weak—a coward. He won't commit despite his bad feelings. Indeed, the following week a Native American family moves into town, and yet again Manny joins in with that nasty crew, just so he can fit in. In this case, I say Manny feels guilty, but, unlike Buster, he does not blame himself.[3]

The preceding four cases show that guilt and self-blame are distinct. Neither is necessary nor sufficient for the other. Nevertheless, they *are* intimately connected, as are other-directed blame and expressions of moral anger in the form of resentment and indignation. How so? Episodes of these reactive attitudes are the affective complements of our blaming in exemplar or paradigmatic cases. They provide the characteristic medium within which we normally express our blame, and they offer a motivational source of our preparedness to blame. Moreover, because we characteristically blame in this way, our conventions for expressing our blame toward others have been built up out of the practices wherein these emotions are given expression. For these reasons, I propose that we theorize about both blame and the negative reactive attitudes by attending to paradigmatic or exemplar cases representative of the phenomena we are most interested in assessing. Thus, in the many familiar cases that come to mind, one self-blames *by way of feeling guilty*. Her guilt provides the motivational engine to respond to the blame of others in ways that express the fact that she does hold herself to account, does appreciate the moral demands of others, is motivated to improve herself morally, to reconcile, and so on. Because of this tight, albeit contingent, connection between

---

[3] For an insightful discussion of the norms of self-blame, see Hannah Tierney (2022), who argues that, *ceteris paribus*, one self-blames wrongly when one does not express their self-blame to those whom they've wronged here. My argument is consistent with hers, but I make a stronger claim here. When there is no inclination at all to engage in any meaningful expressions of self-blame, despite feeling guilt, one does not self-blame at all.

the central cases of self-blame and guilt, we can still make sense of the contention that self-blame and guilt can both be fitting and deserved. Or so I will now argue.

7.4 The Fittingness and Deservingness of Directed Blame and Moral Anger

Set aside for the moment self-blame and guilt. Consider paradigmatic cases of directed blame wherein one blames another, and grant that the blame is deserved. As I have argued, within the context of a conversational theory, directed blaming can be assessed for being intelligible or unintelligible as a means of addressing a blamed party. Just as, in actual conversations, some replies to an interlocutor can miss their mark while others are especially apt, so, too, when blaming, one can blame another in a way that is infelicitous rather than felicitous. Recall the example of Daphne and Leslie (Chapter 2). Daphne directly blames Leslie for her hurtful racist remark about Hispanics. As set out, Daphne's behavior has a meaning and is intelligible as a reply to the salience of Leslie's morally objectionable conduct. It is *fitting*, and its fit is captured on analogy with conversational felicity.

By contrast with the case as described above, imagine instead that Daphne had done none of the above, thought nothing of leaving the coffee shop, kept the planned meeting with their mutual Hispanic friend, but instead angrily told Leslie her breath stinks and then stuck her tongue out at her. In this case, we need not say that Daphne does not blame Leslie. Rather, we might say she does so in a way that is unfitting. Note that if we understand Daphne's blame as expressed through her indignation, we can then also say of her expression of moral anger that it is fitting for its object when it involves a mode of replying meaningfully to Leslie's offense.

Note two things. First, there is a sense in which, if appropriate, Daphne's meaningful reply *accurately represents* Leslie's offense, just as is required of fittingness. Its intelligibility turns on responding to what Leslie really did and to the meaning that it reveals in terms of the quality of her will. (Suppose Daphne misheard Leslie, and Leslie was not talking about hating Hispanics, but about hating her cousin's histrionics.) Second, its fit captures something that is case-specific, a feature of fittingness noted above. For instance, as an expression of Daphne's blame, she cancels plans to get together with a mutual Hispanic friend, and she also cuts short a date already in progress in a coffee shop where Daphne presumes others might have taken offense or been hurt. These details are rendered appropriate means of Daphne expressing her indignation only in light of the prior relationship and shared expectations.

Just now, I offered a way to show that, in paradigmatic cases of directed blaming, deserved blame and the other-directed emotion of indignation, a species of moral anger, can be usefully illuminated in terms of fittingness. What of desert? Can desert be used to help illuminate fittingness in pertinent contexts? Of course, I stipulated that Leslie deserves Daphne's blame. But what about the reactive emotion, given that I have argued that it is not to be identified with blame? Does she deserve to be the target of another's directed moral anger or some other unpleasant emotional response? Here is the key question: Will desert supply an illuminating way to understand the appropriateness of expressing the pertinent emotions, *or is fittingness alone adequate to account for the appropriateness of the emotional response?*

Here is a quick explanation of why Leslie deserves to be the target of these fitting emotions, followed by a slightly more cautious proposal. The conventional resources for blaming and the characteristic motivation that gives rise to blaming practices are built up out of our modes of manifesting our emotions. As Strawson (1962) observed, these are our actual blaming practices because *this is what we are like.* In this way, if blame is deserved, it is deserved as expressed by beings like us with the sort of affect

GUILT AND SELF-BLAME   185

we deploy to hold others to account. So, yes, *if* the blame is deserved, then the directed anger, as a mode of expressing blame, is deserved.

A slightly more cautious reply goes like this. Deserved blame involves justifications for modes of treatment in response to morally objectionable conduct. The justification that desert offers supplies reasons for why, in holding each other to account, certain forms of treatment that would otherwise be unjustified are in these contexts justified. Those forms of treatment are conventionally understood to be not only unwelcome, but potentially harmful. At least this is so in typical cases. Indeed, as I have argued, these harms are even understood to be noninstrumentally good. But the harms involved in blaming that are registered by the blamed are often harms *precisely because* they are understood by their targets as expression of others' moral anger. The sting that is part of the deserved blame—the harm that is deserved—is a harm *constituted* by being the recipient of others' anger. So, in these paradigmatic cases, if the blame of others is deserved, so is their anger as the means whereby that directed blame is expressed.

7.5 An Analog to "The Punishment Should Fit the Crime"

A further feature of deserved blame gives reason to appeal to considerations of fit to better understand deservingness. When it comes to punishment, it is commonplace to note that the punishment should fit the crime. In the case of blame, there is no such pithy statement. Still, it is plausible to suppose that in like manner the blame should fit the culpable wrong. Given the conversational theory, an appealing feature of the fittingness of a blaming reply to blameworthy conduct is that its meaning can be tailored specifically as a felicitous reply. If this sort of fitting reply is what is

186 CLARIFICATIONS AND FURTHER DEVELOPMENTS

deserved, we have an elegant way to evaluate just how it is that one sort of blaming response is the one that is deserved rather than some other.

To illustrate, consider again the case of Daphne and Leslie. Above I suggested an infelicitous blaming response by Daphne, spouting out "Your breath stinks!" rather than the fitting response described. Imagine a different sort of infelicity. Suppose Leslie had also culpably slacked off on some work and left it for others, including Daphne, as they are also coworkers as well as friends. Now suppose *as a response to Leslie's racist remark*, Daphne does none of what I described above. Instead she leaves work she could help Leslie complete for Leslie to do on her own. Suppose it is the sort of work they would cheerfully do together when on friendlier terms, but now she does not. Imagine also she angrily says to Leslie, "You know, you are taxing everyone else in the office by blowing us off!" Suppose that Leslie is upset by Daphne's display of anger, and that she is just as wounded and unsettled by it as she would have been had Daphne's reply been as described above.[4]

Here is the point. Leslie might deserve *this* blame from Daphne just as much as she deserves the blame wherein Daphne confronts her about her prejudicial remark. It might sting just as much, and it might be of equal value in terms of being noninstrumentally good that she is so addressed. Nevertheless, *it is not fitting as a reply to her racist remark*. So, though she might deserve it, it is not what she deserves for the offense in question. As philosophers like Feinberg (1970) might put it, the desert base is not fitted for the one response but is fitted for the other. This helps to show that an analog to conversational fittingness, a kind of intelligibility of replying to a meaningful contribution, is a feature of deserved blame. Hence, we get the result that desert in this domain is a species of fittingness.

---

[4] The argument I offer here is similar to one I offer in Chapter 6 (Section 6.3.1).

7.6 The Fittingness and Deservingness of Self-Blame and Guilt

Thus far, I have argued that in the exemplar or paradigmatic cases of blaming the blameworthy, the directed blame and the directed negative reactive attitudes that express blame can be *both* fitting *and* deserved. However, my argument so far has focused only on the blame of others and on the moral anger involved in resentment and indignation. What of self-blame and guilt? Here I can be brief.

Randolph Clarke contends that we should understand guilt as a pained response to the thought that one is blameworthy (2016: 122–3). I agree. Or at least I agree with the basic proposal that in some way the pained response of guilt is to be understood in terms of an agent's assessment of her own conduct as blameworthy or culpable. We can treat self-blame in like fashion. It is an attitude one adopts toward oneself as a response to her own presumption of blameworthiness. So understood, it seems on its face that we have no need to appeal to any communicative or conversational resources to understand either. But we do. Grant that guilt is a pained response to registering one's own blameworthiness. Still, it is a response that, if properly grasped, involves an appreciation of the kinds of reasons others have for communicating their blame to that person. It also can be understood as the sort of attitude others would prefer or desire that she have in light of her treatment of those whom she wronged. The same applies to her self-blame. In all of these ways, we can understand her guilt and her self-blame in terms of the sorts of actions that would involve fitting expressions. That is to say, as part of a set of practices of holding each other to account, both guilt and self-blame can be assessed for their suitability in responding meaningfully to others in a moral community, and most crucially those one has wronged.

To illustrate, imagine that Leslie receives Daphne's blame as Daphne prefers for Leslie to receive it. Leslie comes to blame herself, and she feels guilty. Plausibly, that requires her blaming herself in a certain way and feeling guilty in a manner that renders certain sorts of conduct fitting expressions of her holding herself accountable. This in turn involves the way she is disposed to respond to others. Suppose instead, drawing upon the example of infelicitous other-regarding blame above, that in blaming herself and feeling guilty *for her hurtful racist remark*, Leslie does not apologize for that. She makes no effort to alter any of her modes of interacting with Hispanics, including her and Daphne's mutual Hispanic friend, and she persists in making racially derogatory remarks. Instead, Leslie self-corrects at work and carries more of the weight to help out Daphne and her coworkers with the more unpleasant tasks. She makes extra efforts to be kind in the workplace, and so on. All the while, what she feels terrible for is her racist remark, not her poor behavior at work. But to this hurtful remark, she signals in no way in her expressions of guilt that she takes a stance toward objectionable racist attitudes. Her holding herself to account involves nothing recognizable to other would-be blamers that would communicate that she has taken a stance against her own culpability. In this case, in some perverse way, Leslie might feel guilty for and blame herself for that remark, but it is not fitting, and it is not what she deserves. She deserves to feel a guilt that tends to and is a response to the nature of the wrong for which she is blameworthy. And she deserves to blame herself and hold herself to account in a way that is fitted for that wrong. The conversational theory of moral responsibility illuminates this in terms of intelligible—and so fitting—responses to the blame of others were others to blame. This applies to cases of self-blame and guilt wherein, as a matter of fact, no one else does blame the blameworthy person.

7.7 Assessing Carlsson's Guilt-Based Theory of Blameworthiness

Andreas Carlsson has recently argued that to be blameworthy is simply to deserve guilt (2017). Identifying guilt with self-blame, he writes, "[To] blame oneself—to feel guilty—necessarily involves suffering" (90). He also argues that other-regarding directed blame cannot credibly be what a blameworthy person most fundamentally deserves. Why? It is a contingent matter whether one who is blameworthy suffers due to the blame of others (99–100). After all, a culpable person might not care at all about the blame of others. It might not bother her in the least. Not so with the guilt involved in self-blame. It is necessarily painful. Hence, what a blameworthy person deserves most fundamentally is to feel guilt. He also denies that we should evaluate guilt in terms of fittingness, since responses can be fitting even when a person did not freely act to bring them about, but this cannot be used to justify aiming to bring about responses that are intrinsically painful. Desert, he argues, requires freedom and is itself distinct from fittingness. It supplies the needed normative warrant of guilt, and it helps justify why we ought to blame others and so seek a response of guilt from them (110–3). Finally, Carlsson rejects Clarke's (2016) minimal desert thesis that agents who are blameworthy deserve to feel guilty *because they are blameworthy* (Carlsson 2017: 91). His objection to Clarke's proposal is that it presupposes a prior understanding of blameworthiness (91). Carlsson instead argues not just that blameworthiness necessarily involves deserved guilt, but that deserved guilt *grounds* blameworthiness. When a person is blameworthy, it is in virtue of deserving guilt.

Carlsson's proposal is intriguing and thoughtfully developed. Much is consistent with the conversational theory. For instance, if we restrict our attention to actual human beings and set aside thought experiments about possible beings without emotion, it is plausible that a person is blameworthy just in case she *deserves* to experience guilt as a response to her wrongdoing. Nothing as set out above is incompatible with this. Consider, for instance, Maria and Double M. Neither were in a position to experience guilt. But this does not mean they did not deserve it. They were simply not equipped to receive something they deserved. Of course, contra Carlsson's proposal, the cases of Maria and Double M show that in

190   CLARIFICATIONS AND FURTHER DEVELOPMENTS

blaming oneself one does not necessarily feel guilty. But Carlsson's contention that guilt is a central concept that can be used to elucidate blameworthiness is not impugned. Nor is it in tension with the thesis developed here that fitting and deserved guilt needs to be understood by reference to the communicative features that would make it salient as a meaningful way of responding to the blame of others.

Nevertheless, there are two points where in my estimation Carlsson overreaches. First, Carlsson's reason for rejecting the contention that other-regarding blame can be used to ground blameworthiness is that it does not *necessarily* involve the suffering of the blamed. Rather, the relation between the potential harms in the blame of others and the person blamed is contingent and indirect (2017: 99–100). So, if a culpable person deserves to suffer for her wrongdoing, it cannot be that what she deserves is the blame of others. This is a point Carlsson shares with Dana Nelkin (2013: 124). This, however, is not a good reason to reject the thesis that we can ground blameworthiness in deserving the blame of others, especially in the form of directed moral anger. To begin, one might simply tweak the thesis in a plausible way and avoid the worries about contingency. We could say that what a blameworthy person deserves most fundamentally is not simply others' blame, but to have a pained response to registering the moral anger expressed in others' blame. Indeed, I suspect this is what most have in mind when they link a desert thesis about other-directed blame to the blameworthy. Of course, this is consistent with its *also* being true that a blameworthy person deserves to feel guilty.[5]

Also, Carlsson and Nelkin assume it is problematic to identify what a person deserves with something that is only contingently related to its being harmful or unpleasant for the person who deserves

---

[5] I take it to be a virtue of Clarke's (2016) minimal desert thesis that his proposal is silent about these matters. That is, nothing in his formulation linking blameworthiness to deserved guilt rules out other things like the blame and moral anger of others also being deserved and also being fundamental to blameworthiness and moral responsibility.

it. I disagree. Not everything a person deserves is something she is assured of getting. Sometimes efforts to give a person what she deserves fail, yet that is no reason to think she does not deserve it. To put the point differently: A person may deserve to be treated in a certain way partly on account of the intended consequence of the treatment. Suppose the intended consequence doesn't come about. It may still be true that she deserved, fundamentally, to be treated in that way. So, for example, the person who deserves to receive the trophy for winning the race might drop dead or turn into a turnip before receiving it. She did not get it, but she deserved to. So one key premise in Carlsson's argument for favoring guilt over the angry blame of others is false. The angry blame of others and the harm or suffering conventionally associated with it can be something a blameworthy person deserves. This is so even if she would not find it unpleasant or regard it as a setback to her interests.

Second, between the deserved angry blame of others, and deserved self-blame and guilt, which is more fundamental? I would say neither. They both have a fundamental role to play if either does. This is borne out by the explanation I offered regarding the aims of the blame of others and of the uptake others would prefer of the blamed. Carlsson, I take, treats self-blame as the fundamental notion; the blame of others is a secondary matter. But in many cases, it is not just that a person deserves to experience the pain of guilt for her wrongdoing. What she deserves is to be confronted by those whom she has wronged and to come to experience guilt as a response. In this way, one of the things that makes it good that she experiences the pain of guilt is that it is an expression of her respect or concern for those who have reason to blame her, and it is so as an apt response to a phase in a moral conversation. For cases of this sort, we cannot leave out of the picture reference to the desert of other-regarding blame. This is just an application of a more general feature of the phenomena that needs to be explained. Accountability is about our relations with each other whereby we hold *each other* to account. Guilt's role, and its value as something

192 CLARIFICATIONS AND FURTHER DEVELOPMENTS

deserved, is connected with our relations of mutual regard and the general demand, as Strawson put it, that we show good will toward one another. So, guilt has its place, but it is not *more* fundamental to accountability than the role played by the blame of others.

7.8 A Final Consideration: How Fitting Guilt Might Come Apart from Desert

In this chapter, I have argued for the thesis that we should understand deserved self-blame as a species of fittingness, and we should as well understand fitting guilt as deserved. I did so by deploying features of the conversational theory to show that we can understand what sorts of blaming and self-blaming responses are deserved in terms of conversational fittingness. So, too, for the negative reactive emotions characteristic of blaming, both the angry blame of resentment and indignation, as well as guilt. A critic might protest that we can assess both blaming practices and pertinent emotions via various norms. One might be a matter of fit, another a matter of desert. Perhaps they co-occur in a certain domain and even have the very same objects, as would be the case if, contrary to my counterarguments, we identify blaming with the pertinent negative reactive attitudes. Still, fittingness and desert are distinct. One is not a species of the other.[6]

I reject this alternative proposal. For one reason, it does not allow us to illuminate what sorts of blaming responses are deserved by reference to considerations of fit. Treating desert as a species of fittingness does, as I argued above. Nevertheless, there is a more cautious qualification of my proposal that does make room for the thought that guilt might after all be fitting but not deserved. Fitting accounts of the emotions in general are well-supported. As guilt

---

[6] Justin D'Arms thoughtfully suggested this proposal. Randolph Clarke and Piers Rawling (2022) have recently defended this sort of view.

is such a pervasive emotion, it would be perverse to think that we could not illuminate a normative assessment of it in terms of fit along with the full suite of human emotions. This supplies a strong incentive to endorse a fittingness account of guilt. But our blaming practices and our folk assessments of guilt both seem subject to considerations of desert. These plausibly turn upon assumptions about free agency or free will as a condition of desert, and so justice, a thesis I defended in Chapter 6. This supplies a strong incentive to endorse a desert-based account of norms bearing on both blame and guilt.

Grant the two preceding points. Should we now assume that in this domain desert and fittingness *must* come together? No. Recall the final results of the preceding chapter. If free will and moral responsibility skepticism are true, no one basically deserves directed blame and the accompanying harms involved in expressions of anger and guilt. Would the emotions in play here then be unfitting? Not at all. Suppose no has free will and that, therefore, as free will skeptics argue, no one deserves the harms of blaming, punishing, and so on. Surely in some way guilt might still accurately represent to a guilty party that her treatment of another was objectionable— say as manifesting ill or insufficient good will toward another. This sort of fittingness as accurate representation would not itself, in the absence of appeal to desert, involve any further judgment that, as desert theorists would have it, it is noninstrumentally good or just to experience the pain intrinsic to guilt. So, my final proposal is this. If persons have free will and are morally responsible, then self-blame and guilt are both things that a moral agent might deserve, even if they are distinct, albeit importantly related, phenomena. If not, guilt and other emotions are still subject to evaluation in terms of fit—*even if they are not deserved*. Since desert on my proposal supplies *pro tanto* reasons for forms of treatment that are otherwise morally problematic, while fittingness alone does not, the forms of treatment that fitting moral anger and guilt can help to justify in the absence of desert are far more limited.

PART III
INTERROGATING THE PROPOSAL

8

The Attenuated Role of the Hostile Emotions

> We are covered in blood girl, you know our forefathers
> were slaves. Let us hope they've found mercy in their
> bone-filled graves.... But there's violence in the eyes, girl,
> so let us not be enticed.
>
> —Bob Dylan, *Precious Angel*

According to some moral responsibility skeptics, negative reactive attitudes of anger are morally problematic. They therefore provide a strong incentive for abolitionism or revisionism about our ordinary concept of moral responsibility (e.g., Caruso, 2012; Caruso and Pereboom, 2022; Flanagan, 2016; Levy, 2011; Nadelhoffer and Tocchetto, 2013; Pereboom, 2001, 2014, 2021; Waller, 2011, 2014, 2015). This is because they are assumed to be so intimately tied to our ordinary understanding of what it is to be and to hold morally responsible that, absent significant revision, we cannot defend the legitimacy of the latter but by way of presuming the good standing of the former. Indeed, many philosophers contend that moral responsibility is essentially connected to these emotions (e.g., Bell, 2013; Bennett, 1980; Shoemaker, 2015, 2017b; Wallace, 1994). I disagree. I disagree both about the contention that moral responsibility is essentially linked to the reactive attitudes and to the contention that the negative ones are as problematic as many take them to be.

Responsibility and Desert. Michael McKenna, Oxford University Press. © Oxford University Press 2024.
DOI: 10.1093/9780197679999.003.0008

198 INTERROGATING THE PROPOSAL

8.1 The Essentialist Thesis and the Hostility Thesis

Call the thesis that the negative reactive attitudes are essential to moral responsibility *the essentialist thesis*. Many have endorsed some variation on this thesis. Strawson (1962) appears to have done so in the following passage[*]:

> Only by attending to this range of attitudes can we recover from the facts as we know them a sense of what we mean, i.e., of all we mean, when, speaking the language of morals, we speak of desert, responsibility, guilt, condemnation, and justice. (1962, as appearing in Watson, 2003: 91)

Following this Strawsonian-inspired thesis, David Shoemaker (2017b) makes the reactive emotions the grounding feature of moral responsibility. What moral responsibility most fundamentally is involves appraisals of agents and their conduct that render fitting an emotional response from those who would hold these agents responsible. R. Jay Wallace (1994) accounts for holding morally responsible for wrongdoing in terms of experiencing an episode of a negative reactive attitude of resentment or indignation, or believing such a response would be appropriate. Macalester Bell defends a view she calls the "hostile attitude account," arguing that the negative reactive attitudes partially constitute blame (2013: 266). More generally, many philosophers writing on moral responsibility understand blame most fundamentally in terms of the appropriateness of a negative reactive attitude.

In what way are these negative reactive attitudes found to be morally problematic? The most passionately argued criticism is that they are hostile emotions. They involve a morally indefensible propensity

---

[*] Note, I say *appears*. As readers will learn, I am skeptical that Strawson intended to endorse anything as modally robust as this.

THE ATTENUATED ROLE OF THE HOSTILE EMOTIONS   199

to cruelty and revenge, seeking the suffering of those at whom they are directed. Call this thesis—the thesis that the negative reactive attitudes are hostile and so morally unjustified—*the hostility thesis.*

Even P. F. Strawson, who was no critic but instead an advocate for the value of these emotions, wrote of the connection between them and a "preparedness to acquiesce in that infliction of suffering on the offender which is an essential part of punishment" (1962, as appearing in Watson, 2003: 90). Bruce Waller, who was a critic, argued that this preparedness to inflict suffering is deeply objectionable. He characterized such emotions, which he took to be central to our understanding of moral responsibility, as "strike-back emotions" (2014: 39–51). And he argued that the fundamental motive in their expression is "even deeper than revenge: it is the powerful desire to 'pass the pain along'" (2014: 43). On his account, in numerous cases one is not all that concerned to pass on the pain to the person who deserves it; anyone will do. Martha Nussbaum argues that if anger can be made intelligible, it is as a means of lowering the status of wrongdoers relative to our own through causing their "pain and humiliation" (2016: 5). On her view, "it is normatively problematic to focus exclusively on relative status. . . . [T]hat type of obsessive narrowness, though common enough, is something we ought to discourage in both self and others" (6).

According to Derk Pereboom, the most salient reason to reject or at least contain these emotions is due to a metaphysical presupposition implicit in them—in particular, the presupposition that those at whom they are directed exercised their free will and so basically deserve to be the target of their expressions (Pereboom 2014: 128–29, 180–82). On his view it's not their morally problematic nature alone that supplies the rationale; the metaphysical assumptions are key. Nevertheless, we have a strong *incentive* to settle this matter given the moral hazards of acting on these emotions.

Frequently expressions of moral anger are intended to cause physical or emotional pain. . . . In extreme cases, it can provide motivation to take very harmful and even lethal action against another.

> The sense that expressions of moral anger are damaging gives rise to a robust demand that they be morally justified. The demand to produce a moral justification for behavior that is harmful to others is always pressing, and expressions of moral anger are typically harmful to others. Moreover, this demand is made more acute by our attachment to moral anger; we often enjoy displaying it, and so we want these displays to be morally justified. We frequently justify expressions of moral anger by the claim that wrongdoers deserve to be their target in the basic sense. From the hard incompatibilist perspective, however, this claim is mistaken. (2009: 172)

Of course, the hostility thesis has ancient roots, dating back to, among others, Seneca, who characterized anger as the "most hideous and frenzied of all the emotions" and "wholly violent," having as its "onrush . . . resentment, raging with a most inhuman lust for weapons, blood, and punishment" (1928, I.1, as quoted in Srinivasan, 2017: 2).

Building upon the hostility thesis, and citing the teachings of Mahatma Gandhi and Martin Luther King, others have argued that the practices that give expression to these negative reactive attitudes are, as Gary Watson has put it, "destructive of human community" (e.g., 1987, as appearing in 2004: 255). Social harmony is often compromised by acting on these emotions; they place distance between those blamed and those who hold the blamed to account (e.g., Nadelhoffer and Tocchetto, 2013; Pereboom, 2014: 180; Waller, 2011). Still others (e.g., Pickard, 2011, 2013), argue that the negative reactive attitudes are deleterious of positive therapeutic outcomes in clinical settings, and more generally in treating persons suffering from various forms of mental illness. A similar problem arises in settings that involve relations where one party is positioned to provide guidance or nurture another whose agency is compromised but can be repaired, or is in an emerging

THE ATTENUATED ROLE OF THE HOSTILE EMOTIONS   201

state of moral development (Brandenburg, 2017). According to a further objection, the negative reactive attitudes are toxic for those who experience them (e.g., Nussbaum, 2016). Efforts to rid oneself of them or to minimize their role in thought and action lead to a more fulfilling life. Finally, many argue that the negative reactive attitudes are sources of epistemic distortion and thereby undermine morality's aims. For instance, Jeanette Kennett and Jessica Wolfendale argue that that these attitudes track and reinforce relationships of privilege and oppression rather than objectionable regard for others' moral standing (2019). In this respect, they simply mislead, and do so from motives of the sort Nussbaum identified, ones involving status. (See also Alicke, 2000; Alicke et al. 1994, 2012; Duggin, 2020; Goldberg et al. 1999; Nadelhoffer, 2006.)

In this chapter, I argue for three interrelated points. First, I will reject the essentialist thesis; the reactive attitudes are not essential to moral responsibility and more specifically to what must be involved in blaming and holding morally responsible for blameworthy conduct. Second, I will also reject the hostility thesis; negative reactive attitudes such as resentment and indignation need not be construed as objectionably hostile or severe and in fact are consistent with morally justifiable expressions that are humane and dignified. Finally, I will advocate for a prescriptive thesis: One should embrace a stance of compassion as a corrective against excessively harsh treatment in the process of blaming. This is compatible with suitable expressions of negative reactive attitudes like resentment.

Before proceeding, I pause to clarify a couple matters. First, some treat the full range of reactive attitudes permissively, and so include such emotions as hurt feelings, regret, and contempt (e.g., Shoemaker, 2015, 2017a). This traces to Strawson (1962). Others wish to restrict them considerably, at least as they pertain to theorizing about moral responsibility (e.g., J. Bennett, 1980; Wallace, 1994). We have no need to settle this issue here. It suffices for present purposes to note that there is some limited range of reactive emotions that have an element of anger in them. The ones

202 INTERROGATING THE PROPOSAL

that Strawson focused upon were resentment and indignation. In moral contexts, these can then be modified as *morally* reactive. Second, there is also some disagreement about how to parse this limited class of negative emotions, the ones deployed in holding persons accountable for blameworthy conduct. Some favor Strawson's use of the terms "resentment" and "indignation" (e.g., Wallace, 1994). (Let's set aside the self-reflective case of guilt.) But others prefer just the more generic notion of "anger" or "moral anger" (e.g., Pereboom, 2009; Shoemaker, 2015). And others (e.g., J. Bennett, 1980) follow Strawson in reserving resentment for reactive responses to personal offenses and rely upon indignation for responses in the domain of accountability when others are morally wronged. In what follows, I will elide all of these finer distinctions and promiscuously write in terms of moral anger while treating resentment and indignation as species of moral anger.

8.2 Resisting the Essentialist Thesis

Consider the following thesis about the relationship between being morally responsible and holding morally responsible, one limited just to blameworthiness and a blaming response[1]:

Necessarily Blameworthy iff Apt Blame: Necessarily, a person is morally blameworthy for performing an action if and only if it is appropriate to hold her morally responsible for performing that action by blaming her.

The pertinent sense of holding responsible and blaming is a matter of a stance or attitude that includes a preparedness to regard or instead treat a person differently in virtue of being blameworthy.

---

[1] As I understand it, being morally responsible for a moral wrong (without an excuse) just is to be morally blameworthy for that wrong.

THE ATTENUATED ROLE OF THE HOSTILE EMOTIONS   203

I endorse some version of the preceding principle (2012). It follows from an important point about the nature of moral responsibility. Being morally responsible *is* essentially related to the conditions for appropriately holding morally responsible. The practices and norms of holding morally responsible set the conditions on the basis of which a morally responsible agent is understood to act well or poorly and be a candidate for assessment in terms of praiseworthiness or blameworthiness.[2]

It bears repeating here that the sense of aptness at issue only provides *pro tanto* reasons. The same applies to the principles to be discussed in what follows. However appropriateness is to be further specified, such as by way of desert (in the fashion of Chapter 3), fairness (e.g., Wallace, 1994), or contractualist considerations (e.g., Scanlon, 1998), it will always be possible that a person whom it would be appropriate to blame should not all-things-considered be blamed. Some other competing reasons might override those reasons for doing so. Imagine as an example that someone deserves to be blamed mildly for a peccadillo but that, due to her present fragile nature, doing so would risk her suicide.

Granting the truth of *Necessarily Blameworthy iff Apt Blame*, here is a principle that should be rejected, despite its apparent Strawsonian bona fides:

Necessarily Blameworthy iff Apt Anger: Necessarily, a person is morally blameworthy for an action if and only if it is appropriate to blame her by responding to her with moral anger.

This principle is often defended along with a corollary that also should be rejected:

Necessarily Blame iff Anger: Necessarily, a person blames another if and only if she responds to the person with moral anger.

---

[2] See Gary Watson's (2014) characterizes Strawson's (1962) view in this way.

204 INTERROGATING THE PROPOSAL

If these two principles are false, then, plausibly, essentialism about the relation between moral responsibility and the reactive attitudes is false, and more particularly, essentialism about the relation between moral blameworthiness, moral blame, and moral anger is false.[3] Why reject these two principles?[4] My argument is simple and relies upon a conceivability claim, one I set forth in in Chapters 2 and 7, but did not develop, as I will here.

> Imagine a world consisting just of rational beings who have complex moral lives, hold each other to account, seek penalties and consider other costs for defecting from various cooperative agreements, and are strongly incentivized to act well and show due regard for the demands of fellow members of their moral community. Yet they have no affect; they are emotionless beings. Or instead imagine beings that have emotions and manifest affect, but they have exceedingly different sorts of emotional profiles, and none of their emotions or any affect associated with them is deployed in the mutual regulation of holding others to account.

Such beings would appear to engage in a set of moral responsibility practices, hold each other to account, and therefore blame each other for blameworthy conduct. But it would be at best misleading to contend that their blameworthy conduct would render it appropriate for them to respond to one another with negative reactive attitudes, understood in terms of moral anger.

One might dig in her heels here and insist on the truth of *Necessarily Blameworthy iff Apt Anger* by arguing that it might still

---

[3] I use the hedge term "plausibly" because there are other reactive emotions like guilt that might serve as candidates for an essentialist thesis (e.g., Carlsson, 2017). Here I assume that guilt should not be construed as a form of self-directed anger (see Chapter 7). I set this issue aside in what follows.

[4] See Pereboom (2021: 41–2) where he also argues against a view like *Necessarily Blame iff Anger*.

THE ATTENUATED ROLE OF THE HOSTILE EMOTIONS   205

be appropriate for such beings to so respond since there are worlds (not their own actual world) in which they were prone to such emotions, and in relevant classes of such worlds they do respond in apt circumstances. I regard this as a desperate response and set it aside in what follows. The actual world for those beings would be one in which, for them, the pertinent attitudes were not appropriate, but wherein, at that world, it is possible that they could be—if they were beings equipped with emotional proclivities that they did not actually possess.

A more credible source of resistance might go as follows: If we were to encounter such beings, it would remain appropriate for *us* to respond with such emotions and in so doing blame them. Hence, *Necessarily Blameworthy iff Apt Anger* is not impugned.[5] This, however, is not sufficient to deflect the challenge on offer here. As I am imagining the sort of cases, these beings would not recognize our responses as modes of blaming. At the very least, it would not be appropriate for us to respond to *them* via directed episodes of these emotions. In any event, it would be odd to think that the role of these emotions helped to capture the essence of blaming and blameworthiness for creatures at such a world, even if strictly speaking it was true that it would be apt for us to respond with anger to such agents and directly blame them were we to have some encounter with them.

Despite my argument against the two preceding principles, a weaker one survives. I doubt anything in Strawson's essay gives reason to believe that he was committed to more.

Blameworthy iff Apt Anger: As human persons actually are, as a matter of contingent fact, a person is morally blameworthy for an action if and only if it is appropriate to blame her by responding to her with moral anger.

[5] Both Justin Capes and David Copp suggested this reply.

206 INTERROGATING THE PROPOSAL

This principle is just *Necessarily Blameworthy iff Apt Anger* without the commitment of necessity, and restricted to critters like us.[6] Note that this weaker principle is consistent with denial of a corollary to *Necessarily Blame iff Anger*, one that drops the modal commitment.

> *Blame iff Anger*: A human person blames another if and only if she responds to the person with moral anger.

I endorse *Blameworthy iff Apt Anger* and reject *Blame iff Anger*.

To explain, on the view I propose, it is a contingent fact that, as the creatures we are and given the moral responsibility practices that as a matter of contingent fact have emerged, a person is blameworthy just in case it would be appropriate (for someone) to respond to her with a blaming emotion. This is so even though there are viable modes of apt blaming that need not involve a reactive emotion of anger, or for that matter any emotional response at all. To illustrate, suppose Marcella is blameworthy for harming a stranger in some minor way, and both of her friends Pat and Leslie are witness to her misdeed. Pat is indignant and expresses a mild degree of moral anger in responding to Marcella. Leslie, however, is not indignant and experiences no episode of anger. Still, Leslie confronts Marcella, demands that she apologize to the stranger, and indicates a commitment to withdraw friendly relations until she does so. Leslie, I contend, blames Marcella, but unlike Pat, not by experiencing or expressing moral anger.[7,8] If so, *Blame iff Anger*

---

[6] I assume none my readers is an alien being or self-conscious robot. My apologies if I am mistaken on this point.

[7] Wallace (1994: 76) disagrees. He would claim that Leslie holds Marcella responsible but does not blame her, whereas Pat does. On his view, blame requires an episode of a reactive sentiment of resentment or indignation (what I am calling anger), and so *Blame iff Anger* is true. I have argued for a more permissive account of blame (2012: 25).

[8] Relatedly, recall also from Chapter 7 (Section 7.3) the case of depressed Maria who blames herself for wronging Martin but has no emotional response due to her depression.

THE ATTENUATED ROLE OF THE HOSTILE EMOTIONS   207

is false. Still, it is true that it would be appropriate for Leslie to experience and direct a mild degree of anger toward Marcella. Hence, *Blameworthy iff Apt Anger* stands.

Perhaps my defense of *Blameworthy iff Apt Anger* is too quick. Pereboom has proposed two cases that look to be clear counterexamples.

> Athena is a parent, and her teenage children misbehave in minor, common, predictable ways; they squabble, fail to clean their room, text their friends when they should be sleeping, Some parents respond with anger, but Athena doesn't, and instead responds from the sense of duty to morally educate, combined with care, but with anger. The angry response is at best optional, in many such cases inappropriate. This is also the case for Basil, a high school teacher, whose students often misbehave in common ways. They come unprepared not having done the assigned reading, distract their classmates by talk not related to class material, and surf the internet instead of participating and paying attention. Basil responds with protest, engaging his students constructively, but not with anger. For both Athena and Basil, the angry response stands to be counterproductive and to undermine forward-looking effectiveness and respect. (2021: 42)

Despite these two provocative examples, properly qualified, *Blameworthy iff Apt Anger* still stands. Note, first, that forward-looking considerations might very well flood the *pro tunto* reasons for a deserved response, resulting in all-things-considered judgments that expressed anger is unjustified. This might be especially so for those charged with the moral development of minors. But if the appropriateness mentioned in the principle can allow for this—and it can—the examples are not decisive. Second, the cases of Athena and Basil might be under-described. As I will argue below, angry responses can be tempered by other laudatory reasons and motivations, and it is consistent with some appropriate ways

208 INTERROGATING THE PROPOSAL

of manifesting anger that one be nurturing and supportive. Maybe Athena and Basil *do* express some anger, but in ways that are not at all counterproductive.

Neither of these two responses are entirely convincing, however, since as a parent or a teacher there does seem to be a special role each plays that favors rising above anger altogether. Let's grant that. It is inappropriate for Athena and for Basil to express any anger at all, and maybe even experience anger privately. Nevertheless, we might say of a slightly revised version of *Blameworthy iff Apt Anger* that a person is morally blameworthy just in case it is appropriate for someone or other to blame her by responding with anger. Maybe Athena oughtn't become angry with her children, but what of the their fellow siblings when one of them treats mom poorly? Or what of the fellow classmates in Basil's classes who have to tolerate the disruption of other unruly students?

While, given the preceding qualification, *Blameworthy iff Apt Anger* is a contingent fact about us as human beings, or instead just a contingent fact about persons in the sorts of moral communities predominant in wide swaths of human cultures, *it is nevertheless a deep fact about us.*[9] Our proneness to these reactive attitudes within our responsibility practices is so thoroughly causally baked into our lives that it would remain, as Strawson might put it, *practically* inconceivable for us to think we could entirely extricate ourselves form a set of practices that made their role central to holding others and ourselves to account.

An appealing way to understand the relation between these reactive attitudes and our moral responsibility practices might be cast as follow. As it happens, humans evolved with a collection of emotions. It is a contingent fact that because of this we are so disposed to respond in various ways in pertinent social contexts.

---

[9] I proposed this in earlier work (2012: 112), but see also McGeer (2013: 169), who builds on the "criterial significance" instances of blaming that involve expression of these emotions.

THE ATTENUATED ROLE OF THE HOSTILE EMOTIONS   209

Nevertheless, these are the proclivities we have. And while our dispositions can be modified in various ways, and while there is much variety in how they can be expressed, there is no getting around our being built that way—or at least this is so for the majority of us.[10] It is natural to expect that some of these proclivities would be recruited in the service of practices designed to hold others and ourselves to account in moral contexts (cf. McGeer, 2013: 171–2). What *is* essential for our having a set of moral responsibility practices is that there is some set of practices of holding to account, including means of signaling our demands and expectations, of registering disapproval, and a commitment to altered regard and treatment to those who depart from our demands and expectations. What is contingent and so not essential is that the practices we have are built up out of our emotional repertoires.

Consider by comparison the emergence of a natural language built from the sounds we are able to make with our voice boxes. It is not as if as a matter of metaphysical necessity humans simply *had* to construct the languages on planet earth so that in their most basic form they are designed to be spoken. Nevertheless, it is only to be expected that there is a deep but contingent connection between the natural languages we find and the resources and limits of the human vocal range for expressing those languages. The same, I say, for the relation between our moral responsibility practices and our emotional repertoires.

The preceding argument for downgrading *Necessarily Blameworthy iff Apt Anger* to *Blameworthy iff Apt Anger*, while rejecting *Blame iff Anger*, suggests that, as in comparison with the essentialist thesis, the link between moral responsibility and the pertinent emotions might permit more plasticity regarding ways these emotions are expressed in the service of holding members of

---

[10] For some counter-evidence, Pereboom notes (2021: 6) Jean Briggs's (1970) study of the Utka Unuit of Canada's northern territory, who express anger only very infrequently.

210 INTERROGATING THE PROPOSAL

our moral community to account.[11] If so, it helps to pave the way for an argument that the characteristic modes of expressing the reactive attitudes need not be as hostile or burdensome as some critics seem to suggest. I turn to this issue.

8.3 Resisting the Hostility Thesis

Now consider the objection that the reactive attitudes are morally objectionable because they are hostile. We can start with a point that makes it harder to rebut this objection. There are stronger and weaker ways to understand the appropriate reactive response in principles such as *Blameworthy iff Apt Anger*. After all, episodes of emotions can be appropriate even when fully concealed from others. Some who defend accounts of moral responsibility assume that the appropriateness at issue in sizing up a justification for an episode of a reactive emotion only needs to concern a mere private episode of it. This is often cast in terms of the *fittingness* between the emotion and that to which it is a response (e.g., Graham, 2014; Hieronymi, 2004; Shoemaker, 2015; Smith, 2007). Modes of treating one who is blamed is a *further* matter. Recall this passage from Shoemaker, quoted in Chapter 6.

> I want to insist on the crucial distinction ... between the fittingness of various sentimental responsibility responses and the appropriateness of harsh treatment of offenders. The latter is a distinctively moral response and simply does not bear at all on whether we have reasons of fit of the former. The latter does of course bear on whether we have all-things-considered reasons to respond to people in certain ways, where these are a weighted

---

[11] I do not claim that a rejection of *Necessarily Blame iff Anger* and *Blame iff Anger* entails this result. I am simply pointing out that once we appreciate that the relation at issue is contingent but deep, it invites considerations about how flexible the connection might be.

THE ATTENUATED ROLE OF THE HOSTILE EMOTIONS   211

> function of reasons of fit and moral reasons.... The real question, then, is whether the practices of harsh treatment to offenders are also necessarily and essentially responsibility responses.... But I cannot see that they are, once this distinction has been highlighted. (2015: 223)

I disagree; our responsibility responses include our outward behavior, not just the occurrence of our inner sentimental lives. This way of understanding the debate makes it harder to see what critics of the reactive attitudes are concerned to resist. It also makes it harder to see why two of the more familiar ways of explaining the sense of appropriateness at issue are cast in terms of desert or fairness (cf. Carlsson, 2017). Treatment of blameworthy agents is the sort of thing that is best captured as a weighty matter, one in which appeals to desert or fairness seem to have force. While admittedly it might be undeserved or unfair for others to think unwarranted angry thoughts about us privately, it does not carry the weight that differential, hard, unwelcome treatment does. (Consider, e.g., the quotation from Pereboom in the previous section.) It is moreover simply far more plausible to say that what a blameworthy agent deserves when she deserves blame, or instead what would be fair as a response to her, is something that can count for her as unpleasant or unwelcome *for her to experience*.[12] One cannot experience another's privately concealed emotional responses. Hence, it is best to focus just on directed blame. I therefore propose that in formulations like *Blameworthy iff Apt Anger*, we presume that the philosophically interesting thesis is about directed manifestations of these emotions.

Before proceeding, it also bears mentioning that the communicative understanding of directed episodes of moral anger is consistent with the essentialist thesis. However, subtracting the

---

[12] In Chapter 7, this point was central to my criticism of Feinberg's contention that what is most basically deserved are emotional responses.

212 INTERROGATING THE PROPOSAL

essentialist thesis, the elements of the communication-based theory make it easy to appreciate the relationship of contingency between the reactive attitudes and blaming. These emotions are natural vehicles for modes of communicating moral demands, expectations, protest, and the like. Their characteristic expressions gave rise to conventional means of communicating what is involved in holding another responsible. However, what is crucial is not the *experiencing* of the emotion itself but instead a sincere (rather than feigned) means of communicating pertinent moral or ethical considerations when holding a culpable wrongdoer to account.

This helps to account for what some might think of as counterexamples to, or instead problematic cases for, the essentialist thesis. Suppose, for instance, a person is severely depressed and so has a flattened affect, perhaps she simply is not positioned to feel or to be angry at all, yet when she witnesses serious wrongdoing, thinking that she should, she musters the resources to behave in the ways that characteristically signal moral anger and in doing so blames the wrongdoer. Those committed to the essentialist thesis, and especially to *Necessarily Blame iff Anger*, have to argue that this person is engaged in hollow or insincere blame, not the real thing. Not so given the communicative resources I have identified above.

Consider instead some recent work on moral responsibility and the high-functioning autistic. Some have argued that *if* the autistic person cannot recognize certain emotions in others, then they cannot be morally responsible in the accountability sense. The rationale is that without recognition of these emotions, they cannot grasp the moral considerations figuring centrally in this kind of moral responsibility. One way to resist this consequence is to deny the antecedent (e.g., Shoemaker, 2015; Stout, 2016). But given a rejection of the essentialist thesis, a communication-based theorist can easily account for how a high-functioning autistic person can remain *within* the domain of being a morally responsible agent in the accountability sense, even if it is true that autistic persons are not able to recognize these emotions in others. All that is required

THE ATTENUATED ROLE OF THE HOSTILE EMOTIONS   213

is that the person is able to adopt alternative interpretive means of grasping what is involved in the conventions that give characteristic expression of reactive emotions of moral anger.[13] Although the cases of the depressed person and autistic person are strictly a digression from the main point of this section, they help make vivid a point I will now develop regarding the variability of the ways moral anger might be made manifest in one's conduct.

With these preliminary considerations in place, I turn to a rejection of the hostility thesis. Note that the principles considered here, such as *Blameworthy iff Apt Anger*, are expressed in normative terms. The right-hand side of each biconditional is characterized in terms of appropriateness. This is in contrast to dispositionalist formulations sometimes attributed to Strawson (e.g., Bennett, 1980; Fischer and Ravizza, 1993). For instance, on a dispositionalist proposal, a person would be blameworthy for some course of action just in case others in the moral community would be disposed to blame that person. Such versions have been properly rejected (e.g., Fischer and Ravizza, 1993, 1998; Wallace, 1994; Watson, 1987). Some might be inclined to dismiss the hostility thesis simply by appeal to the normativity specified by these principles. The appropriate response, one might claim, to a blameworthy person will not permit expressions of anger that are excessive or unwarranted. This is built into the propriety constraints. But this is far too quick of a dismissal of the worries raised by philosophers like Waller, Nussbaum, Pereboom, Watson, Pickard, Kennett, and Wolfendale. Those who press the hostility thesis contend that there is a misfit between any claim of an appropriate response to (putative) blameworthy conduct and an episode of moral anger. This is because these emotional responses involve tendencies toward morally indefensible means of response—to hostility, or to strike back, to seek suffering, to take pleasure in the harm caused to others, or,

---

[13] Admittedly, this places extra burdens on the autistic person and so might be grounds for mitigation. But so is being sleep-deprived.

214 INTERROGATING THE PROPOSAL

as Nussbaum puts it, the humiliation of the indicted. It is this objection that needs addressing.[14]

So, how might one reject the hostility thesis while showing deference to the reasonable concerns of its advocates? Curiously, those who endorse normative formulations such as *Necessarily Blameworthy iff Apt Anger* have devoted little attention to the fact that their thesis *also* includes a dispositional element. After all, as moral anger is an emotion, it has a dispositional profile, one that involves characteristic stimulus conditions and manifestations. This is why it is natural to theorize about the emotions in terms of eliciting conditions and action-tendencies (e.g., Frijda, 1987). But there is a risk in conceiving of these dispositional features as too mechanical or restrictive. Unlike the dispositional properties of inanimate objects—such as chunks of salt that either will or will not manifest the property of solubility when placed in water in such-and-such circumstances—the dispositions at issue, when manifested, are those expressed by *rational beings*. They are not merely static, passive mechanisms but are, as Julia Annas (2011: 8–15) might put, active dispositions of persons capable of exercising intelligence and skill in their expression. As such, principles like *Blameworthy iff Apt Anger* are about persons who are able to exercise some degree of rational control and so variability over *how* their own emotional responses are manifested. They are also often able to exercise some control over whether they are manifested at all rather than masked, or even finked. This is especially so when we keep clearly in mind that we are primarily interested in the directed cases that are expressed in how we act in our interactions with a person whom we are blaming.[15]

---

[14] They might grant that there are empirical questions about consequentialist considerations that could be marshalled against their thesis. However, most, I take it, think the consequentialist considerations lean rather heavily against the instrumental value of the role of moral anger (e.g., 2012).

[15] For a similar point developed with quite different resources, see Victoria McGeer (2013: 173–5). See also her (2019) wherein she distinguishes between the mere

THE ATTENUATED ROLE OF THE HOSTILE EMOTIONS   215

Of course, two points must be granted, one about the nature of these reactive emotions, another about their risks. First, there is no denying that moral anger involves action-tendencies that aim to regard and treat negatively the person at whom one's anger is directed. When discussing anger, Aristotle wrote of "an impulse, accompanied by pain, to a conspicuous revenge for a conspicuous slight" (Aristotle, 1954, 92/1378a–b). Something along these lines is part of what the pertinent form of anger is. This leads to the second point. Given that anger does involve such tendencies, it also must be granted that there are moral hazards that come with accepting its role in our practical lives rather than trying to expunge it. It is for these reasons that, as noted above, Waller speaks with some plausibility of strike-back emotions seeking to pass on pain, sometimes just to anyone it all. It is also for these reasons that Nussbaum describes them as aiming at the humiliation of their target, and that Pereboom notes how, when harming another, anger is often expressed with pleasure. But one might counter that these hazards are due to a *misapplication* of the proper role of moral anger in our lives, a role that can be constrained by our efforts to exercise some control over how and when we express and act upon them.

The immediately preceding point is sufficient to rebut the hostility thesis. Among competent moral agents who are possessed of some degree of self-control and awareness, there is a great deal of room for exercising control over overt expression of reactive attitudes like moral anger, especially when expressed in the context of directed blame. While some features of our emotional responses are less subject to direct rational and voluntary control, others are more flexible. Even tendencies to have certain thoughts or impulses, say violent ones, can be corrected or constrained by focusing on other thoughts or considerations that help one to temper

---

dispositions of agents and the acquisition of intelligent skills of agents to respond to reasons in acting as responsible agents. Those skills will *also* apply to control over expression of one's emotions in holding another to account by expressing one's anger.

one's anger (e.g., see Mele, 1995: 106). We have the resources to self-regulate our impulses limiting the severity of their expression. Often we should. But that is consistent with actually expressing them, and so with not completely suppressing them. Indeed, there are numerous cases we encounter on a daily basis wherein people do just this. It's called being civil. On a communication-based view, that sort of self-regulation is consistent with *persisting* in expressing and communicating one's justified sense of moral anger, but by means that can be tempered, humane, and even compassionate.

An analogy with the dispositions of inanimate bits of nature might be useful. Consider the disposition of an enzyme in the process of digestion, lactase, which is enlisted to break down the sugar in milk, lactose. Lactose is disposed to provide a healthy and pleasing source of nutrients for those who can digest it. But its disposition to do so without compromising healthy digestion relies on its working in tandem with another substance, the enzyme lactase, which masks what would be a harmful effect of the lactose. The disposition of the latter substance helps play a regulative role in salutary manifestation or expression of the former. When one cannot produce lactase, the system goes wrong, and an effect that is otherwise beneficial is now compromised. So too, one might say, for the dispositions involved in moral anger. They might well have risks if pertinent hazards go unchecked. But when coupled with other dispositions, such as a commitment to respect the dignity of the blamed, they can be expressed in moderation.

Shifting from the passive dispositions of inanimate matter to the active dispositions of intelligent creatures makes the point even stronger (cf. Annas, 2011). Competent adult persons are capable of consciously deploying techniques of self-regulation, techniques that enlist various character traits so as to regulate the role of others. Indeed, there is a rich literature on the unity of the virtues devoted to explaining how certain active dispositions left unchecked by the proper role of others lead to the development and expression of destructive rather than salutary character traits—that is, lead to vices

THE ATTENUATED ROLE OF THE HOSTILE EMOTIONS   217

and vicious conduct rather than virtues and salutary conduct (e.g., see Vacarezza, 2017).

My contention, then, is that the dispositions, and in particular the "hostile" action-tendencies, that accompany the moral anger involved in blaming are not per se objectionable. They are so only when not held in check by other psychological resources available to competent ethical agents. If so, then the reason that the hostility thesis fails is not because of its descriptive claim. It might be true that these emotions do involve dispositions to seek, as Strawson contends, the suffering of offenders. It is rather that, from the mere fact that these dispositions might play a role in how we respond to and blame others, it does not follow that they must play this role by means that are morally or ethically problematic. They can be tempered and so held in check.[16]

In "Responsibility and the Limits of Evil," Gary Watson concludes by contrasting the ideal of love exemplified by figures like Mahatma Gandhi or Martin Luther King, Jr. with what he called the "retributive sentiments" (1987, as appearing in 2004: 257–8). Watson contended, contra his understanding of the Strawsonian thesis, that figures like Gandhi and King held others to account by standing up for themselves, confronting their oppressors, urging and demanding considerations for themselves and others. But, he remarked, "they manage, or come much closer to managing, to do such things without vindictiveness or malice" (258). Watson takes the ideal exemplified by King's and Gandhi's modes of holding others to account as *in opposition to* the sorts of propensities involved in responding to those we blame with moral anger. I suppose in some sense it is. Love and compassion involve very different action-tendencies than does anger. Of course. But Watson then goes on to write the following about his expressive

---

[16] My argument shares some affinities with Macalester Bell's (2013) excellent work assessing the moral significance of contempt.

218   INTERROGATING THE PROPOSAL

(I say communicative) interpretation of Strawson and the lives of the likes of King and Gandhi:

> Hence, Strawson's claims about the interpretation of responsibility and the retributive sentiments must not be confused with the expressive theory itself. As these lives suggest, the retributive sentiments can be stripped away from holding responsible and the demands and appeals in which this consists. What is left are various forms of or reaction and appeal to others as moral agents. (258)

It is at this point that I think Watson gets wrong what we are able to learn from Gandhi and King. Perhaps Gandhi and King really did have it in them to reliably hold the blameworthy to account by means that involved no expression of moral anger at all. I am doubtful.[17] But even if they were able to take such a saintly path, a more realistic one is in keeping with their teachings of nonviolence. It is consistent with making moral protests of the sort that animated these men that, in standing up for themselves, confronting others, urging and demanding moral recognition, they might communicate moral anger. What, I say, these heroic figures showed to be within our reach is a means of stripping away vindictiveness and excessive malice so as to give tempered expression to our moral anger. This is entirely consistent with treating with love and compassion the very people with whom one is angry. It is consistent with calling them to account as culpable wrongdoers, a point

---

[17] I offer a confession. I was sure that if I combed through the writings of Gandhi and King I would find evidence that some of their moral admonishments to those who had harmed their people would reveal some expression of moral anger. But in a collection of Gandhi's numerous political writings (1996), and in a nearly seven-hundred-page collection of King's writings (1986), I could not find nothing to support my suspicion. Totally pissed me off.

On a more serious note, Meena Krishnamurthy contends that we can find anger expressed in some of King's public presentations: https://historyofphilosophy.net/transcript/king-krishnamurthy, n.d. Thanks to Derk Pereboom for the reference.

THE ATTENUATED ROLE OF THE HOSTILE EMOTIONS   219

anyone with maturing children or fallible intimates should be able to appreciate.

Hence, I contend, the modes of holding morally responsible and blaming exemplified by Gandhi and King are consistent with civil expressions of moral anger. Indeed, even this "gentle" form of blaming can be regarded as costly and burdensome to those blamed, so that this sort of blaming might persist in carrying the characteristic sting or force that Pamela Hieronymi rightly notes is a feature of pertinent cases of blame. Two things permit this level of flexibility or variability. One is that the dispositions involved in episodes of these emotions are the dispositions of rational beings who can exercise some degree of control over how these emotions are expressed in outward conduct. Another is the fact that, on a communication-based theory, our social practices permit for a good deal of plasticity in how these emotions figure in meaningful forms of blaming behavior.[18]

Before proceeding, I pause to register an argumentative path I'll not pursue here but leave open. Above I claimed that the hostile action-tendencies accompanying moral anger are not per se objectionable. In this section, I have only meant to establish that the strong reasons to think they are objectionable stem from a failure to recognize that they can be effectively modulated and so used to express moral demands in a morally acceptable fashion. I have not, however offered a positive defense of their value. In that case, one might say, they are not per se objectionable because they bring with

---

[18] Note that my argument in this section differs from the sort that Shaun Nichols (2007) advanced in response to the emotion-replacement proposal of philosophers like Derk Pereboom (2001, 2014). Pereboom argues that sadness is a better response to moral wrongdoing than anger. Nichols argues in reply that moral anger has pro-social benefits that responses like sadness lack. Cast in this way, Nichol's proposal can be understood as one in which the benefits of persisting in practices that express moral anger outweigh the risks. This might be correct, and it seems to be an open empirical question. My argument, however, is rather that the features of expressing moral anger that Pereboom and other critics take to be so morally problematic in the first place, and as a reason to seek a replacement strategy at all, are simply not morally problematic in the way the hostility thesis contends.

220 INTERROGATING THE PROPOSAL

them important goods. I'll not explore this in this chapter except to note that there are two viable ways to develop that point. One is to argue that the harm associated with being the target of deserved forms of moral anger in blaming might be noninstrumentally good insofar as it delivers to a culpable wrongdoer something she deserves (see Chapter 3). Another is to argue that it is inevitable for creatures like us that we will experience moral anger, and so even if there are preferable responses to wrongdoing, say ones that are more effective at correcting bad behavior, civilized expressions of moral anger do have the value of holding others to account for what they've done, promoting moral improvement of wrongdoers, and incentivizing others to act well (see Pereboom, 2014: 180–2).

8.4 An Ethical Prescription: Blame Should Be Attenuated by Compassion

The preceding argument for resisting the hostility thesis provides an alternative to the intriguing diagnosis Hannah Pickard (2011, 2013) has recently offered of how practitioners in clinical settings hold patients responsible for their wrongdoing while not blaming them, and why they are right to do so.[19] These patients, Pickard contends, are responsible for their wrongdoing, but they are not to be treated as if they are morally blameworthy via a blaming response. It is inappropriate to blame patients in clinical settings when they engage in moral wrongdoing. Nevertheless, holding them responsible is fully justified. Her reasoning is precisely that the angry reactive emotions are not warranted in such settings. Of course, it might be that in certain clinical settings, for special cases, Pickard is correct as a matter of successful psychiatric care: any treatment must be washed clean of expression of all anger. But

---

[19] That is, blaming them in the sense that is at issue here, which Pickard characterizes as affective blame.

THE ATTENUATED ROLE OF THE HOSTILE EMOTIONS   221

I propose that in a wide variety of the settings she has in mind, her actual target ought to be harsh, hostile, or punitive blame, rather than a kind of blame, emotionally valanced though it may be, that is tempered by compassion or understanding. This is in opposition to the way Pickard thinks of compassion and its relation to (angry) blame. She writes,

> Compassion and empathy push the negative emotions constitutive of affective blame aside. They simply cannot comfortably co-exist. (2013: 1147)

Of course, Pickard equates angry blame with hostile or punitive blame, as per the hostility thesis. But this is just what I have disputed in this chapter. Once the hostility thesis is denied, there is room to argue that, insofar as the patients Pickard discusses are morally responsible for their wrongdoings, when they have no excuse, they are indeed blameworthy and as such apt candidates for angry blaming responses, albeit responses tempered by compassion.

Similar remarks apply to Derk Pereboom's (2001, 2014, 2021) important proposal for an alternative emotional response to moral anger, one that involves expressing sadness and disappointment. Pereboom advocates a response of sadness rather than anger as an effective and justified alternative, given his skepticism about a desert-based conception of moral responsibility. But a middle-ground position, one that rejects the sort of skepticism Pereboom advances, favors measured or tempered expressions of moral anger, expressed civilly, and with appeal to further resources like compassion to help limit the more excessive modes of expressing anger. Indeed, in many cases, it might be hard to distinguish when such a response in one's treatment of a blamed person is distinct from a response of sadness.

I will now develop this proposal by drawing on some recent work by Daphne Brandenburg. Brandenburg (2017) has proposed a distinct stance for some agents who are exempted from

222 INTERROGATING THE PROPOSAL

wrongdoing due to an incapacity. In these cases, the agents who have done wrong were incapacitated in some respect and so lacked the agential resources needed to act well. Hence, we can grant that they were not blameworthy for what they did at the time. But it might remain true that these agents were sufficiently developed that they were then able to *develop* these capacities, and they might have even been aware of this when as exempted agents they acted wrongly. In these contexts, Brandenburg argues, the Strawsonian proposal for adopting an objective stance toward these exempted agents is misguided. But so also is seeing them as fully competent agents from the interpersonal stance we adopt toward candidates who are capable of being fully responsible, and so *not* exempted. Such cases include clinical settings or the rearing of children, especially adolescents. In these contexts, there is a sense in which we persist in seeing these persons as morally responsible agents, and so we need to distinguish a different stance from either the objective or interpersonal to capture the sort of expectations and sense of moral responsibility at issue. Brandenburg proposes a *nurturing stance*, since the stance identifies one sort of aim we should adopt toward such agents, which is meant to nurture and so support the acquisition and laudatory exercise of pertinent agential abilities.

The nurturing stance need not be construed merely as an aspirational one for those we hope one day *will be* morally responsible agents but now are not. No. It's a stance toward those who do possess at the time of wrongdoing some of the capacities needed to undertake efforts of moral development and improvement and to take responsibility for past conduct with the aim of personal and moral development. So, in this sense, these agents *are* morally responsible for aspects of themselves. Although she does not make it explicit, it seems Brandenburg intends to restrict the justified grounds for adopting this stance. I take it she conceives of the nurturing stance as justified *only* as applied to those who sit precariously between a status wherein all that is warranted toward them is the objective stance and the full interpersonal stance involved in seeing one as a

THE ATTENUATED ROLE OF THE HOSTILE EMOTIONS   223

fully, morally responsible agent. There is good reason for this. To adopt a nurturing stance toward another seems to involve an assumption of moral superiority, of unwelcome paternalism, or of a clinical relation of caregiver to patient. It thus risks moral condescension and a failure to respect the autonomy, worth, or dignity of those whom others might seek to nurture.

Despite the risks identified in the preceding paragraph, I propose to expand the justified application of Brandenburg's nurturing stance to all members of the community of morally responsible agents. While it takes focusing on the sorts of cases Brandenburg considers to identify the stance as a distinct one, I propose that it is warranted as a stance we might take to *any* morally responsible agent (cf. Vargas, 2013; McGeer, 2019). The risks of presuming moral superiority, or of disrespecting the dignity or autonomy of those toward whom we might adopt this stance are risks of *misapplication* of the stance. Adopting a nurturing attitude toward friends and those we love, to mutually respected peers in various settings, or even to strangers in unexpected encounters, is entirely consist with respecting them and doing so without any sense of moral superiority. It's a matter of conceiving of our relations with others so that it is always an open possibility that a person might be supported with an aim toward moral improvement.[20]

Suppose it is an inescapable natural fact about our natures that we are inclined toward reactive attitudes like moral anger. Nevertheless, if we are enticed to act with too much hostility when, as Dylan phrases it in *Precious Angel*, the violence is in our eyes, embracing a general policy of adopting a nurturing stance when one is able to do so can help count as a corrective to poor, cruel, or vengeful expressions of our moral anger. This ethical prescription

---

[20] Jeannette Kennett helpfully noted one source of support for my proposal: Kant's commitment to both duties of respect and duties of love. In personal correspondence, Mark Timmons concurs, and notes that Kant writes of balancing one's duties of respect with one's duties of love. See, especially Kant, *The Metaphysics of Morals* (1797/2017: 6:448).

is of course one that it is not always reasonable to expect of victims, especially of severe personal harms or losses. But as a guiding aim to live well, it provides a resource for one to seek measured means for proper, warranted, appropriate, fitting, deserved, or fair expressions of one's angry blaming responses to those who are, after all, *worthy* of blame.

9

Power, Social Inequities, and the Conversational Theory

> In general, we demand some degree of goodwill or regard
> on the part of those who stand in these relationships to us,
> though the forms we require it to take vary widely in dif-
> ferent connections. The range and intensity of our *reactive*
> attitudes toward goodwill, its absence or its opposite, vary
> no less widely.
>
> —P. F. Strawson "Freedom and Resentment" (1962)

I turn now to an interrogation of our moral responsibility practices in light of worries about various forms of social injustice. We can begin by asking, How should we understand the social and relational dimensions of moral responsibility? Understood in one way, this question has an obvious answer: Sociality is essential to moral responsibility. So it is for P. F. Strawson (1962) and numerous others embracing a broadly Strawsonian approach to theorizing about moral responsibility.[1] On this approach, moral responsibility

---

An earlier draft of this chapter was originally published in 2018, as "Power, Social Inequities, and the Conversational Theory of Moral Responsibility," in K. Hutchison, C. Mackenzie, and M. Oshana, eds., *Social Dimensions of Moral Responsibility*, 38–58. New York: Oxford University Press.

[1] Gary Watson (2014: 17) offers the clearest expression of the thesis that sociality is at the heart of Strawson's theory. For those adopting a Strawsonian approach, see, for example, Bennett (1980), Darwall (2006), McKenna (2012), Oshana (1997, 2004), Russell (1992, 2004), Scanlon (2008), Shoemaker (2015), Vargas (2013), Wallace (1994), and Watson (1987).

Responsibility and Desert. Michael McKenna, Oxford University Press. © Oxford University Press 2024.
DOI: 10.1093/9780197679999.003.0009

226 INTERROGATING THE PROPOSAL

is essentially interpersonal because being responsible is conceptually connected to holding responsible, which in turn is understood in terms of social practices. Hence, responsibility turns out to be a deeply social phenomenon. This is intimated in the passage from Strawson's seminal paper "Freedom and Resentment," quoted above. Granting this obvious answer, in this chapter, I argue that there are further considerations that should lead us to be suspicious of the role of sociality in helping to set the conditions for moral responsibility.

9.1 Strawsonian Theories of Responsibility and the (Dubious?) Demand for Good Will

On Strawson's own proposal, *being* morally responsible in the sense of being either praiseworthy or blameworthy is most fundamentally about the quality of will with which an agent acts—whether it is from good or ill will. How is this thesis conceptually linked with considerations of sociality? Standards for an agent's acting from a reasonable quality of will are understood by reference to the expectations of the moral community positioned to hold responsible. The community makes the moral demand that agents show a sufficient degree of good will. Deviations from these demands then render fitting reactive responses such as praise or blame in the form of outwardly manifested emotions like gratitude or resentment. In this way, the fittingness of praising and blaming in social practice signals the scope of praiseworthiness and blameworthiness. One involves surpassing the standards set down by the basic demand for good will; the other involves falling below them.

In this chapter, I am concerned with the requirements of sociality in light of the Strawsonian enterprise. More precisely, I will focus upon a strikingly neglected topic within the literature on free will and moral responsibility: the social and relational dimensions of moral responsibility in light of both social inequities and asymmetrical relations of power.[2] How do and, perhaps more importantly, how *should* these factors influence our moral responsibility practices and judgments? By drawing upon the conversational theory of moral responsibility, I intend to expose a rather unseemly dimension of our moral responsibility practices. To foreshadow what will come, I call attention to Strawson's remark that, in general, we demand some degree of good will or regard on the part of those with whom we are variably related. This widely shared assumption is often heralded as one of the deepest and most celebrated insights in Strawson's paper (e.g., Watson, 2014). Of course, in a certain respect it is undoubtedly true, given that it is qualified with "in general." Nevertheless, it masks much that is a source of worry, and so perhaps should not be celebrated without caution. After all, not all *do* demand a reasonable degree of good will from pertinent others. For some, there is little point in doing so because there is little reason to expect that their demands will even register at all among those whose authority is liable to have great sway over them. For many others, the forms good will can be expected to take will be settled by standards they have no part in shaping.

In what follows, I will focus primarily upon disparities regarding the forms good and ill will can be expected to take. By drawing upon the conversational theory, I will argue that many agents who are morally responsible for their conduct, even when they do act from a reasonable degree of good will, operate in contexts that are morally unfair to them as agents. Or, at any rate, there is something morally suspect about the social conditions facilitating exercises of their agency when they act in ways that are morally praiseworthy (and also morally blameworthy). This is because, as the conversational theory reveals, quality of will is to be identified and explained by a community of interpreters who take some kinds of actions as indicative of good will and other kinds as indicative of lack of good

---

[2] A recent corrective is the excellent collection edited by Katrina Hutchison, Catriona Mackenzie, and Marina O'Shana (2018).

will. Since some in this community are socially empowered, in contrast with others who are socially disempowered, the conditions for what signals good and ill will are liable to arise from potentially unjust social circumstances.

9.2 The Conditions for Moral Responsibility

Consider the conditions for moral responsibility. Examining these will help assess the influences on moral responsibility of asymmetric relations of power and various forms of social inequities. I will assume in what follows that we can set aside worries about free will and moral responsibility skepticism. Perhaps, contrary to my own position, skeptics like Derk Pereboom (2014) and Galen Strawson (1986) are correct that because no one has free will no one is morally responsible, at least in the sense that requires basic desert. I leave that as an open question. But the issue before us is about potential effects on responsibility due to *special* conditions of our sociality. Hence, it will be most useful to assume free will and moral responsibility realism and then proceed by raising questions about unique social and relational conditions in which these can be attenuated, compromised, or extinguished.

Some Strawsonians hope to exhaust the conditions for moral responsibility by focusing upon quality of will alone, or instead quality of will and a general capacity for engaging in adult interpersonal relationships.[3] My own view is that this attempts to do too much with too few resources. I prefer a mixed theory. Moral responsibility as I understand it requires at least two conditions that are neutral between Strawsonian interpersonal theories and other competitor proposals: a *control condition* and an *epistemic condition*, as I acknowledged in Chapter 2 (Section 2.4).[4] These

---

[3] See Bennett (1980), Russell (1992, 2004), and more recently Shoemaker (2015).

[4] This is a widely shared thesis. For example, see Fischer and Ravizza (1998), Haji (1998), McKenna (2013b), Nelkin (2011), Sartorio (2016), and Wolf (1990).

conditions apply both to the conditions for being a morally responsible agent—which concerns the *status* of some but not all persons—and also to the conditions in which a person who *is* a morally responsible agent is morally responsible *for* something, such as an action, an omission, or the consequences of one of these things.

Attending to the control and the epistemic conditions gives rise to several interesting philosophical issues regarding the influence of significant social inequalities and asymmetric relations of power. The control condition invites worry about coercion and duress, especially in contexts of interactions between members from disparate groups whose social status and power are asymmetrically distributed. A further and more subtle possibility here concerns domination in the sense Phillip Pettit (2001) understands it. In such cases, a person's options might be constrained in light of the mere prospects that others are easily able to exercise domination over that person, with no repercussions. Hence a person self-regulates in ways that are liable to diminish her freedom.[5] These factors can sometimes serve as grounds either for mitigating or instead excusing otherwise blameworthy behavior on the part of those who are disadvantaged by the pertinent disparities. Naturally, they can also promote *greater* degrees of freedom for those advantaged by these conditions, and so too a potentially greater range of conduct for which one ought to be regarded as accountable.

In the case of the epistemic condition, the social and relational variables at issue raise worries about disproportionate access to education, complex sources of information, or, for that matter, the opportunity to attend to matters of moral and political concern with sufficient care—people working three jobs to make ends meet,

---

[5] I am grateful to Dave Shoemaker for pointing this out. Also, as Katrina Hutchison has pointed out in her comments on this chapter, there has been a considerable amount of work on this topic in connection with the topic of relational autonomy. See, for example, Baier (1985), Christman (2004), Friedman (1997), Meyers (1989), and Oshana (2006).

230 INTERROGATING THE PROPOSAL

for instance, can perhaps be excused for failing to stay abreast of efforts to properly regulate the banking industry. Hence, some appeals to ignorance or limited understanding as grounds for mitigation or excuse from blameworthiness are far more compelling than others.[6] Those massively disenfranchised and without the power to guide the aim of various inquiries will be far more likely to merit some form of mitigation or excuse in certain contexts, although it should be noted that, ironically, they are often the same group of people far less likely actually to be excused. Likewise, of course, those with *greater* access to epistemic resources are liable to bear a greater degree of blameworthiness for their conduct since the charge "You should have known better" will apply more liberally.

The considerations mentioned in the two preceding paragraphs provide ample resources for exploring the social and relation dimensions of moral responsibility in light of extreme disparities in relations of power and significant social inequities. A further variable, however, concerns quality of will. Some Strawsonians apparently think that a quality of will condition on moral responsibility is encompassed by the control and the epistemic condition already identified.[7] When, for instance, an agent knowingly and freely does morally wrong, this alone, some might contend, is sufficient for her

[6] Another set of issues relevant to the epistemic condition and to problematic practices of holding responsible relates to what Miranda Fricker calls "epistemic injustice." To suffer epistemic injustice is to be subject to prejudicial exclusion from knowledge practices on the basis of one's social group membership. Epistemic injustice encompasses testimonial injustices, such as discounting the credibility of a person's testimony due to identity prejudice, and hermeneutical injustice, which is "the injustice of having some significant area of one's social experience obscured from collective understanding owing to hermeneutical marginalization" (2007, 158). For another who has also developed the notion of epistemic injustice, see Charles Mills (2007). Thanks to Elinor Mason for the latter reference.

[7] The textual evidence is not decisive, but there is some reason to think that Strawson himself (1962) endorses this view, since when he gives his list of pleas that would defeat judgments of responsibility (and acting from objectionable quality of will), they naturally parse into control and epistemic categories. Also, Fischer and Ravizza (1998) endorse a Strawsonian account of responsibility and seem only to identify a control and an epistemic condition on responsibility.

having a morally objectionable quality of will and so being morally blameworthy. But, as I set it out in Chapter 2 (Section 2.3), quality of will is a *further* condition over and above the control and epistemic conditions. In the case of blameworthiness, what is involved is either an ill will or an insufficiently good will.[8]

Recall, quality of will is a matter of the value of an agent's regard for others and for salient moral considerations. When we hold morally responsible, what we are reacting to, or what we are prepared to react to, is an agent's quality of will as manifested in her conduct. Eventually, we will scrutinize the quality of will condition as a locus of concern regarding social inequities. However, before doing so, we will first consider an especially illuminating application of the epistemic condition in evaluating cases of putative blameworthiness. Are those ignorant of largely unrecognized moral wrongs due to conditions of oppression blameworthy for participating in and benefitting from those conditions? Is their ignorance exculpating? This will help cast a light on the particular issue I wish to consider.

9.3 Excusing Morally Ignorant Oppressors?

In her superbly argued "Responsibility and Reproach," Cheshire Calhoun (1989) confronts a challenge for feminists faced with questions about how to respond to social oppression when carried out or at least perpetuated by seemingly innocent participants in the oppressive practices. Is reproach warranted in such cases? If so, it seems that these apparently innocent participants are not innocent

---

[8] To explain: A person might do morally wrong, might do so knowingly and freely, and yet not be blameworthy because she does not act from a morally objectionable quality of will. Suppose, for instance, she acts in the context of a moral dilemma and so cannot avoid wrongdoing. In that case, if she harbors no poor regard for anyone, and if she shows sufficient regard for all involved, then she might do wrong, but she is not blameworthy. Cases like this, I maintain, show that quality of will is a further condition on blameworthiness for wrongdoing, beyond a control and an epistemic condition.

232 INTERROGATING THE PROPOSAL

after all but instead blameworthy. If not, it seems that feminists are not entitled to "use moral reproach as a tool for effecting social change" (1989: 389). Each horn comes at quite a cost.

Consider the first horn—that the seemingly innocent are blameworthy after all. As Calhoun rightly notes, many individuals who are, as she puts it, "morally unflawed" (389) unknowingly commit wrongdoing through participating in oppressive social practices that strongly disfavor women. Yet they do so by means that appear to arise from nonculpable ignorance. How so? In contexts in which some moral knowledge is not widely shared, which Calhoun calls "abnormal moral contexts" (396), it is not just the unsavory, like pimps and other misogynists, who are prone to harm women by means of various oppressive practices, but many well-meaning men (and some women, too). Calhoun mentions parenthetically "male bias in psychological and other theories, the design of female fashion, the use of 'he' neutrally, [and] heterosexual marriage" (397). Even if one wished to dispute any of these as significant moral wrongs, it is beyond question that various shared social practices regarded widely by many as morally neutral do after all contribute to morally wrong forms of oppression that undermine women's autonomy. To think that reproach *is* warranted even for those Calhoun refers to as "morally unflawed" is, it seems, to think that these moral agents are after all culpable for engaging in what they take to be perfectly innocent behavior. But how could that be? We cannot expect even the most virtuous among us to have access to all the best information about morality. Presumably, we're all vulnerable to moral blind spots at the limits of our current social and cultural settings.

Now consider the other horn—that in these contexts the seemingly innocent are indeed as they seem to be, innocent. If so, it appears that feminists are not entitled to reproach—by which I take it Calhoun means moralized blame. The cost of thinking that reproach is *not* warranted because these parties are not blameworthy means that feminists must let too much pass. The oppression

POWER AND SOCIAL INEQUITIES 233

identified is after all deeply harmful and far-reaching. Failing to reproach, Calhoun argues, comes dangerously close to endorsement and so to participating in the modes of oppression that feminists correctly see as deep forms of moral wrongdoing.

Calhoun offers an elegant solution to this dilemma. She distinguishes between reasons to blame in light of blameworthiness, and reasons to blame as a means of effecting social change. A person could be entitled to blame those who are not blameworthy, say in the context of excused wrongdoing, given *other* powerful moral considerations. A significant need to achieve social reform is such a reason, according to Calhoun, and, moreover, failing to reproach is highly likely to signal endorsement or sanctioning of the moral order (400–5). (Of course, it should be clear that the reasoning at issue here applies to other cases as well, like that at issue in claims of white privilege or class privilege.)

Some might be inclined to downplay Calhoun's proposal as perhaps correct but no more than a pedestrian application of a simple point: Blameworthiness merely provides a *pro tanto* reason to blame. All blameworthiness ever establishes, we might suppose, is that a wrongdoer is deserving of something, blame—and all desert ever provides is a *pro tanto* reason for some sort of response. But there can be reasons other than desert for treating a person a certain way, and these reasons can override the *pro tanto* reasons. Or these other reasons can instead do duty to justify a treatment like blame when the desert-based reasons are altogether absent. For instance, young children who are not yet morally responsible agents are not yet blameworthy for their conduct. Hence, they do not deserve blame—granting the near truism that only the blameworthy deserve blame. But we might have good moral reason to blame them as a means of training them up into becoming morally responsible agents who will eventually deserve blame (and praise). So, too, it can be argued, we can have reasons to blame those who are not blameworthy for participating in oppressive practices because it is in the service of an overriding social good.

234 INTERROGATING THE PROPOSAL

While this might be true, there's nothing especially philosophically illuminating going on here.

To downplay Calhoun's proposal in this way would be to misunderstand the striking philosophical point she brings into relief. Her argument, as I understand it, is not *simply* about overriding reasons to ignore considerations about what a nonculpable wrongdoer does not deserve (blame). It is, rather, about the *special social setting* giving rise to those overriding reasons and how that social setting shapes not only the moral landscape but our moral responsibility practices as modes of responding to that moral landscape. (It is this point in particular that I wish to draw upon in my own proposal as I shall develop it below.) As Calhoun puts it, the sort of moral wrongdoing at issue in these kinds of cases occurs at the social rather than at the individual level (394). This occasions a special class of moral reasons that can then be "turned back on" our responsibility practices in the hope of refashioning them.[9]

Think about it this way. The architecture of our responsibility practices is, so to speak, built up out of a stock of accessible bits of moral knowledge. Good moral reasoners, being fallible creatures and so lacking moral omniscience, rely upon this stock as a resource for engaging with others in ways that can give rise to blameworthy as well as praiseworthy behavior. But if moral knowledge, like all knowledge, is dependent upon background social conditions rendering pertinent truths accessible or instead inaccessible, then some forms of moral knowledge will sometimes be, so to speak, outside the reasonable scope of even a well-meaning person's epistemic radar. Of course, perhaps a few elites at the fringes of moral knowledge might be better positioned, but their understanding cannot be expected to be accessible to most others.[10] As such, the moral landscape will be affected insofar as even morally virtuous agents

---

[9] Calhoun never explicitly states this last point, but, as I read her, it is clearly an intended implication.

[10] This is how Calhoun understood the feminist community at the time she penned her essay (397–8).

POWER AND SOCIAL INEQUITIES   235

will be liable to participate unwittingly in wrongdoing.[11] And, moreover, because of this our practices of holding morally responsible will be likewise affected insofar as this sort of epistemic limitation will do two things. First, it will provide legitimate grounds to claim nonculpable ignorance as a basis for excusing conduct that contributes to oppression. Second, it will limit the moral community's resources and so impede the moral community from deploying the very machinery of our blaming practices that could be used to correct these sorts of wrongs.

These special features of our social setting and the pressure they place on our own practices of holding morally responsible provide reasons for justifying blame even when directed at those whose wrongdoing, due to epistemic considerations, is excusable—that is, even at those who do not deserve blame.[12] Doing so allows for the possibility of moral reform. This, I take it, is precisely an application of what Manuel Vargas (2013) has in mind in writing of *building better beings*. We modulate our responsibility practices with the aim of encouraging people to be more alive to moral reasons. By blaming those wrongdoers who are not blameworthy in these contexts, we thereby allow for the possibility of making accessible this sort of moral knowledge. *We bring it to light.* This in turn can help to refashion our responsibility practices in such a way that those failing to act properly in light of this moral knowledge would no longer be able to claim nonculpable ignorance. Then they could after all be regarded as blameworthy and so not excused. There is, in this sense, a feedback loop that helps us bootstrap our

---

[11] This is how I think of many of the issues regarding the moral status of nonhuman animals.

[12] This is not to deny that there might be countervailing reasons for proceeding in this way. In correspondence, Pereboom has rightly warned of a backfire effect, especially if the reproach in blaming is harmful in any way. Those who are the targets of such blame might respond in ways that worsen the moral landscape, seeing those who blame them as adversaries. Pereboom favors moral counseling that does not inflict harm. Fair enough. Although the risks of a backfire effect might be diminished by tending to modes of blaming cast from the sort of nurturing stance proposed in the preceding chapter.

236 INTERROGATING THE PROPOSAL

moral responsibility practices to be better positioned to hold accountable those who unwittingly do engage in wrongdoing that contributes to oppression.

9.4 The Role of the Conversational Theory and the Demand for Good Will

In the next section, I will draw upon Calhoun's proposal to help cast a critical light of a different sort on our moral responsibility practices. But consider first a key ingredient of the conversational theory (as set out in Chapter 2). Grice (1957) distinguished speaker from sentence meaning. When we interpret a speaker in actual conversation, our interpretive goal is to understand what the speaker meant by what she said, not just what the sentences mean that the speaker used to convey what she meant. Often these go together, but they can come apart. We can, for instance, use the sentence "That was a good meal" to mean the meal was terrible by making use of sarcastic cues and the like and relying upon our audience to cooperatively receive our expression as we intended it. So, while conventions regarding sentence-types help shape what we mean to say, they do so in ways consistent with variation that allows for particularizing our own intended meanings and departing from the conventional meanings assigned to sentence-types. An analogous point applies to interpreting the actions of morally responsible agents, and it *also* applies to interpreting the praising and blaming responses of those holding responsible when they react to those blamed (or praised). A shove, for instance, might characteristically show ill will, but in some contexts could be taken to express solidarity or playful aggression (say on a basketball court). Why is this important for what is to come? Consider our ability to function in an interpretive space where others are equipped to see us as acting with good will. And consider our ability to communicate to them our reactive assessment of them when they do not. We rely

POWER AND SOCIAL INEQUITIES   237

upon an expectation that we share enough interpretive resources to facilitate successful communication. And one kind of resource is just social authority—being positioned to have one's interpretive scheme do the work in settling meaning. This resource, as it happens, is usually not evenly distributed.

Given this observation, and in the light of the conversational theory as I have deployed it thus far, consider this passage from Strawson:

> We should think of the many different kinds of relationships which we can have with other people—as sharers of a common interest; as members of the same family; as colleagues; as friends; as lovers; as chance parties to an enormous range of transactions and encounters. Then we should think, in each of these connections in turn, and in others, of the kind of importance we attach to the attitudes and intentions towards us of those who stand in these relationships to us, and of the kinds of *reactive* attitudes and feelings to which we ourselves are prone. In general, we demand some degree of goodwill or regard on the part of those who stand in these relationships to us, though the forms we require it to take vary widely in different connections. The range and intensity of our *reactive* attitudes towards goodwill, its absence or its opposite vary no less widely. (1962)

Note Strawson's observation about the variability and particularity of our relationships. He focuses on how much we care about how others regard us in their interactions with us (their quality of will) and our demand for goodwill on their behalf. This extends to our reactions to those who fail to meet the demand when we hold them responsible via a reactive attitude. Note also his observation that the forms we require the demand for good will to take vary widely. Compare this with the preceding point about the particularity of speaker meaning in relation to generic sentence meaning. Now let us inject into this picture a fact about non-ideal human

238 INTERROGATING THE PROPOSAL

communities. Those who make the demands for a reasonable degree of good will and those prepared to react to departures from those demands are not all equally empowered. If we add familiar facts about significant social inequalities and asymmetric relations of power, we bring to light a set of considerations that are not necessarily so flattering to a Strawsonian understanding of our responsibility practices.

9.5 Something Insidious Rooted in Our Responsibility Practices?

Looking through a critical lens, focus yet again on Strawson's remark that, in general, we demand some degree of good will or regard on the part of those who stand in varying relationships with us. As it happens, it is a contingent albeit inescapable fact that some who express a demand for good will are taken to have an authority that others lack. As noted above (Section 9.1), there are some who take their own social status to be so limited that they do not demand that they are shown a reasonable degree of good will—at least in relation to members of comparatively advantaged groups. In some cases, they do not see any point in even making the demand. Others do, but they have no part in settling the interpretive standards regarding what plausibly counts as expressions of good will. In this way they are, in a certain sense, outsiders to those positioned to exercise a greater degree of moral authority.

Consider, for instance, etiquette or manners. While standards of etiquette or manners are usually not directly regarded as relevant to morality (however, see Buss, 1999), drawing upon these conventions in how one comports oneself can often be a *vehicle* for showing or instead failing to show deference or respect for others, which is a matter of morality. In this way, especially as understood through the lens of the conversational theory, superficial conventions of etiquette can function as a way of manifesting

POWER AND SOCIAL INEQUITIES   239

morally significant behavior. However, the social conventions constituting what counts as polite behavior—such as pausing to hold a door open for someone, refraining from interrupting another who is speaking in certain social contexts, how one behaves while dining in certain settings rather than others, the cutlery one uses, when one begins to eat, and so on—are all established by social contexts wherein those empowered set the expectations. Departures from expected behavior can be taken to show lack of respect or concern for the feelings of others—such as hosts. The upshot is that those who act in such contexts have available to them resources for displaying good or ill will, but those resources are themselves structured and constrained by some rather than other groups empowered to set expectations and "police" departures from expected behavior. Of course, if this were limited just to matters of etiquette, there would be little interest here. But my contention is that these interpretive pressures on the conversational context of action are ubiquitous. They pervade nearly every aspect of our social lives. Those marginalized by existing power structures—cultural, social, and economic—live out their lives shouldering the burdens of acting in a context in which much of the interpretive framework signaling what counts as constituting good or ill will is settled by others whose lives are in some way alien, inaccessible, or unwelcoming to them.

Return to Calhoun's insight. Special social contexts can provide reasons to blame some who are not in fact blameworthy in order to achieve social change. Her focus was on social structures involving massive disparities in social advantage that supported forms of wrongdoing: contributing to oppressive social conditions through forms of moral ignorance that were exculpating. These social structures helped support the *perpetuation* of the oppressive conditions by deploying the very responsibility practices that, were they exercised by better-informed moral agents, would have instead functioned as a tonic in correcting those oppressive conditions. Calhoun's proposal shows us how to alter our resolution and look upon our responsibility practices critically so as to determine whether their design is in certain respects deleterious. This is what I intend to do in this section.

There is, however, a significant difference between the cases I wish to focus upon and the ones Calhoun was interested in. Calhoun focused on cases of moral *wrongdoing*. She argued that in these special sorts of contexts moral ignorance really was excusing. (She then argued that reproach could be warranted anyway—a conclusion I agree with.) My interest is different. I am interested primarily, albeit not exclusively, in cases where well-intentioned moral agents, those Calhoun would describe as morally unflawed (I would prefer a different term), do *not* engage in moral wrongdoing at all. Instead, they act well. They do right. In doing so, moreover, they act in ways that *do* show adequate moral regard for others. These agents *do* meet reasonable demands for good will. Indeed, they might even be regarded as praiseworthy. My claim is that, in many of these cases, those who act well often do so in contexts in which the resources for interpreting their quality of will are framed by the interests of others—sometimes, even often, quite innocently so. (An example is forthcoming in the next paragraph.) Yet these framings have power insofar as a comparatively socially disadvantaged yet fully competent moral agent, in acting from good will, will be responsive to that interpretive framework. The standards the empowered set for signaling compliance with the demand for good will are shaped by those whose status is in some manner or other dominating. And this can happen, as in the sorts of cases Calhoun has in mind, even when the parties in positions of domination are all well-meaning and innocent of any wrongdoing. In such cases, the parties involved need not be individually culpable for any particular conditions resulting in these asymmetric social conditions.

To return for just a moment to a superficial case of etiquette, imagine a young provincial boy from an impoverished family off to college at some very elite school. Through his talent and good

POWER AND SOCIAL INEQUITIES 241

fortune, he comes to find himself at "high table" dining with a so-phisticated class of people, all well-meaning and welcoming him. He tries his best to display grace and gratitude, somehow managing to comport himself well in dining and conversing with these elite, even managing to be able to talk a bit about high art, like a recent opera production he was lucky enough to attend. Suppose, all going smoothly, his hosts later think so well of him, and he, too, about himself. Here's the thing. He showed good will (not necessarily *morally* good will, but good will), and were he in various ways to have departed from these forms of etiquette, he could have been *accurately* regarded as an ass—as having shown disrespect for his hosts or other company. Nevertheless, the conventions deployed to discern his good intent, the cues he was aware of as potential signals of disapproval (even if only possible and never actually on display), all arise from a world where the persons setting those in-terpretive conditions are the ones empowered to do so, while he comes from a world as an outsider. Were he later to feel some pride for being a bit of a success, he might also, not unreasonably, feel degraded and in some way burdened by his disadvantaged place. It is not that there is a type of oppression of which he is a victim, al-though maybe there is that, too. It is rather that his own exercises of responsible agency are shaped by conditions that still are liable to leave him feeling alienated.[13]

My contention is that *this is everywhere*. Our lives are rife with circumstances like this. Academics reading this will naturally think of the familiar dynamics of what counts as appropriate behavior in conferences or colloquia settings, how to maneuver in a graduate seminar, or, for that matter, when and how to show deference in responding to a referee. In philosophy settings, there are modes of

---

[13] Michelle Ciurria (2022) has rightly characterized this case as a kind of double-bind, and she has drawn upon cases of this sort to argue that the reactive attitudes and our re-lated responsibility practices involve conditions for oppression. Ciurria sees these forces as so deep as to entirely impugn them. I am not committed to such a radical indictment, but I grant that there are reasons to consider her proposal carefully.

242   INTERROGATING THE PROPOSAL

argumentation, styles of asking questions, or knowing when to shut up that are simply settled by those empowered. Even when one is at one's best and is regarded as showing the best quality of will in her dealings with others, the means of showing that are by conventions shaped by an elite few.[14]

What more is there to say about this observation? Think about the social conditions informing Calhoun's proposal. Special social circumstances—what Calhoun called "abnormal moral contexts"—set a baseline for forms of conduct regarded as acceptable in a way that shields us from accurate moral knowledge. In the cases Calhoun had in mind, certain sorts of moral wrongs, such as those involving gender disparities, were not recognized by most in the moral community, and so objectionable moral behavior was not seen as such. Here, something similar is going on, a baseline for deploying an interpretive scheme regarding what counts as signaling good and ill will is set in place by a set of background cultural practices. Participants to the practices, both those who are comparatively advantaged and those who are not, cannot be

---

[14] Here is another example suggested to me by Elinor Mason, who permitted me to quote her from our personal correspondence. Mason writes,

> [A]s we welcome our new students this week . . . I am deluged with inadvertently rude emails. It is a constantly frustrating aspect of my job that, as a woman, it is very hard to give critical feedback to students about anything other than their work. So, for example, the terrible emails they write (which are, of course examples of them getting the etiquette rules wrong: sometimes through social disadvantage, but sometimes the opposite—some of our students are so over-privileged that they think everyone else must be the servant class). I feel like it is part of my job to tell my personal tutees how to write to their professor. But I am always met with instant hostility. So I can't do my job as well as I should be able to do, because my good will in correcting them is perceived as bitchiness or something. If a man did it, it would be perceived as avuncular good advice. So in Fricker's terminology, I am suffering a sort of epistemic injustice. But (and I take it this is part of your point), the particular way in which I am not taken seriously affects my *responsibility*, because I cannot undertake certain things trusting that my will is going to be read correctly. I cannot do my job as well as a man.

The special irony of this case is that when I received her comment, I was having the very same dealings with one of my students, and my experience is pretty much exactly as Mason predicted it would be. Indeed, in all of my years of teaching, over twenty-five now, I've *never once* had my similar corrections be treated in an unwelcome manner.

expected to have antecedently fashioned these by reference to some morally ideal standard. They come to be taken as given background conditions of the cultural milieu in which agents get trained up into the moral community and learn to function. But as it happens, these interpretive schemes, and the conventional meanings they assign to patterns of action, have baked-in forms of bias that serve as the basis for even well-intentioned people to engage with each other. Moreover, since on the conversational theory the interpretive enterprise involves efforts to understand the particularized meaning of an agent's actions, moral agents rely upon the interpretive community being inclined to interpret them well. Those disadvantaged due to significant asymmetries in relations of power then risk alienation by defying or departing from these conventions, both in attempting to act with good will and in reacting to others when holding them accountable. Hence, our moral responsibility practices—our actual practices as they normally function—are in a sense morally tainted, or at least they are morally dubious. At the very least, they need to be assessed from a critical distance. Perhaps an example will help.

Consider a more serious matter than one simply about etiquette, one that does after all have moral import. In a comical exchange in the opening pages of E. M. Forster's *Howards End* (chapter 2), Meg discloses to Aunt Juley her sister Helen's secret—that Helen and young Paul Wilcox are in love. This is taken by Aunt Juley and Meg for apparently different reasons to be a crisis of the first order. Why? The reader is left to infer that two young people being in love is nearly tantamount to an engagement. It seems someone who has Helen's interests at heart is needed to go size up the situation by visiting Helen at the Wilcoxes' estate where she is staying. Meg and Aunt Juley debate who is suited for this task and how to proceed, with Meg delighted for the news and Aunt Juley wary. The relative social positions of the two families are a central factor in these considerations (we are led to believe that young Paul Wilcox comes from a much wealthier family). In explaining herself with youthful

244 INTERROGATING THE PROPOSAL

exuberance, Meg remarks that if Helen had fallen in love with a shop assistant or penniless clerk, it would not matter. Nothing other than Helen's being in love counts—although perhaps a very long engagement might be needed. To this, pleading to be the diplomat, Aunt Juley then remarks to Meg:

> Now, just imagine if you say anything of that sort to the Wilcoxes. I understand it, but most good people would think you mad. Imagine how disconcerting for Helen! What is wanted is a person who will go slowly, slowly in this business, and see how things are and where they are likely to lead. (Forster, 1910/1986: 10)

Of course, as the reader soon learns (only pages later), Helen's relationship with Paul Wilcox quickly falls apart. Nevertheless, this lighthearted opening exchange is very revealing. While Meg and Aunt Juley both have something morally important at stake—the well-being of Helen—they are alive to what would and should count as proper decorum in assessing the situation. Why is this relevant to the current topic? As the reader learns, Meg and Aunt Juley's situation is influenced by asymmetric relations of power shaped by wealth, gender, and social status.[15] They are simply not suitably positioned to exercise much power over the Wilcoxes given their place in the social life of that time. Revealingly, it never occurs to either that one might just go as relative moral and social equals and speak plainly with the Wilcoxes about the prospects for this young couple. Instead, to show good will and act well (alive to "what most good people would think"), what is needed, as Aunt Juley remarks, is the discretion of one who can signal to these people what is expected of proper folks. Hence Aunt Juley promises just to visit and discretely look about, making no mention of engagements or anything of the sort.

---

[15] As it happens, we learn that the Wilcoxes apparently have considerable wealth. Moreover, we learn in a prior letter from Helen to Meg that Mr. Wilcox (Sr.) had found occasion to say "the most horrid things about women's suffrage," but "so nicely" (1910/1986: 506), leaving Helen to feel terribly ashamed for saying she believed in equality.

POWER AND SOCIAL INEQUITIES   245

This might seem a curious example for me to pick from *Howards End*, given the famous scene, featured prominently in Angela Smith's (2006) work on moral responsibility, when Meg confronts her Henry (Mr. Wilcox, Sr.) for blindness to his own moral hypocrisy in being so unforgiving of Helen for her adultery.

> "Not any more of this!" she cried. "You shall see the connection if it kills you, Henry! You have had a mistress—I forgave you. My sister has a lover—you drive her from the house. Do you see the connection? Stupid, hypocritical, cruel—oh, contemptable!— a man who insults his wife when she's alive and cants with her memory when she's dead. A man who ruins a woman for his pleasure, and casts her off to ruin other men. And gives bad financial advice, and then says he is not responsible. These, man, are you. You can't recognize them because you cannot connect." (Forster, 1910/1986: 243–4)

A critic at this point might object that I have gotten it wrong: Meg's performance in this famous scene places on full display that, disproportionately disempowered or not, Meg has equal moral footing in the moral responsibility game for holding to account those she blames—in this case this ass, Henry. But, as I see it, this deepens my point rather than cuts against it. Why are we to regard Meg as a heroine in *Howards End*? It is in part because she is able to act well as a moral agent—as a morally responsible agent—holding to account others who would tarnish her sister or judge her cruelly. But her acting so well is to be regarded by us as heroic partly because she takes her role as a moral agent by operating within a social context in which she and her family are socially disadvantaged. That is, her moral agency is "against the odds" and yet she is able to hold others to account despite her marginalized social position. The earlier lighthearted story gives us a window into the world into which Meg, Helen, and Aunt Juley enter, and we see them socially disadvantaged in the circumstances in which they are

246 INTERROGATING THE PROPOSAL

initially to engage the Wilcoxes. Apparently, as they see their own circumstances, they are expected to operate within the conventions taken to bear on what counts as showing good will, and so on.

9.6 Conclusion

In works like *Beyond Good and Evil* (1886/1966) and *Genealogy of Morals* (1887/1967), Nietzsche famously argued that our moral responsibility practices were benighted. They concealed ugly facts about our nature and our true motivations. Although I have come at it by very different means, I, too, have attempted in this essay to cast a critical eye on these practices. I have no interest in drawing the sorts of conclusions Nietzsche wished to draw. But I have been at pains to scrutinize an element of Strawson's project that, to the best of my knowledge, no one has ever even considered looking upon critically—the demand for good will that according to Strawsonians serves as the foundation for our moral responsibility practices. Drawing upon the conversational theory of moral responsibility and attending especially to the interpretive dimension to our perceptions of what counts as good and ill will, I have argued that our moral responsibility practices are tarnished or in some way benighted.[16] They have baked into them problematic moral assumptions placing pressure on those who are comparatively disadvantaged given significant asymmetries of power in the social relations between disparate groups.

When I first encountered this dimension of the Strawsonian enterprise, and when it occurred to me that my conversational theory

---

[16] To be clear, I take it as a problem of *any* Strawsonian approach if the demand for good will is uncritically accepted as a foundation for our moral responsibility practices. Focusing on the conversational theory as a way of bringing this to light is helpful albeit not required to make the point. Why helpful? The theory explicitly attends to a community's interpretive resources as a strategy for discerning the "conversational" significance of an agent's actions (as a way of identifying the quality of her will). This makes it easy to reflect upon how those interpretive resources can be asymmetrically shaped.

assumed and absorbed wholesale these problematic elements of our responsibility practices, I took it to be a damning criticism of the Strawsonian enterprise and of the conversational theory. But, upon reflection, I do not think it is. Indeed, I now take it to be an advantage of the conversational theory that it helps to bring these facts about our responsibility practices into clear focus. Bear in mind that the point of a Strawsonian theory is to *explain* our moral responsibility practices and not necessarily to endorse them. So, as a descriptive resource, I think it just helps in getting something correct. As a diagnostic resource, I also think it is useful; we are pointed in the direction of what needs correcting. But what about as a prescriptive resource? Here I must say, the Strawsonian program and my conversational theory are completely silent.

In the opening section of this chapter, I asked how both social inequities and asymmetrical relations of power affect our responsibility practices and judgments. Drawing upon the conversational theory, I hope I have been successful in the preceding discussion in helping to answer that question. But I also asked, noting this to be the more important question, how *should* social inequities and asymmetrical relations of power affect our responsibility practices and judgments? So far as I can tell, to this normative question, Strawsonians have little to offer, nor do I from the resources of the conversational theory. Perhaps we might learn from Calhoun's proposal for how we ought to respond to those in abnormal moral contexts acting from some forms of nonculpable moral ignorance. With an eye to reform, she argues that we ought to treat these parties as if they are culpable. Maybe something similar is called for here in thinking about revising our responsibility practices in ways that more equitably reorient the standards for what counts as signaling good and ill will.[17]

---

[17] This project comes down squarely within the boundaries of the approach Manuel Vargas (2013) advocates. He argues that we should evaluate our existing moral responsibility practices with an eye to improving the way agents best respond to moral reasons.

10

Wimpy Retributivism and the Promise of Moral Influence Theories

In this penultimate chapter, let us return to the issue of retributivism. How minimal can we make it out to be while still treating it as a genuine desert thesis applicable to both blame and punishment? Consider *wimpy retributivism*. Wimpy retributivism is wimpy in its reluctance to act on its convictions that the morally blameworthy deserve blame and the criminally culpable deserve punishment. Wimpy retributivists fear overreach. They worry that they might blame and punish more often and more harshly than is necessary. They hold out hope that some consequentialist theory—such as Manuel Vargas's (2013) *moral influence theory*—might help bolster their resolve, providing them with supplementary reasons to give the blameworthy and the criminally culpable at least something of what they deserve. Being wimpy, the wimpy retributivists' anxieties do not end there—surprise, surprise! Timid as they are, they also fear that their assumptions about the blameworthy and the guilty might be faulty. Maybe the range of agents who possess free will and are morally responsible is much more limited than ordinary thought suggests. Or maybe *no one* possesses free will, and so no one is morally responsible (in at least one important sense). Maybe as an upshot no one deserves *any* blame or punishment. What then? The wimpy retributivist hopes that some variation on a moral influence theory can keep her skeptical worries in check and

Responsibility and Desert. Michael McKenna, Oxford University Press. © Oxford University Press 2024.
DOI: 10.1093/9780197679999.003.0010

somehow help her muster the courage to do what needs to be done when it is time to blame or punish.

Wimpy retributivism contrasts with *hard-ass retributivism*. Hard-ass retributivists are confident in their convictions that, because the blameworthy deserve blame and the criminally culpable deserve punishment, those who have standing to blame and punish are fully warranted in doing so. Hard-ass retributivists are equally confident in their commitments to free will realism—be they compatibilists or libertarians—and thus to the prospect that most persons are free in the sense required to be morally responsible for what they do. They do not suffer from any anxiety that there are broad theoretical reasons to worry that most or all blame and punishment might not be deserved. Consider, for instance, John Martin Fischer's admirable hard-ass characterization of his own view, semicompatibilism:

> [A] semicompatibilist need not give up the idea that sometimes individuals robustly deserve punishment for their behavior. . . . That is, a semicompatibilist need not etiolate or reconfigure the widespread and natural idea that individuals morally deserve to be treated harshly in certain circumstances, and kindly in others. We need not in any way dampen down our revulsion at heinous deeds. (Fischer et al., 2007: 81–2)

This is a far cry from the wimpy position I shall explore here.

Wimpy retributivism and hard ass retributivism are at dif ferent ends of a spectrum on a continuum of views. While I do not wish to endorse unqualifiedly a full-throated version of wimpy retributivism—or for that matter any form of retributivism—in what follows I will explore the view and argue that some version of wimpy retributivism can profit from an alliance with a moral

---

An earlier draft of this chapter was originally published as "Wimpy Retributivism and the Promise of Moral Influence Theories," in *The Monist* 2021, 104 (4): 510–25.

250 INTERROGATING THE PROPOSAL

influence theory. Moreover, I will argue that if we think in terms of a continuum, it is better to err on the side of wimpy retributivism rather than any variety of hard-ass retributivism. I will conclude by considering the prospect that the difference between wimpy retributivists and various abolitionists about retributivism might come to very little in practice.

10.1 Retributivism and Shretributivism

What is retributivism? To begin, retributivism bears on moral responsibility, but only in the accountability sense. In the accountability sense, a person is a morally responsible agent just in case she is a candidate for being held to account for blameworthy conduct by way of blame, and for being held to account for criminally culpable conduct by way of punishment.[1] As explained in Chapter 2, holding another person to account by blaming or punishing involves alterations in interpersonal interactions that can be costly for the person who fails to comply with pertinent moral demands and expectations. In such cases, an agent is characteristically an apt target of a range of other-directed reactive attitudes. For our purposes, we will restrict our attention to overt expressions of anger directed at the blamed. These expressions can take on the character of sanctions and shade into episodes that are punitive. As I will understand it, retributivism is a theory about the justification of these potentially costly responses of *both* blame and punishment.[2] Consider, then, the following desert thesis:

---

[1] Such a person is also an apt target of responses for praiseworthy and meritorious conduct as well.

[2] Many take retributivism to be restricted to matters of punishment, a point I will take up below.

DT: A person deserves blame just in case she is blameworthy, and she deserves punishment just in case she is guilty of criminal wrongdoing.

DT captures the most essential feature of retributivism, whatever else a fully developed retributivist thesis might come to. As set out in Chapters 3 and 4, the desert at issue is basic at least in the minimal sense that it does not concern any more fundamental normative consideration, such as might be offered by appeal to contractualist or consequentialist justifications. When a person deserves blame or punishment in this sense, she deserves it *just because of her conduct*, and for no further reason.

Desert's being normatively basic means that we cannot find something more normatively fundamental in terms of which we can account for it, but it can still be rendered intelligible. One promising way to do so, as argued in Chapter 6, is in terms of a relation of *fit* between a desert-base and a deserved response. A familiar picture, which I offer as a toy model, might be captured with the following example. Yogi freely lies to his friend Booboo, fully aware of what he is doing. He deceives Booboo about the whereabouts of the most prized picnic baskets so that he, Yogi, can raid from the best ones without having to compete with Booboo for the goodies. So he sends Booboo off on a wild goose chase. As a result, Booboo goes hungry. Yogi's freely and knowingly doing morally wrong supplies the desert-base, let us grant, that then renders it fitting that Booboo blames him in a way tailored to the significance of Yogi's wrongdoing. In this case, Booboo takes up the specific details of Yogi's deception. In angrily confronting Yogi, he points out what in particular made this hard on him. Suppose as the recipient of the blame, Yogi finds it unpleasant, feels guilty, and recognizes that Booboo's manner of blaming is a fitting response to what he did—indeed, fitting just because of what he did and for no other reason. A normative evaluation of Yogi's circumstance might be put this way: Yogi deserved *that* response. All things being equal, that alone is sufficient to justify Booboo's blaming him.

What more can be said to help us understand what basic desert comes to? Here we can merge the axiological theses regarding the basic desert at issue with respect to blame (Chapter 3) and punishment (Chapter 4):

> *ADT*: When a person deserves blame, the harm in blaming her is noninstrumentally good, and when she deserves punishment, the harm in punishing her is noninstrumentally good.

Understandably, some find ADT objectionable because it holds that sometimes harming a person is good, regardless of instrumental considerations (e.g., Scanlon, 1998: 274). However, as I argued in Chapter 3, one benefit of an axiological thesis over non-axiological desert theses is that the goodness implicated in giving the blameworthy what they deserve supplies a favoring reason for one positioned to blame or punish. This offers a reason to follow through and do whatever is involved in blaming or instead punishing.

On the view under consideration, retributivism supplies a justification for *both* blame and punishment. How do they differ? Here we can rely on work done in Chapters 3 and 4. First, punishment as a response to criminal conduct involves an intention to harm or in some way cause a setback to the interests of the culpable; it aims to do this. It is an intended sanction. This need not be so for blame, or so I have argued. In blaming, one might knowingly but not intentionally harm the intended recipient of one's overtly expressed blame. In such a case, one might merely aim at interpersonal engagement, moral protest, expressing a demand that the blamed party register the legitimacy of one's feeling unjustly wounded or the reasonableness of one's reactive anger (see also Shoemaker, 2015). Second, punishment involves a greater range of harms than those that are involved in blaming. In short, the harms of blame are limited to the welfare interests a blamed person has in reasonably being able to expect the good will of others. Blame involves a (partial) withdrawal of expected good will. Punishment involves more. It can involve fines and other penalties, incarceration or sequestration, imposed burdens or tasks, and corporal punishment and even capital punishment.

What about criminal culpability? How does it differ from mere blameworthiness? I treat *crime* as a moral and not a legal notion. To be criminally culpable is to be *morally* responsible for a crime. Recall from Chapter 4, crime, as I characterize it, is a moral wrong sufficiently egregious to justify others in interfering in the performance of such conduct. It is, moreover, sufficiently morally objectionable that it justifies others in responding to such wrongdoing by means that go beyond the harms involved in blaming—that is, it justifies punishment.[3] While all criminally culpable conduct is blameworthy, not all blameworthy conduct is criminally culpable.

Both friends and foes of retributivism might find my characterization too far a departure from standard formulations (e.g., Walen, 2020). They might restrict retributivism to a theory of punishment and not apply it to deserved blame. They might also insist that, at the very least, we need to add a condition of proportionality so that the nature and severity of any deserved costly responses match the nature and severity of wrongdoing. They might as well protest that retributivism is not just concerned with harm of the guilty, but *suffering*, where suffering involves a phenomenology as to how any received harms might be experienced by a deserving recipient. Finally, they might continue, for the retributivist, the suffering is not just noninstrumentally good, but intrinsically good;

---

[3] The term of art introduced here, "crime," does not track ordinary usage. For instance, children punished by a teacher or parent need not be thought of as committing a crime as we usually use the term. My formulation is only meant to parse those moral wrongs that would justify any form of punishment from those where this is not so. We might then think of crimes within the ambit of the law, consistent with how we normally use the term, as ideally capturing a proper subset of *moral* crimes. I say "ideally" since not all legal crimes are morally wrong.

254   INTERROGATING THE PROPOSAL

the suffering *itself* can be something that merits our aiming to bring it about by punishing.

This last point bears further attention. Recall our appeal in Chapter 3 to Korsgaard's (1983) distinction between extrinsic and intrinsic goods. Extrinsic goods depend for their value on their relation to other things, whereas intrinsic goods do not. For example, a flower's beauty might be a function of its rarity. Yet its value is not an instrument for the promotion of something else of value. So, its value would then be extrinsic. A real hard-ass about the value of deserved suffering might make the suffering in itself valuable—intrinsically— that is, regardless of its relation to anything else. But a more cautious desert-based theorist or retributivist can argue that any value in the suffering of the culpable must be as it relates to, for example, an expression of concern for the moral wrong done, perhaps in the service of a means of expressing guilt or remorse, as I argued in Chapter 4. On this sort of view, deserved punishment's aim and the value that it supplies is not brute suffering or harm for its own sake.

I set the preceding reservations aside and will gladly forgo the label "retributivism" if pressed. Call the formulation set out thus far *shretributivism*. Fine by me. At any rate, my focus is on two essential features in play in various respectable formulations of retributivist accounts of punishment: the basic desert thesis, DT, and the attendant axiological thesis, ADT.

10.2 Minimal Retributivism

In Chapters 3 and 4, I already sought relatively minimal commitments in terms of the nature and the severity of deserved responses. How minimal can we go while still retaining a bona fide desert thesis for blame and as well for punishment? By contrast, Galen Strawson (1994) has characterized true moral responsibility as the sort that would make intelligible deserving eternal suffering in hell. Less extreme retributivist theses might still be quite harsh.

Kant (1797/2017: 6: 333), for instance, remarked that if society were about to dissolve itself, it would still have a strict obligation to execute all murderers before meeting its own end.

Recall my proposal for deserved blame as set out in Chapter 3. Perhaps some desert theses for blame license harsh interactions, strong expressions of anger, and great interpersonal costs, such as long-lasting ostracization. But instead focus on deserved responses of blame wherein all that is a candidate for desert is a tempered angry response resulting in some social discomfort due to withdrawal of some degree of good will from others and some degree of guilt for a bit of blameworthy conduct (e.g., Bennett, 2002; Nichols, 2013, 2015; Scanlon, 2013). Is there a principled way to argue for a theory of deserved blame that seeks minimally costly blaming responses? Here the conversational theory helps. It accounts for blame by reference to communicating moral demands and expectations, protest, and the like. These modes of communicating come with costs that can amount to what a blameworthy person deserves, and yet they can be quite mild.

Now consider punishment. Analogous remarks apply. Some proposals for basically deserved punishment justify exceedingly harsh treatment for exceedingly harsh crimes, including capital punishment, hard labor, and solitary confinement. But focus on deserved punishment wherein all that is a candidate for deserved punishment is some meaningful sanctions that are nevertheless by comparison far less severe. In Chapter 4, I argued that basically deserved punishment might be structured around communicating not only the moral demands and expectations of those holding a wrongdoer to account, but also communicating expectations about the nature and degree of guilt a person ought to accept given her culpability. Such modes of punishment would remain consistent with environments that were otherwise conducive to promoting the wrongdoer's reform and well-being.

At this juncture even my most charitable readers might be pushed to their limits. Surely, it might be protested, there has to be

256 INTERROGATING THE PROPOSAL

some sense of proportionality! You cannot issue fines for murder, or community service for violent assault. But if we introduce reasonable proportionality requirements to make the punishment fit the crime, and the blame fit the misdeed, we'll ratchet upward the lower end of the range of deserved costly responses. Eventually, the minimal retributivists' range of responses will begin to converge on the range of the harsher full-throated responses, at which point it won't be so minimal after all. Fair enough. The minimal retributivist needs in *some way* to accommodate considerations of proportionality. Two ingredients should suffice while still allowing her to reject a version of retributivist proportionality wherein the wrongful harms to others require proportionately harmful responses.

First, the relation of fittingness identified in the preceding section, the one relating a desert-base to a deserved response, can do some heavy lifting. Recall Booboo's blaming response to Yogi, a response fitted for the particular wrong Yogi did to Booboo. We can suppose that in Booboo's response he did not fume at Yogi for his dorky looks, or for his failure to clean up around the dwelling they share. It was tailored to Booboo's being caused to go hungry, his sense of uncertainty about counting on Yogi to coordinate on future picnic-basket-raiding plans, and so on. Moreover, some responses from Booboo, perhaps because so gentle, just would not convey the sense that Booboo was genuinely upset to have been tricked into being so hungry. Some might be exaggerated, and so treat Yogi as if he were blameworthy for slaughtering Booboo's children, and so on. Proportionality can in this way be captured in terms of whether the response conveys the meaningfulness of the particular wrong done and the proper sense of one's being wounded. Booboo's aim in no way needs to be thought of as extracting from Yogi a harmful cost that measures proportionately to the cost to Booboo. By appeal to considerations of fittingness as involving a kind of meaningfulness or intelligibility, some sense of proportionate deserved responses can be retained. These responses can remain far weaker than would follow from a strict requirement of proportionality measured in terms of the degree of harm involved in wrongdoing.

Second, along with her commitment to a core desert thesis like DT, the minimal retributivist can also endorse a moral principle of compassion extrinsic to the norm of desert, placing a significant limit on retributivism—in particular a limit on the upper end of any substantial harmful responses to the more egregious forms of criminal wrongdoing. She can grant that many gruesome crimes render fitting exceedingly costly responses, even by the more restrictive standards suggested in the preceding paragraph. But based on considerations of compassion, and as part of our shared humanity, she might argue that there is a limit on how much one should ever pay back—literally retribute—for extreme departures from morality. If any efforts to seek such retribution would outstrip our sense that each person merits respect or dignity as a person, then the possible deserved responses can be ruled out.[4]

This completes my presentation of minimal retributivism—minimal shretrubitivism—wherein the theory on offer preserves a commitment to a core desert thesis, DT, and a core axiological thesis, ADT. It also seeks some sense of proportionality in what counts as a deserved response for blameworthy and criminally culpable conduct. One might think that here we have arrived at wimpy retributivism, as in contrast with hard-ass retributivism. But not so fast. On the sliding scale suggested above, minimal retributivism still allows one to be a hard-ass about its implementation. Given the limits placed on deserved responses, one can now be a hard-ass about supplying a deserving person with the full measure of what she deserves—by these comparatively minimal standards. And one would remain confident that a significant range of persons really do act freely and are morally responsible for what they do. So, we are not yet at the position of the genuinely wimpy retributivist. We can get a lot wimpier.

---

[4] Kant places a similar restriction on punishment in his Doctrine of the Right (1797/2017: 6:363).

10.3 From Minimal to Wimpy Retributivism

The wimpy retributivist begins with the presuppositions of the minimal retributivist. Then, based on a range of considerations relevant to her epistemic humility, she retreats further from her commitments to robustly blaming and punishing those who deserve either.

To begin, consider a feature of retributivism in any defensible form. The desert identified by even the hardest of hard-ass retributivists should only supply a *pro tanto* reason to blame or punish a person who deserves either. All-things-considered reasons are beyond their reach. Suppose a hard-ass retributivist is fully committed to the judgment that a murderer deserves to be capitally punished. If doing so would cause the destruction of the world, then all-things-considered that murderer should not receive what she deserves. The wimpy retributivist capitalizes on this fact and allows her anxieties free rein, leading to reservations about whether, all-things-considered, she ever ought to blame or punish, even by very minimal standards.

Consider first the wimpy retributivists' concerns about holding to account by blaming or punishing those who, it can be granted, *are* blameworthy or criminally culpable. Start with blame. One factor speaking in favor of caution about harmful blaming practices, even in cases of very minimal responses for peccadilloes, is that a recipient of blame might internalize it in ways that for her will be experienced as extremely painful. Maybe Yogi's far more sensitive than he lets on, and Booboo's mild rebuke risks leaving a scar, causing Yogi considerable and lasting pain, something Booboo himself would never wish on Yogi. Maybe Yogi had thought that there were at least some goodies in the area he tricked Booboo into exploring, and so he really had no idea that the harm to Booboo would be so great. So maybe while deserving some blame, Yogi deserves even less than would occur to Booboo. Or instead, rather than focus on worries about how the blamed might receive a blaming response, the wimpy retributivist might also fret about how the blamer dispenses her blame and manifests her anger in blaming. A familiar aspect of our expressions of anger is that often we are unaware of how excessive we really are. Our anger can cloud our perception of how harsh these instances might be. Mere uncertainty about the prospect that such reasons apply to a given case can give the wimpy retributivist reason to err on the side of caution, and so blame less often and less harshly despite the favoring reasons for blaming.

In the case of punishment, the risks are much greater. Even the more humane means of punishing prescribed by the minimal retributivist might be internalized by a culpable person in a way that leaves a psychic wound far beyond what even a hard-ass retributivist might judge as deserved in a given case. Likewise, even those who intend to punish in ways meant to be minimal might not fully grasp how harsh their punishments are.

But these considerations, as significant as they are, pale in comparison with the numerous other reasons various abolitionists about punishment have featured (e.g., Kelly, 2018). As noted above, the pertinent notion of crime at issue here is a moral not a legal one. Nevertheless, when faced with the options of punishing, one needs to deploy available resources, and these will be supplied by the law and the legal institutions as they are, not in some idealized arrangement. A wimpy retributivist might note that the penal system in the United States and similar nations, relying as it does on crude forms of incarceration and not much more, is ghastly and would go no way toward supplying the sorts of humane means of deserved punishment proposed in the preceding section. Moreover, the wimpy retributivist might point out, the process of implementing criminal trials is broken in ways that violate reasonable standards of fairness. A familiar criminological fact about the United States is that minorities and the poor routinely receive inadequate representation in the process of standing trial (Hinton et al., 2018). So, there is just pervasive distributive injustice baked into the system. There are as well grave concerns about policing practices and who among

260 INTERROGATING THE PROPOSAL

a population even get singled out for criminal prosecution in the application of the law. This, of course, is setting aside which criminal laws are morally defensible to begin with. Finally, the wimpy retributivist might be persuaded that unjust states cannot claim to have the authority to use force against their citizens, and so the entire legal and penal system would be illegitimate insofar as it is a mechanism for enforcing the demands of an illegitimate state. It then becomes an open question whether a nation like the United States is legitimate, and, if not, what sorts of justifications would be left for retaining any elements of the currently existing penal system. These considerations taken together can lead the wimpy retributivist to agree with abolitionist that for *practical* reasons in non-ideal circumstances, legal punishment in its current form is morally indefensible, even if those guilty of crime—in the moral sense—deserve to be retributivistically punished. In the absence of such legal resources, there seems to be few to no options for *morally* punishing those who, it might be granted, deserve to be punished.

So much for the wimpy retributivists' reservations about the practices of blaming and punishing. What of her further concerns about the proper scope of those held responsible—those who, it is assumed, are blameworthy or criminally culpable? Here she has two different types of concerns.

First, grant that free will skepticism is false and free will realism is true; some persons act of their own free will and so possess whatever sort of control is required to be morally responsible for what they do in the accountability and desert-entailing sense. Nevertheless, the wimpy retributivist remains concerned that the proper scope of persons who do act freely and are morally responsible for what they do is far narrower than is characteristically assumed. In this respect, she has piecemeal rather than global skeptical worries about the underlying empirical facts accounting for why, in a wide range of cases, many engage in moral wrongdoing. On those various occasions when we find reason to hold to account by directly blaming—whether it be a chance encounter with a stranger or instead a coworker, a close friend or intimate—how often are we ignorant of a condition like depression, anxiety, duress, addiction, or perhaps an impulse disorder? Might one of these have played an excusing or a mitigating role in why a person acts as she does? Setting these sorts of concerns aside, situationists argue that situation can play a stronger role in determining behavior than agents or observers are aware (e.g., Doris, 2002), and while this might not be a reason for global skepticism about moral responsibility (McKenna and Warmke, 2017), it is consistent with raising worries that, in a range of cases, a person's agency might be far more compromised by situational factors than is available either to her own conscious awareness or to those positioned to blame.

When we turn from reservations about blameworthiness to questions about the criminally culpable, the prospects for mistaken attribution of responsible agency are greater. A familiar fact about the penal system in the United States is the striking number of those incarcerated suffering from various forms of mental illness, addiction, and other behavioral disorders (Bronson et al., 2017; James and Glaze, 2006). How many in that population who in fact did commit crimes possessed sufficient control over their conduct to be genuinely responsible for it? It's likely that our ignorance here is vast and an upshot is pervasive injustice.

Second, the wimpy retributivist also worries that maybe free will skepticism is true. Of course, as a retributivist, she is committed to free will realism. But commitment to a controversial metaphysical thesis about the nature of persons is consistent with some degree of uncertainty about it. Free will realists are divided between compatibilists and libertarians about the satisfaction conditions for free will, the latter requiring the falsity of determinism and the former rejecting that requirement. Regardless, they are united in agreeing that most normally functioning persons have free will and are, as well, morally responsible agents. In an earlier time, some compatibilists argued that any metaphysical reasons to think people

262 INTERROGATING THE PROPOSAL

lacked free will arose from simple confusions (e.g., Schlick, 1939). That people possessed free will, it was thought, was a no-brainer. But in our own time, the range of free will realists, compatibilists as well as libertarians, rightly argue as if they themselves take it to be an open question whether people really do possess free will. But surely, if it is an open question, and if these realists have any respect for their skeptical adversaries, it would amount to breathtaking hubris simply to disregard the live prospect that free will realism might after all be false. In my own work, I have always granted that it is an open philosophical question whether anyone has free will. If pressed and asked to assign a degree of credence to my conviction that free will realism is true and free will skepticism is false, on a good day I'd go in for a 0.8. Given this, based on considerations of epistemic uncertainty, am I and are other free will realists obliged to refrain from harmful blaming and punishing? Derk Pereboom, a free will skeptic, puts it succinctly.

> [S]uppose it is unclear which prevails—retributivism or the objection. Then a case can be made that the plausibility of the objection makes it illegitimate to justify actual punishment policy retributivistically. Punishment—in particular, punishment designed to satisfy the retributivist goals—harms people. If one aims to harm another, the justification must meet a high epistemic standard. (2001: 161)

In this context, Pereboom was considering a slightly different objection than simply the objection that free will skepticism might be true. Nevertheless, the line of reasoning applies here, too (see also Caruso, 2020; Vilhauer, 2009).

Here, finally, we have arrived at wimpy retributivism. What drives her retreat is the risk of the moral hazards in unjustifiably harming those whom we blame or punish. Is her retreat warranted? Has she argued herself into quietism with respect to our responsibility practices of blaming and punishing?

10.4 Enter the Moral Influence Theorist

Wimpy retributivists need a hero, someone to save them from their retreat into quietism.[5,6] Enter the moral influence theorist. A moral influence theory offers a consequentialist justification for our practices of blaming and punishing. J. J. C. Smart (1961) famously developed a version of this view, arguing that we can justify harmful practices of blaming and punishing to the extent that they play a salutary role in influencing both wrongdoers and the wider community of responsible agents to morally improve. Smart's initial proposal met with a considerable amount of resistance, since it seemed so easy to supply counterexamples. For example, sometimes it can be just as consequentially beneficial to punish an innocent person as a guilty one, in some cases maybe even more beneficial. But in more recent times, several philosophers have developed consequentialist justifications for our practices of holding responsible that avoid the apparent shortcomings of Smart's proposal.[7]

Perhaps the most thoroughly developed and influential proposal has been put forth by Manuel Vargas in his aptly titled *Building Better Beings* (2013). Key to Vargas's proposal is that the practice of holding to account can overall have a consequentialist rationale while standards internal to the practice need not be understood in consequentialist terms. Hence, we can rule out punishing the innocent because it is opposed to an internal normative feature of our actual responsibility practice, and yet we can still commit to a "modest" teleological justification of the practice as a whole

---

[5] With the title to this section, I pay homage to the 1973 Bruce Lee film, *Enter the Dragon*. And, yes, I do intend to suggest that Manuel Vargas and other moral influence theorists like Tori McGeer, Dick Arneson, and Anneli Jefferson are the bad-ass Ninja master heroes of this unfolding saga.

[6] I suggest the following as a theme song by Bonnie Tyler, "I Need a Hero," to capture their predicament: https://www.youtube.com/watch?v=1mzUvDokTLE

[7] For an excellent defense of Smart's proposal, see Arneson (2003) and Milam (2021).

264   INTERROGATING THE PROPOSAL

insofar as, overall, it aims to build better beings.[8] A crucial feature of Vargas's *agency cultivation model* is that we get justifications for the overall framework of our practices only to the extent that, by and large, such practices really do support the moral improvement of rational agents. Where the practices cannot be so justified, there we have a reason to be revisionist and seek more effective means of holding responsible—hence we can build better rather than worse beings. Vargas's proposal dovetails nicely with my suggestions for the forms of blaming and punishing advocated by the minimal retributivist. The more excessive forms of treatment—especially those that would be deleterious to an agent's ability to take responsibility for her past misdeeds—would be precluded.

The details of Vargas's view I highlighted just now all have to do with a justification for our practices of holding to account by blaming and punishing. A different question concerns how a moral influence theory might account for the conditions for *being* a morally responsible agent. Vargas (2013) decoupled these issues. He did not build into an account of the conditions for being a morally responsible agent a dimension of influenceability. This seem to be one source of difficulty for views like Smart's. But other moral influence theorists, such as Victoria McGeer (2014, 2015) and Anneli Jefferson (2019), have argued that a Smart-inspired constraint on being a morally responsible agent is the prospect that by being a recipient of blame or punishment, an agent is susceptible to "scaffolding" as a kind of restructuring of one's agency to be more ideally responsive to the proper scope of moral reasons. The challenge for such views is that, as a strict requirement of morally responsible agency, those not so susceptible to moral improvement are

---

[8] See Vargas (2013: 171–81). It bears mentioning that I am coopting Vargas's (2013) proposal in ways that depart from his own treatment of desert. Vargas (261–5) treats desert as nonbasic and as part of the internal standards that can then be justified on consequentialist grounds, a wise move, and he might be correct to do so. Here I am exploring a more robust retributivism that embraces basic desert, which in earlier work Vargas rejected rejects. More recently, Vargas (2019) is prepared to embrace a more robust desert thesis.

not morally responsible agents at all. It is not just that there is in these cases no good justification for holding them responsible by blaming or punishing. It is that they are not the kinds of agents that are responsible at all. Consider a case of a person who commits a grievous moral wrong but who has so hardened her heart that she is no longer capable of being influenced by any form of morally defensible punishment. Jefferson and McGeer face a challenge in accounting for whether and how this person is blameworthy and criminally culpable for her wrongdoing. Vargas doesn't. Here I'll not attempt to adjudicate this disagreement. I only note it as one that will prove illuminating momentarily.

Now, how might some version of a moral influence theory be able to rescue the wimpy retributivist? One might think that the proposal is a nonstarter, and for two reasons. First, consequentialist justifications for blaming and punishing practices are typically thought of as alternatives to desert-based justifications like retributivism. A moral influence theory is what one goes in for if she wants to justify blame and punishment in the absence of considerations of basic desert. That was clearly Smart's (1963) view. Second, basic-desert-based reasons are *pro tanto* reasons to blame or punish a person just because of what she did and not for any other reason, such as consequentialist considerations. So, now, how can a moral influence theory help bolster any retributivist theory that at its core is committed to basic desert?

Key to arranging this odd alliance I am now proposing is the distinction between the reasons that might be supplied to a blameworthy or criminally culpable person to justify blaming or punishing her, and the reasons that might be supplied to the person who blames or punishes. It is a requirement of retributivism in any form that if a person deserves blame or punishment in the basic sense, absent such defeaters as "the world will explode," her deserving such treatment is all that is needed to justify to the blameworthy person her being so treated. No consequentialist considerations are required. But remember, for one positioned to

266 INTERROGATING THE PROPOSAL

blame or punish, reasons of desert count as *pro tanto* reasons. And any noninstrumental good that accompanies such reasons of desert also only supplies *pro tanto* reasons in favor of following through and giving the deserving what they deserve. None of the wimpy retributivists' worries or anxieties concerned reasons to discount the legitimacy of these reasons supplied by desert. They were just meant to weigh in the scales overall so as to settle whether, all-things-considered, a potential blamer or punisher has sufficient reason to act on reasons of desert.

My proposal for the wimpy retributivist can now be easily stated. The reasons for the wimpy retributivist to be wimpy and recoil from blaming and punishing those who deserve to be blamed and punished have to be weighed against the positive value of engaging in a set of practices of holding to account, as is featured in moral influence theories. These overall costs can, although need not always, outweigh the reasons giving rise to the wimpy retributivists' reluctance to act on her retributivist convictions. Moreover, the less taxing the retributive costs are, the more easily the reasons supplied by the moral influence theorist can help move the wimpy retributivist all the way to action. The harsher the deserved treatment is, the more the moral influence theorist will have to demonstrate the clear payoff despite the increased risks of moral hazards. This itself, by relying upon a moral influence theory, will favor minimal retributivism in our practices.

An upshot of the wimpy retributivist view offered here is that it changes the stakes in the dispute noted above between Vargas's more conservative proposal and the more radical alternatives of Jefferson and McGeer. Vargas might be right to worry that a moral influence theory on its own should not place constraints on who should count as a morally responsible agent and who should not. We risk getting the extension wrong. Regardless, if a moral influence theory is introduced as a supplement to a retributive theory that *independently* assesses an agent as blameworthy or criminally culpable, we can rest assured that we will only attend to agents who retain that status regardless of consequentialist considerations. But with that held fixed, along with Jefferson and McGeer, the justification for who among those individuals we ought all-things-considered treat as such agents is bolstered when we supplement reasons of desert with considerations about the prospects that we might aid in their moral improvement. Hard cases, like the criminal with the hardened heart, will remain hard. In such cases, we might decide that, all-things-considered, some other policy is best for how we should handle them.[9]

On the current proposal, it is open to the wimpy retributivist to be wimpier as the risks of the pertinent moral hazards increase. Recall our previous assessment of the differences between blame and punishment. Blame need not involve an intention to harm, whereas punishment does, and the harms involved in punishing are much greater and more varied. Insofar as the harms of blaming are limited to compromising the welfare interests a blamed person has in being able to expect the good will of others, one might have less incentive to supplement one's reason to blame with further consequentialist considerations.[10] While there are moral hazards, they are not as great as those involved in punishing. Naturally, the more severe the punishments, the greater the risks. This leaves open an attractive option for the minimal retributivist: Give in to her wimpy inclinations *only* for punishment. In that domain, commit to a policy of not punishing retributivistically unless her reasons for doing so can be supplemented with the sorts of consequentialist considerations highlighted by the moral influence theorists. When it comes to blaming the blameworthy, suppress any wimpy inclinations and boldly stand prepared to blame on retributivist reasons alone, at least in keeping with the commitments of the minimal (albeit not wimpy) retributivist.[11]

---

[9] Thanks to Anneli Jefferson for help in clarifying this point.

[10] Thanks to Phillip Robichaud for help in clarifying this point.

[11] I confess that I find this an attractive proposal insofar as I would be prepared to commit to retributivism at all. Perhaps it also bears mentioning that this proposal,

268 INTERROGATING THE PROPOSAL

A residual worry remains. The wimpy retributivist is committed to minimal retributivism but remains uncertain. Maybe, contrary to her own convictions, her commitment to free will realism is false. If so, no one does deserve blame or punishment. Then, were she to blame or punish, wouldn't she do an injustice, blaming and punishing those who do not deserve to be blamed or punished? Shouldn't this prospect force her to remain a quietest? How does a moral influence theory help here? In reply, note that the prospect that wrongdoers would be blamed or punished who did not deserve to be blamed or punished should not be conflated with the stronger thesis that those wrongdoers deserve not to be blamed or punished. Not deserving x is a weaker thesis than deserving *not-x*. In the unwelcome scenario in which the wimpy retributivist is wrong to believe that anyone deserves blame or punishment, she would not thereby be committed to acting in ways that the wrongdoers deserve not to be treated. Desert in this context would no longer apply. Rather, in such a situation, wherein retributivism is no longer justified, given her reliance on a moral influence theory, there will be other consequentialist reasons that will then function as the primary rather than the supplementary reasons to blame or punish. Of course, for the wimpy retributivist, this is simply an open possibility that she believes she cannot discount due to her epistemic humility. She believes that retributivism *is* justified, but the resources of a moral influence theory offer her "back-up" reasons to justify her blame or punishment should it turn out that her minimal retributivism is morally indefensible due to lack of free will.[12]

---

while arrived at by quite different means, is very close to one developed by Paul Russell (1995: 137–53), who in turn drew upon H. L. A. Hart's (1968) efforts to distinguish justifications for punishment (in legal contexts) from mere blame.

[12] I am indebted to Tom Christiano, Tim Kearl, and Phil Robichaud for pressing me on the issue of how the wimpy retributivist should countenance the prospect that free will realism might be false and hence retributivism fails. Robichaud remains unpersuaded

10.5 Conclusion

I'll conclude with a few bold albeit undefended assertions. To begin, reflect on a familiar range of cases involving morally objectionable conduct, the sort at issue in blameworthiness and criminal culpability. Consider minor matters like Yogi's wrongdoing, as well as serious violent assault. I propose that the sorts of treatments my wimpy retributivist would advocate will, for a vast range of cases even if not all, look nearly indistinguishable from the sorts of responses to wrongdoing favored by abolitionists about retributive blame and punishment. If this is so, then much of the difference between them will turn not so much on dramatically different sorts of treatment, but on the justifications available to those who respond to moral wrongdoing. Retributivists will require, where various other theorists will not, a condition of free will, and that condition will play a *justifying* role. To those who are, by the retributivists' lights, blameworthy or criminally culpable, the wimpy retributivist will be able to justify any deserved hard treatment allotted to them by pointing out that they acted freely and in so doing settled the grounds for their treatment; they brought it on themselves. That's a significant normative difference, for sure, but not the one that most highlight when contrasting the difference between retributivists and abolitionists about retributivist punishment. This is a substantial payoff for the wimpy retributivist over that of the hard-ass retributivist.

But, it might be protested, the right kind of retributivist to be is the hard-ass retributivist. There are lots of moral hazards, and the wimpy retributivist is too quick to overlook one that matters, too—which is not giving a deserving person the full measure of what

---

that one could believe something is justified while retaining residual doubts that one is correct about the matter. But as odd as it might sound, there are many perfectly ordinary cases like this. Unless we require certainty for justified belief, this is just part of being an epistemically fallible agent.

270 INTERROGATING THE PROPOSAL

they deserve.[13] Maybe so. But here, too, if we are measuring risks and assessing the costs and benefits of different theories, we need to weigh the risks of blaming and punishing too little those who rightly deserve more from the countervailing risks of blaming and punishing too often and too harshly those who deserve less. That's a tradeoff friendly to the spirit of the moral influence theorist, and I myself am willing to pay that price. If so, I contend, between the hard-ass and the wimpy retributivist, with some aid from a moral influence theory, wimpy retributivism is the better view.

What about the wimpiness? No one wants to be wimpy. Agreed. But that's just marketing. A more edifying label is *cautious and compassionate retributivism*. Let's go with that.

---

[13] As David Shoemaker notes in personal correspondence, this is surely what victims might point out when we opt for less extreme responses. Don't we owe it to them to give the culpable the full measure of what they deserved?

11

Conclusion

Let's collect results. The overall arch of my argument naturally divides into three parts with three chapters for each part. The first sets out the basic proposal, integrating the conversational theory with a basic desert thesis for both blame and punishment. The second builds on the basic proposal, clarifying and expanding upon it. The third scrutinizes the view and asks some critical questions about potential shortcomings of the conversational theory's appeal to basic desert. Parsed in this way, here is a brief tour of the ground we covered in each chapter.

Part I: The View

We began in Chapter 2, "Directed Blame and Conversation," by clarifying what directed blame is according to the conversational theory. This included the sorts of harms characteristic of pertinent blaming practices. Blame, so understood, gives rise to normative questions about when this sort of blame is appropriate. In Chapter 3, "Basically Deserved Blame and Its Value," I explored an answer to those questions in terms of a thesis wherein directed blame and the harms characteristic of it could be what a blameworthy agent basically deserves. A central element of the basic desert thesis I defended is that the harms a blameworthy person deserves in being blamed can be noninstrumentally good. In this respect, the basic desert thesis I defend is more demanding than characterizations of desert that do not endorse a claim that it is in any way good that the culpable are harmed or suffer (e.g.,

Responsibility and Desert. Michael McKenna, Oxford University Press. © Oxford University Press 2024.
DOI: 10.1093/9780197679999.003.0011

272 CONCLUSION

Scanlon, 2008). Regardless, I argue that it has advantages that non-axiological versions lack.

In developing this axiological desert thesis, I also argue that the severity of what is deserved in blaming is far more limited than in comparison with others who advance various retributivist theses. And by no means is it the case that what a person deserves is just suffering *qua* suffering as something that would be intrinsically valuable as such. Key to my proposal, linking tightly Chapters 2 and 3, is that the harms that are deserved are constituted by the communicative nature of blaming. The blaming and the harms involved in blaming are a matter of the modes of those in a moral community altering interpersonal practices in ways that have a conversational character. They engage the (putatively) culpable via altered forms of unwelcome treatment and regard, thereby communicating demands and expectations, perhaps protest, and, crucially, seeking a response in the form of an apology, expression of contrition, or at least acknowledgement.

Chapter 4, "Punishment and the Value of Deserved Suffering," draws upon Chapters 2 and 3 to develop a conversational theory of punishment. There, too, I argue for an axiological thesis—that it is noninstrumentally good that the criminally culpable get the harmful punishment they deserve. But as with my efforts in regard to deserved blame, so, too, with deserved punishment: It is consistent with a basic desert thesis for punishment that what is deserved is relatively limited. I thus resist the familiar retributivist contention that the culpable deserve to suffer the same degree and kind of harm that they have wrongly caused. In developing the view, I updated my overall theory of moral responsibility (from 2012) by reconsidering the role of guilt, when understood as a pained response to recognizing one's responsibility for wrongdoing. Guilt, I argue, is the preferred uptake others seek when they blame the blameworthy. This applies to punishment as much as blame. But, unlike mere blame, the wrongs that justify punishment are of a sort that no longer warrant us leaving it to the culpable to come to experience guilt under their own steam, so to speak. (In the case of mere blame, this is at least a live option.) Justified punishment, conceived as issuing from the conversational theory, is a kind of communicative intervention that means to participate in helping to bring the agent to experience fitting guilt. The conversational character of punishment can, then, be treated as a means of engaging the criminally culpable, and expressing *with them* the sort of expectations for what sort of guilt is fitting and deserved given the meaning of their criminality. Punishment, I argue, can then be understood and justified as a means of others in the moral community holding accountable by providing external conditions that a person guilty of a crime should register as a proper environment for her to give outward expression to her guilt. In short, she should see it as a deserved treatment suited for and expressive of the guilt she accepts.

Part II: Clarifications and Further Developments

Having a thorough account of deserved blame and punishment before us, Chapter 5, "The Free Will Debate and Basic Desert," turns to the question of how this sort of desert thesis bears on the free will debate. Many philosophers writing on the metaphysics of free will, though not all, take the free will debate to be limited to the sort of control uniquely presupposed by basic-desert-entailing blame (and punishment). I begin by attempting to explain why it is thought that desert is so special in this regard. Put briefly, I suggest that it is because free will seems to do grounding work as the basis for justified blame (and punishment) that cannot be done in the absence of basic desert. When all that is required to justify blame or punishment is basic desert, the agent's freely exercising her own agency settles whether she brings on herself the prospect of unwelcome, deserved treatment. In this way, it is up to her whether she deserves these unwelcome forms of treatment. Other justifications

274 CONCLUSION

that make the basis for justified blame or punishment also depend on, say, contractualist arrangements with others, or overall utility, or fair arrangements with others. And this diminishes the direct control it seems a free agent can have regarding whether she ought to be blamed or punished. Having offered a rationale for why it seems to many that basic desert is essential to the free will debate, I resist this rationale and argue that other normative bases for justifying blame and punishment might also require robust conditions of agency that thereby implicate free will. If so, it is at least a viable option to justify our blaming and punishing practices without appeal to basic desert, and yet the freedom required by these justifications might still leave it as metaphysically puzzling whether anyone could possess and act from such freedom under conditions of determinism. Hence, the free will debate is not held hostage to the legitimacy of basic desert as the normative foundation for our practices of blaming and punishing.

Chapter 6, "Fittingness as a Pitiful Intellectualist Trinket," begins by beating up a bit on P. F. Strawson (1962) for his ungenerous assessment of his libertarian contemporaries. I focus especially upon his dismissal of their (alleged) attempt to appeal to an intuition of fittingness. According to Strawson, they appealed to it in order to fill a justificatory gap between their metaphysical proposal and the normative basis for harmful blaming and punishing practices. Strawson claimed that their appeal amounted to no more than a pitiful intellectualist trinket. In response, I argue against Strawson that he himself needs the notion of fittingness in just the way that figures in Joel Feinberg's (1963) appeal to it to help him account for deserved praise and blame, reward and punishment, as well as resentment and indignation. So, while we might spot Strawson his particular objection to the way libertarians of his time made use of fittingness (though I don't think we should), fittingness per se, I argue, actually helps Strawson make sense of the relation between a morally objectionable quality of will and appropriate resentment or indignation. Such moral anger is rendered appropriate when

CONCLUSION 275

it is a fitting response to ill will (or a lack of a sufficient degree of good will). The worry, however, with this way of understanding Strawson's argument is that we can still ask what basal reasons are required for fitting morally reactive anger. And it is at least open to critics of Strawson to counter that one of the fittingness bases for such anger is that an agent who acted with an objectionable quality of will did so freely. If so, are we not back in the arena of asking whether a robust freedom condition is embedded in the rational constraints on fitting moralized anger? If so, Strawson's argument has not carried us so far after all.

The dispute, I then argue, turns on whether and how we can differentiate mere fittingness from desert when desert is construed as a species of fittingness—a thesis I also advance along the way. Following a suggestion of Feinberg's, I contend that the fittingness at issue is a matter of desert. But then, arguing against Feinberg, I show that what is basically deserved in response to a blameworthy agent is a form of *treatment* expressing a reactive emotion like resentment. It is not just the emotion itself, which is how Feinberg thought of it. This, I argue, is what helps to differentiate between mere fittingness and desert. In the case of mere fittingness, what is most basically fitting *is* the attitude, where expressions of it in forms of treatment are only derivatively fitting. Not so for desert. But, along with granting this thesis, I also argue that deserved blame and punishment thereby require stronger freedom conditions as part of their desert-base, and this is what justifies a blaming or punishing response. Hence, theorists seeking to advance the overall style of argument first suggested by Strawson have a choice to make between two different ways of moving forward. One is to account for the normativity of our reactive attitudes in terms of mere fittingness, and the other is to do so in terms of desert. The former has the seeming advantage of avoiding the thorny metaphysical problems Strawson hoped to side-step. But one has to pay the cost of a kind of normativity that is limited just to explaining the propriety of our emotional responses to morally objectionable conduct. It cannot

276 CONCLUSION

do the work of supplying the normativity needed to justify our practices of directed blaming and punishing. Desert supplies that, but at the high cost of having to take on the traditional debate about the freedom of the will in face of the prospect that determinism might after all be true. While I favor the latter strategy, I do not argue for it here. I just leave it as an open question.

In Chapter 7, "Guilt and Self-Blame," I revisited my prior account (2012) of self-blame as well as my assessment of guilt. In earlier work, I built self-blame from the resources I used to account for other-directed blame (second- and third-personal). Thus, to self-blame, I argued, was just to address and converse with oneself in the way one addresses and converses with others when it is another that one blames. Guilt, I then reasoned, was the first-personal version of resentment or indignation. That is, it was a form of self-directed moralized anger, at least in morally salient contexts. But this was all bollixed. For one thing, it gets wrong the empirical facts about guilt. Guilt is not a form of anger; there is no strike-back action tendency, for instance, as there is with anger. And the phenomenology just does not align with such an assumption. The relevant action-tendency in the case of guilt is reparation, repair. And it is just implausible that when we blame ourselves we confront ourselves as if conversing. In some cases, okay, but not in the typical case. My earlier mistake, I now argue, was that I did not attend enough to my own contention that our responsibility practices are a dynamic affair that relate blamer and blamed. Self-blame and the characteristic attendant reactive emotion of guilt, I now argue, is better seen as a desired or even virtuous response to the warranted blame of others were they to engage in directed blaming behavior at all. It can then be understood as a *response* to the blame of others, and then guilt is seen as the salutary *uptake* in recognition of the moral anger of others, a point I developed by drawing upon Colleen Macnamara's excellent work. In developing the view, I took up two issues that others working on these topics favor. One is that to self-blame just is to experience guilt. Another is that guilt can be appraised in terms of mere fittingness rather than in terms of desert. I reject both of these. As regards the relationship between guilt and self-blame, I argue by appeal to cases that one can self-blame in the absence of guilt, and that one can experience an episode of guilt and fail to self-blame. If so, the relationship between the two is contingent—contingent but deep. As for treating mere fittingness as a competitor to desert as an account of the appropriateness of blame, I further develop the proposal I set out in Chapter 6.

Part III: Scrutinizing the Proposal

Chapter 8, "The Attenuated Role of the Hostile Emotions," turns to both a criticism and a defense of the role of moral anger in theorizing about moral responsibility, and especially in theorizing about both directed blame and punishment. The criticism comes in the form of a rejection of what I call the *essentialist thesis*, which I treat as a Strawson-inspired thesis that the morally reactive attitudes, or perhaps a special subclass of them, are essential to the practice of holding morally responsible. I reject that thesis. The relation between this full range of emotions and our moral responsibility practices is, I argue, contingent but pervasive and deep. It might be, as a matter of what is practically conceivable and given the way we are, that we could not wash our practices clean of a commitment to the legitimacy of these emotions as resources for holding members of the moral community to account. (I doubt this.) Regardless, it is not essential to moral responsibility per se. It is possible that there could be beings who hold each other morally responsible in the accountability sense and yet they do not make use of emotions at all in doing so. But now, having established this, I also argue that the actual role of these emotions in our actual moral responsibility practices is not benighted in the way some free will skeptics and abolitionists about retributive punishment claim. According to the *hostility thesis*, pertinent forms of moral

278   CONCLUSION

anger are deeply ethically problematic because they encourage the sort of hostility giving rise to vengeance, cruelty, and taking pleasure in the suffering of others. I argue that this indictment of moral anger is misplaced and is advanced only by attending to unjustified and unvirtuous expressions of moral anger, expressions that are not properly modulated by salutary dispositions to temper one's expressions of anger with considerations of justice and compassion. So, I contend, moral anger can play a positive role in a defensible theory of moral responsibility.

Chapter 9, "Power, Social Inequities, and the Conversational Theory," turns a critical eye on the conversational theory itself and for that matter any Strawsonian communication-based theory. The worry for any such approach is that the theory on offer risks taking the existing relations of privilege and power for givens in helping to understand the standards for demanding a "reasonable degree" of good will in our mutual relations with each other. Strawson treated it as a bedrock feature of our moral responsibility practices that we all demand a reasonable degree of good will on behalf of fellow members of the moral community. But what the conversational theory makes clear, as do other communication-based theories, is that what counts or signals good will rather than ill will is itself determined by an interpretive medium for assessing the meaning or significance of actions within a shared social setting. Those standards, I argue, are settled by those who are empowered, and often at the expense of those who are instead oppressed, exploited, or just ignored. One problem among others made clear by these reflections is that often well-meaning people operating within these interpretive frameworks will bolster or reinforce these dysfunctional relationships. How then to respond? Here I turn to Cheshire Calhoun's work, where she considered similar problems for feminists who were critical of existing practices with built-in sexist upshots often perpetuated by some who might be morally innocent because ignorant of the moral landscape feminists laid bare. I fail in this chapter to offer any prescriptive advice. But I do argue

CONCLUSION 279

that it is an advantage of the conversational theory that it helps to make these problems especially vivid.

Chapter 10, "Wimpy Retributivism and the Promise of Moral Influence Theories," revisits the topic of retributivism, treating it as a thesis that applies to blame as well as punishment. The goal of this chapter is to push further on a theme introduced in Chapters 3 and 4: Seeking as minimal of a desert thesis for blame and punishment as is consistent with still being considered a respectable contender in a proper theory of moral responsibility. A motivation in earlier chapters, extended to this chapter, was to avoid an implication that seemed to be suggested by free will skeptics and other abolitionists about retributive theories of punishment—that what is deserved when one deserves blame or punishment can properly be regarded as, at times, quite severe. I contend that this creates an unfair dialectical disadvantage for free will realists and those who defend some version of a retributivist or at least a basic desert theory. Otherwise, intuitions get tested in contexts involving the freedom that could help to justify, for example, eternal suffering in hell. By minimizing as dramatically as is consistent with a respectable desert thesis the severity and nature of what is deserved, I have argued that we can thereby get to a level playing field and so still treat it as an open question whether anyone possesses free will. Free will realists thus do not have to negotiate the visceral revulsion to judgments about deserving extreme forms of hard treatment. In this chapter, I attempt to push this point to (and perhaps past) reasonable limits by moving from what I called minimal retributivism to wimpy retributivism. Wimpy retributivism begins with a minimal desert thesis as advocated in Chapters 3 and 4, and it adds further elements regarding epistemic uncertainty about the severity of our blaming and punishing responses, as well as the accuracy of our assuming that persons in the moral community possess and act from sufficient freedom as is required to basically deserve potentially harmful blame or punishment. If these epistemic uncertainties have a rational basis, then should we not

280 CONCLUSION

err on the side of refraining from directed blame and punishment? Otherwise, don't we risk directly blaming or punishing those who do not deserve the degree of blame or punishment we might allot to them? Might they not deserve any blame or punishment at all? This, I contend, risks driving the wimpy retributivist to quietism about appropriate directed blame and punishment.

However, I then argue, a moral influence theory like the one advanced by Manuel Vargas could be deployed to help save the wimpy retributivist from quietism. Consequentialist reasons could, on my proposal, be treated as a supplement to, rather than a competitor of, desert-based reasons for blaming and punishing. The basic proposal is that reasons about the overall advantages of blaming and punishing can help tip the scales for the wimpy retributivist to treat her *pro tanto* reasons of desert as enough, when supplemented, to justify all-out judgments to persist with our very minimal variety of retributivism. In this way, I close the penultimate chapter with an effort to leave as limited a version of basically deserved blame and punishment as might be consistent with a bona fide theory of moral responsibility. But does that mean that the case is made for deserved blame and punishment? No. Not at all. Let free will skeptics and other abolitionists about retributive punishment make their best case. I do not wish to deny that they will succeed in showing that no one has free will. I regard it as a genuinely open metaphysical question whether anyone has free will. If no one has free will, then make the retributivism or the basic desert thesis as wimpy as you can imagine it. Still, no one would basically deserve any harmful directed blame or punishment.

* * *

Given my fly-over of the terrain we have covered in Chapters 2 through 10, here I will just briefly comment on several themes that have emerged.

CONCLUSION 281

Strawson's Influence: While clearly my proposal is Strawsonian in many respects, I wish to resist too strong of an allegiance to Strawson. In the arena of moral responsibility (not so much as it applies to the free will debate), I fear that Strawson has reached the status of near sainthood. This is unhealthy and clouds clear thinking. I have seriously challenged Strawson's proposal on at least three fronts. First, I reject Strawson's extremely strong reliance on the reactive attitudes as a resource for theorizing about moral responsibility. Of course, they are relevant, and it would be reckless to ignore their role. But Strawson overstates their importance. Second, I also strongly disagree with Strawson's disparaging dismissal of his libertarian contemporaries. In doing so, he skated over an important normative relation—fittingness—that would have helped him improve his own position. Moreover, in failing to attend to it, he failed to see that he could not so easily avoid the metaphysical problems about the freedom requirements for moral responsibility. Third and finally, I develop a worry about the demand for good will that Strawson treats as central to the standards we employ in assessing a will as either good or ill. We ought to be more critical about the role of this demand as it is manifested in our actual practices.

Essentialism about the Role of Moral Anger: Unlike others who theorize about moral responsibility by attending to moral anger and other related reactive attitudes, I argue that the relation between moral responsibility and these emotions is contingent. Moral anger, or instead the more refined notions of resentment and indignation, are not essential to holding morally responsible for blameworthy conduct, and are not essential for blame or punishment. Their absence is consistent with stringent practices of holding others to account by means that involve costly practices, sanctions, and punishment. I do not wish to deny that it is useful to theorize about moral responsibility, and especially blame and punishment, by reference to these emotions. But their status is still, as

I have put it in various places, contingent but deep. Note that this does problematize various approaches to moral responsibility that make these emotions the central focus of developing a full theory. Consider, for instance, Shoemaker's (2017b) response-dependent view that treats being morally responsible and blameworthy in the accountability sense as being grounded in the fittingness of pertinent forms of anger. I say it problematizes Shoemaker's view rather than refutes it since it seems to me there are ways to preserve a response-dependent view while conceding the modal point I advance in this book regarding the nonessential nature of the reactive attitudes in relation to moral responsibility. I leave this as a topic for another occasion.

Fitting Fittingness for a Theory of Moral Responsibility: In earlier work (2012, 2013a), I tossed about the word "fitting" pretty liberally when developing the conversational theory. I was not alone in appealing to this relation. But I did so uncritically, and I also think I was not alone in this respect either. In more recent times, fittingness has been treated with far more care, and some have appealed to it as a competitor to an appeal to desert (basic or nonbasic). I have stuck my neck out and have not only tried to clarify what fittingness is but I have also attempted to defend the claim that desert is a species of fittingness, one that requires more stringent satisfaction conditions. In doing so, I have argued that the reasons supplied by desert are stronger than reasons supplied by mere fittingness because the former can discount or silence reasons of other sorts that might counsel acting in opposition to what is recommended by desert-based considerations. Not so for mere fittingness. Perhaps I go too far. Perhaps desert and fittingness are just different relations, and in some distinct domains they share the same grounds. Nevertheless, I offer the proposal as one that is worth exploring further.

Scrutinizing Moral Anger: Set aside my rejection of the essentialist thesis mentioned above. I have also tried to take a highly critical approach to moral anger as the relevant mode of expressing blame and punishment. Unlike free will skeptics and other abolitionists about retributivism, my intention is not to establish the illegitimacy of the role of moral anger but to clarify its limited role and show what correctives are needed to deflect the legitimate concerns of critics who instead essay for suppression or elimination of these emotions to justified means of responding to moral wrongdoing and criminal conduct. Properly modulated moral anger can be expressed aptly in our moral responsibility practices by agents whose virtues help make room for considerations of justice and compassion.

Minimalism about Harmful Blame and Punishment: I have essayed throughout for a desert thesis that treats very gently both the nature and the severity of what a blameworthy or criminally culpable person might deserve. My goal throughout is to help put a basic desert thesis—or, as some would call it, a retributivist thesis—in the best light by avoiding as much as possible forms of (allegedly) justified treatment that could present as cruel, vindictive, or just uncaring. Abolitionism about basically deserved blame and punishment, sometimes based on arguments for skepticism about free will, is quite forceful and appealing, and one of its appeals is that it favors ideals of compassion, love, and solidarity. For those committed to a basic desert thesis, I at least want to explore the best case for justified forms of treatment that also make room for these humane ideals.

Engaging Free Will Skeptics and Abolitionists: I have not directly argued against free will skeptics and abolitionists about basically deserved blame and punishment. In particular, I have not engaged those who make their case by arguing that no one has the free will required for basically deserved blame and punishment. In these pages, I have not tried to show where any of their arguments fail, nor have I discharged any arguments for free will realism. That is, I have made no argument to the effect that any actual persons possess the freedom that, I contend, is presupposed when we judge that a person basically deserves blame or punishment.

284 CONCLUSION

Nevertheless, I do believe that I have engaged this audience. What, I propose, I have offered is a shared arena of dispute, making clear what basically deserved blame and punishment come to, at least by the lights of the conversational theory. Identifying a level playing field and a shared arena for having the debate about free will helps avoid parties talking past each other. I have frequently now referred to Galen Strawson's 1986) contention that true moral responsibility would allow us to make sense of deserving eternal suffering in hell. What I have offered in this book falls far shy of that, and I regard that as an advantage of my proposal. But, granting that, we can now ask what sort of conditions of freedom ought to apply to what, on the conversational model, can credibly be basically deserved.

* * *

I'll wrap up by registering two limitations of this book.

First, I began in the Introduction by promising a theory on moral responsibility and desert, and, in doing so, I made use of words like "praise" and "reward," but I then I had little of substance to say about them at all. That's a shortcoming, no doubt. A complete theory of moral responsibility that integrates it with the norm of desert simply must account for positive evaluations as well. This book is representative of a syndrome, maybe a disease even, in work on moral responsibility theory. It is obsessed with the negative cases, of blame and punishment, as well as anger and guilt. The explanation for why is obvious enough. The risk of unjustified harms to others gives philosophers good reasons to wring their hands about our harmful practices of blaming and punishing. Maybe unjustified praise and reward are problematic, too, but they seem to rank lower in what should occupy our concerns. This is my rationale for the distinctly negative focus in this book. Nevertheless, something ought to be said about the positive cases. Here, I can only offer a promissory note. I'm working on it.

CONCLUSION **285**

Second, I have remained entirely silent about the topic of free will. I am a free will realist. That is, I believe that some adult persons—most in fact—possess free will and act freely, and they do so most of the time. Well, at any rate, at least fairly often. I am also a compatibilist. I believe that this freedom is compatible not only with determinism but also with forms of indeterminism suited for a fully naturalistic account of the springs of human action and agency. This book, like my earlier work on moral responsibility (2012), is intended to be entirely neutral as regards the metaphysics of free will. I have offered an account of both blame and punishment and suited it for a basic desert thesis. I fully grant that a necessary condition for desert as such to apply to any person is that she acts of her own free will. When libertarians, compatibilists, and free will skeptics debate the nature and the reality of free will, what they are debating, at least as many see it, is the control condition for moral responsibility. But to get clear on that, we need to know what moral responsibility comes to and what sort of normativity is involved in evaluating justification for directed blame and punishment. Advancing the conversational theory of moral responsibility and fitting it for a basic desert thesis is what I have offered here.

The book on free will is next up on my agenda. It's coming, unless I get a visit from the Grim Reaper.

APPENDIX

The Signaling Theory of Blame as a Competitor Proposal

Consider a forceful challenge to the conversational theory's account of blame. In "Moral Torch Fishing: A Signaling Theory of Blame" (2019), David Shoemaker and Manuel Vargas explicitly cast their innovative and provocative theory of blame as a competitor.

> [S]uppose something like McKenna's conversational account (2012), Smith's protest account (2013), or Fricker's communicative account (2014), were best construed as offering a broadly functional account of blame. If so, they would be competitors to the present proposal and they would have to be assessed in the usual fashion: We would highlight the comparative advantages of our account, the competitor functionalist theorists would highlight the virtues of their accounts, and then we would determine which account has the greater net balance of virtues and vices. (597)

Given these remarks, the signaling theory merits considering carefully here. That aside, Shoemaker and Vargas make a compelling case for the thesis that blame *is* better understood in terms of a signaling function rather than as any communicative function (594). Moreover, Shoemaker and Vargas have also expressed specific doubts about whether the conversational theory as I have developed it in earlier work (McKenna, 2012, 2013) can account for such phenomena as overt blaming in the absence of the blamed (Shoemaker and Vargas, 2019: 591 2), or instead self-blame for failing to live up to ideals one sets for oneself (593, n. 27). These are cases that I claim can be accounted for in terms of family resemblance to directed blame.

A.1 The Signaling Theory of Blame

Shoemaker and Vargas maintain that their signaling theory of blame easily handles the striking variability in the modes of blaming. On their view,

For helpful comments on an earlier draft, I am especially indebted to David Shoemaker.

288   APPENDIX

> blame is essentially . . . a costly response to norm violations defined most fundamentally not by any particular content—e.g., a mental state or activity—but by a function, namely, the signaling of the blamer's commitments [to the pertinent norms], including a commitment to enforcement of those commitments. (2019: 582)

Their functionalist proposal fares well, they maintain, where other accounts of blame have to engage in what they call "fancy dancing" (583) to accommodate various cases of blame, like blaming the dead, or overtly blaming in the absence of the blamed, blaming oneself, blaming dispassionately (without any particular emotion). Fancy dancing involves "ungainly fixes" (581) to account for some of the diverse forms of blame.[1] The conversational theory I have proposed here and in earlier work promises to account for cases like private blame, overt blame in the absence of the blamed, or self-blame via family resemblance and by departures from paradigm cases. According to them, in some cases it falls short. If so, their account by contrast appears elegant and so to be preferred. As they put it, they don't need to dance fancy (591).

To appreciate their theory, consider the central case Shoemaker and Vargas use of torch fishing, wherein men in a tribal community in Micronesia engage in a highly costly ritualized fishing practice. The enterprise yields less calories in terms of yellowfin tuna than what it takes participants to prepare for and execute their expedition. This is in stark contrast to their typical means of fishing that is by comparison highly energy-efficient. This seemingly irrational practice, however, is shown to be rational insofar as the payoff for those who are adept at it is the signaling of their work ethic and ability to provide amply for their families. This in turn yields dividends in terms of such things as marriage and community status (Sosis, 2001, as cited by Shoemaker and Vargas, 2019: 581–2). The unifying functional role of blaming is like that, they argue. It is a matter of signaling to others a commitment to various norms and the enforcement of them, where the practice of doing so is costly, but the payoff is shown to be rational via one's relation to one's community. "At its core," Shoemaker and Vargas contend, "blame is moral torch fishing" (587). Understood as such, "the significance of torch fishing is less about the fish and

---

[1] Some might prefer a more traditional description of the burdens of a theory of blame in terms of whether the theory can deliver extensional adequacy without recourse to ad hoc maneuvers, as David Brink noted in correspondence. Fair enough. But here I will take Shoemaker and Vargas's challenge to involve two possibilities. One is that competitor proposals fail to capture extensional adequacy at all, or instead only by ad hoc means. Another is that they succeed on this score, but are inelegant, so their plausibility rests on which proposal has the virtue of theoretical elegance and simplicity. This is an important point, since Shoemaker and Vargas are at pains to make clear at various junctures that they do not wish to deny that competitor proposals might very well be able to accommodate various cases that, they contend, might require "ungainly fixes."

APPENDIX 289

more about what the fishing signals" (582). Likewise, we are to reason, the significance of blaming is less about the target of the blame—the presumptively blameworthy actor—and more about what it signals to others within the wider community.

It is easy to see why the signaling theory appears to pose a significant threat to the conversational theory. According to the conversational theory, blame's fundamental nature *is* about the very thing Shoemaker and Vargas's signaling theory plays down: the fish—that is, the actual engagement with the blameworthy in cases of directed blame.

Resting an account of the fundamental nature of blame on signaling rather than communication has huge theoretical appeal if it can be successfully carried off. This is the heart of Shoemaker and Vargas's case for it as an advantage over "all the leading theories of blame" (2019: 583). Signaling can function as an omnipresent feature of blame in the full range of instances of blame, from directed blame, to overt blame expressed to third parties, blaming the dead, private blame, self-blame, dispassionate blame, hypocritical blame, and hypothetical blame (582–3). How so? A signal is something that is a relatively reliable indicator of something or other that can but need not convey information to other recipients. My blushing red can signal my embarrassment whether or not anyone is around to recognize it, and whether I have any intentions at all with respect to communicating anything to anyone. If one is committed to norms and to their enforcement of them, and if these are properly internalized, then a case of self-blame or of private blame can count as a signal, perhaps unintentional or even unconscious, of one's commitment to pertinent norms that have been violated.[2] By contrast, any communicative theory, including the conversational theory, cannot make use of such a simple proposal. The signaling theory therefore offers an especially elegant proposal just because all other extant accounts of blame *do* shoulder the burden of accounting for some range of blaming cases that do not fit well with the basic contours of the theory. In this way, competitor theories by contrast appear inelegant. Hence, so the charge goes, they need unseemly fixes and fancy dancing.

Add to the preceding theoretical virtue detailed above Shoemaker and Vargas's explanatory claim—plausibly, a grounding claim—and it is easy to see why the signaling theory has strong appeal. The many kinds of blaming they identify have signaling in common, *because that is what blaming most fundamentally is* (585). It is a signal to others of one's commitment to various norms, and a signal of one's preparedness to enforce them. Here is how

---

[2] At least I'll grant this point. In correspondence, Randy Clarke has expressed skepticism about how something imperceptible is a signal. He might be right. A more cautious proposal would treat such cases as expressions that, when perceived, count as signals. I think Shoemaker and Vargas could easily accept this slight modification.

290   APPENDIX

they express their core thesis when describing what we are doing when we blame:

> What I'm doing most fundamentally is signaling that I'm a member of a particular moral tribe, someone who cares about a set of norms and their breaches, someone who is disposed to police the norms, and more. (587)

The reason this grounding claim appears to carry so much force is that surely there is something right about it. Our responsibility practices in their entirety, at least the swath of them regarding our relations of accountability, do indeed serve this signaling function. And they often provide the social glue that supports our moral lives together.

Note that Shoemaker and Vargas's proposal offers an alternative way to resist Miranda Fricker's challenge (discussed in Chapter 2) to analyses of blame cast in terms of necessary and sufficient conditions. Recall, she argues that any such attempt to capture blame's full extension will only supply a thin rather than thick specification. Offering a functional characterization of blame, Shoemaker and Vargas contend, *does* unify blame's extension, and it is not thin, in the sense of being uninformative about numerous key cases.

There is one further point of clarification needed before turning to an assessment of Shoemaker and Vargas's signaling theory, the *costliness* of the signal. Recall the fisherman engaged in torch fishing. You cannot look at a person and simply perceive directly that they are hard and able workers. Even in typical work settings, one's work might blend in well with others and so make it hard to discern how much is really to the credit of a particular person. But with torch fishing, the hard-to-perceive trait is signaled via that special activity. Key, however, is that the actual signal involves real costs, ones that on their face are seemingly irrational and cry out for some explanation. In contrast, consider my love of peanut butter. You cannot read that off of just a simple gander of me. But my frequent decision to reach for it in the cupboard, my choice of peanut butter ice cream, and so on, is a reliable signal of it. Yet that signal costs me nothing (save a few extra unwanted pounds). It is not costly in the relevant way. Shoemaker and Vargas rightly contend that blame is *costly* in various paradigmatic cases (586). In cases of angry protest, for instance, one exposes oneself to a commitment to enforce violated norms like promise breaking. This itself might commit one to further costs down the line. Moreover, as Shoemaker and Vargas explain, all sorts of unpleasant emotions get stirred up, there are risks to the stability of relationships, and those blamed might respond in unexpected and further emotionally taxing ways. There are also risks exposed in sending dishonest signals. The same for misplaced blame. There are, moreover, all sorts of costs of being a *moral agent* capable of blaming generally. It is a tall task to come to be a member of the moral community capable of effective blaming. And there are as well costs of continually updating the techniques whereby one manifests blame overtly. All of this

APPENDIX   291

makes blaming, at least in the accountability sense, and at least in many central cases, a costly affair, albeit one that has clear social advantages.

A crucial feature of these costly signals according to Costly Signaling Theory, as Shoemaker and Vargas explain, is that they are *hard to fake* (Bird et al., 2001, as cited by Shoemaker and Vargas, 2019: 586). It is easy to appreciate why. The point of such a signal is to convey hard-to-discern valued information that has a benefit for those who genuinely possess the property that is signaled (like being a hard worker). This makes the information prized by others who want to identify these individuals. But if the signal were easy to fake, then too many others would seek the same payoff by faking, and the value of such a signal would be diminished for those who prize the relevant information. Hence, the signals can only become part of a stable social system when they are hard to fake.

Note a key conceptual point regarding the relation between the costliness of the signal and its being hard to fake. The latter should not be thought of as a constitutive ingredient of the former. Being hard to fake is not what makes the signal costly. Its being hard to fake is what makes the signal effective in playing a relevant role in a stable social system, as seems to be the case with various instances of blame. Indeed, angry blame *is* hard to fake, as Shoemaker and Vargas note, so much so that professional actors have a hard time being fully convincing when attempting to capture attitudes, facial expressions, and bodily cues (586). And its being hard to fake likely does help to explain why it does seem to play such a successful role in our blaming practices and in our signaling our commitment to pertinent norms. Regardless, its being hard to fake is not part of what makes it costly.

A.2 Problems for the Signaling Theory

Having set out the signaling theory, I turn now to an assessment of it when understood as a competitor to the conversational theory. To begin, why think, as Shoemaker and Vargas do (597), that the conversational theory when construed along functionalist lines is a competitor to the signaling theory? Grant that it is *a* function of blame—a unifying function that organizes and explains blame's extension—that agents signal a commitment to various norms and their enforcement. Often this sort of signaling *is* costly. Grant also, as Shoemaker and Vargas maintain (586-7), that there are various social benefits to this costly practice wherein the payoff explains the otherwise seeming irrationality of the costly endeavor of engaging in various modes of blaming. The conversational theory tells us that the function of blame in the central cases of directed blame is to hold individuals to account in response to culpable conduct. It tells us that it achieves this function through means that can take on a meaning and that have, in paradigmatic cases, a conversational

292 APPENDIX

character. Does this characterization stand in opposition to the signaling theory? Does the one functional role exclude the other? One thought is that the conversational theory and the signaling theory are natural allies. At least in central cases, one who blames, when sincere, is committed to the norms presumed to be violated, and it is made perspicuous by the activity of directed blaming itself that one engaged in blame is committed to an enforcement of those norms.

If there is any significant variation between them, it is that, in contrast with the conversational theory, the signaling theory does not fully capture all that is going in the central cases of directed blame wherein one *does* enforce such norms.[3] In those cases, in answer to the question, "What is this blamer doing?" it would seem to under-describe the case to report that she is signaling to pertinent others her commitment to various norms and her enforcement of them. Rather, she is actually enforcing them. What seems to be left as a divide between these two proposals is just the grounding claims. Perhaps Shoemaker and Vargas want to claim exclusive rights here. But I cannot see why. Each captures something important. Grounding can be complex, after all.[4]

However, as Shoemaker and Vargas present it, there are problems with their proposal. According to them, blaming is *essentially* a costly response to norm violation. No doubt, they offer good reasons for why in a range of cases it is. But it is manifestly clear that blaming is very frequently not even remotely costly to those who blame.[5] It costs them nothing when they do so from the comfortable vantage point of a community of others who widely share their commitments. Moreover, some who blame do so from positions of privilege and authority that shield them from almost any risks of holding to account others who violate the norms that help support their comfortable status.[6]

But perhaps this is an uncharitable assessment of their case for the costliness of blame. Recall the costs of coming to be an adept blaming agent, and the informational costs of updating the effective or felicitous means of blaming, and so forth. These costs will still apply even if there is no risk of blowback.[7] Won't this insulate Shoemaker and Vargas from the prospects of the sorts of counterexamples on offer here? No. Consider your own speaking skills. It was

---

[3] Thanks to Carolina Sartorio for help in clarifying this point.

[4] Shawn Wang (2021) has recently argued for just this position. Wang explores the proposal carefully, while I only gesture at it here. However, a full theory of blame that treats the signaling and communicative functions as mutually supporting can easily handle what otherwise appear to be significant problems.

[5] See, for instance, Kogelmann and Wallace (2018) who note that much blame is indeed cheap rather than costly.

[6] Indeed, this point is on display in Kate Manne's (2018) diagnosis of the logic of misogyny. I take up a related topic in Chapter 9, "Power, Social Inequities, and the Conversational Theory."

[7] Thanks to David Shoemaker for suggesting this in comments on an earlier draft.

APPENDIX   293

damn hard for you to have come to be a capable speaking agent, and it is often taxing on you to come to update your linguistic mastery. Language changes and you have to change with it. Granted, all of that is costly. But is it costly for you to share pleasantries with the checkout clerk at the grocery store, or order a beer at a bar? Surely not. So, too, for blaming. Not all of it is costly.

In reply, Shoemaker and Vargas could instead claim that, of course, not *all* cases of blaming are costly for blamers.[8] Indeed, I agree. That is what they should say, and this is entirely consistent with a functionalist proposal. In offering a characterization of their view above, I granted that perhaps *often* blaming is costly. Formulated as such, I endorse their proposal. But they contend that blame is *essentially* costly. If this implies that *all* instances of blaming are costly, that is false. Suppose instead it doesn't. If they thereby are only committed to the more plausible contention that blame is often or sometimes costly, then they'll need to accommodate cases that fall outside the scope of the central cases they focus upon wherein blame is costly. Won't this also require, as they put it, fancy dancing? In any event, they'll then need to explain why these "inexpensive" cases are also cases of blame but do not share this important feature that they say plays the central role in a unifying account of blame's diverse modes. If so, and if, as they contend, the signaling theory competes with the conversational theory, we'll need to weigh overall costs. Which proposal does better at explaining pertinent cases that are *not* among the exemplar or paradigmatic cases? Moreover, which proposal starts with better—say more theoretically useful or illuminating—exemplar cases? Will they be cases where the blaming is not really so much about the person blamed, or will they instead be cases of directed blame that instead emphasize that relation?

One might protest that this criticism misses the mark insofar as the costliness at issue is the special one at play in Costly Signaling Theory, and not the commonsense one.[9] Such seemingly inexpensive signals are costly *because they are hard to fake*. They might contend that the sorts of cases I have in mind here are costly in this sense. This, however, would be a mistake. As explained above, on a credible way to understand the proposal, being hard to fake cannot be what makes a signal costly. What makes it costly is that, well, it is actually costly. It comes with burdens that involve actual setbacks, as it is with the torch fishermen and as it is in many clear cases of angry blame.

Turning to issues of normativity, consider the relation between what blame is, as Shoemaker and Vargas characterize it, and the norms that would justify blame, especially directed blame. Strawson (1962) chided his compatibilist adversaries for characterizing our blaming practices as activities that exploited rather than expressed our nature. And he also objected to justifications for these practices in terms of utility because they supply the wrong kinds of reasons for

[8] Thanks to Dana Nelkin for suggesting this.
[9] Thanks to Randy Clarke for suggesting this.

294 APPENDIX

blaming (and punishing). But surely if what we are really most fundamentally doing in blaming a person is signaling to preferred others one's allegiance to some norms, any appeal to a justification for what we are *actually* doing will only supply the wrong kind of reason to blame that person. A right kind of reason will instead supply a justification for holding her to account that is concerned with the blameworthy party and her lack of regard for others, and so on.

One might reply that Shoemaker and Vargas are offering an account of the nature of blame, not its norms.[10] Agreed. But the sorts of justifications that are viable candidates for supplying the right kinds of reasons are built upon presuppositions about what one is actually doing in blaming. Whatever those presuppositions are, plausibly, they are *not* about promoting some aspect of the blamer's interests, such as signaling to relevant others that she is committed to various norms. The natural Strawsonian thought is that we do not merely exploit but also express our natures when we hold others to account by blaming them. What we are actually doing is about standing in a relation to *them*, expressing our demand or expectation of their showing us or others a reasonable degree of good will. The conversational theory, or for that matter any of the other communicative theories, takes this or something close to it as the focal point for theorizing. The signaling theory as Shoemaker and Vargas cast it does not. For them, its unifying feature is, as they themselves put it (587), most fundamentally a matter of moral tribalism.

If left without supplementation by something like the conversational theory, the signaling theory has the distinctive character of a debunking account of the phenomena it purports to explain. Religion, Freud contended, is really driven by infantile desire for a powerful father figure; veracity of religious belief is not part of the deep explanation. Likewise, when we learn, as Shoemaker and Vargas contend, that even in the central salient cases of directed blame, blame's fundamental nature is really a matter of signaling to others commitment to various norms—for the purpose of social gains—it defeats the presumption implicit in what a sincere blamer takes herself to be doing when she holds to account someone who has wronged her or others. Imagine that someone was clear-eyed in a moment of directed blame in such a way that she might announce as she blamed another "what I am most fundamentally doing is signaling that I am a member of a particular moral tribe" (Shoemaker and Vargas, 2019: 587). Her report, if sincere, would undermine the legitimacy of her blame.

Shoemaker and Vargas object to my earlier contention (McKenna, 2012: 117) that we can explain blaming overtly in the absence of the blamed by reference to how we would respond to and converse with the one blamed were we in the presence of the blamed. The problem with this proposal, they

---

[10] Thanks also here to Randy Clarke for suggesting this and for helping me to clarify this point.

APPENDIX   295

contend, is that when we blame overtly in the absence of the blamed, we do so in ways that are radically different from how we blame in the presence of the blamed (Shoemaker and Vargas, 2019: 592). Suppose over morning coffee Ozzie remarks to Harriet something about a coworker's questionable efforts to avoid a tax burden for their company. In doing so, he overtly expresses his blame to Harriet. Clearly, in Ozzie's mode of expressing his blame to Harriet, he is not going to express himself to her as if she is his target, or as if this colleague were present at the kitchen table. Of course, Shoemaker and Vargas are correct about this. But their criticism is off target. To say that we can understand overt blame in absence of the blamed by reference to how we would respond directly to the blamed is not to imagine that we would do or say or act in all of the same ways whether the blamed were present or absent. Rather, we can understand intelligible or reasonable indictments expressed to another in terms of whether, were the blamed present, it would be fair or deserved or fitting or reasonable to address her in some manner or other were we to blame her directly. That will inform how we understand our blaming in their absence.[11] The point of treating certain cases of blame as paradigmatic—in the case directed blame—and then considering departures from the central cases as related by way of family resemblance just is to allow for intelligible variation.

Finally, it also bears mentioning that Shoemaker and Vargas's competitor proposal to the others they consider is not without its own *prima facie* burdens to explain away cases that seem for them not to fit well with the thesis that what one is most fundamentally doing is signaling to others one's norm commitments. Imagine Ozzie and Harriet know each other quite well and have long shared commitments to various norms—such as ones about attempts to evade taxes. What exactly is Ozzie doing in signaling a norm commitment to Harriet while the two are alone there in the kitchen? He knows well she's on his side. How costly is it to him? What gain is he to achieve by his activity given that he is already quite secure in his solidarity with Harriet? The conversational theory tells us that there is a kind of communicative interaction going on, and it is not the same as, but is similar in some ways, to central cases wherein someone like Ozzie would direct his blame at his culpable coworker directly.

One might protest that the questions I raise here are orthogonal to the point of the theory. The theory is about why we blame, what explains the phenomena, and its fundamental nature. It is not about the reasons that an agent blames, nor the gains the agent might actually consider in doing so. *Of course* Ozzie does not have accessible to his consciousness any such consideration,

---

[11] Michael Zimmerman (2022: 66–9) has recently criticized my conversational theory on similar grounds. I take what I say in response to Shoemaker and Vargas here to be sufficient as a reply to Zimmerman as well. Zimmerman approvingly refers to Vargas's earlier criticism (2016), wherein Vargas raised a similar criticism to the one by Shoemaker and Vargas I discuss here. See also my earlier (2016) reply to Vargas.

296 APPENDIX

and it plays no role in his own intentional action. The theory does not mean to account for such matters.[12] But Shoemaker and Vargas are not entitled to claim as much as a way of discounting the contention that they, too, have some explaining to do. On its face, such cases seem to have nothing to do with the point of signaling to others one's norm commitments. So, then, how should a proper theory explain such cases? It's a fair challenge to put to Shoemaker and Vargas's functionalist proposal to point out that the cases on their face, not themselves serving the pertinent function, seem at odds with the explanatory resources supplied by the theory.[13]

Consider the following diagnosis of how Shoemaker and Vargas came to treat their important and insightful proposal as a competitor to communicative theories rather than as a potential ally. It is one thing to raise the question of why a practice has emerged, what general purpose(s) it serves, and what justifies it as a whole. It is quite another to then ask about the nature and justification of applications of it. By analogy, consider Vargas's well-known two-tiered approach to understanding the nature and justification of our moral responsibility practices (2013, 2015). The practice as a whole has a consequentialist justification, and this tells us much about its nature, while specific applications of it, such as blaming, might be justified in nonconsequentialist terms.[14] So, too, here we might think that asking why we have such a practice at all does appeal to a costly signaling explanation, and this does tell us something genuinely illuminating about its nature. But then, when it is said, as Shoemaker and Vargas do, that what I am doing right now in blaming is most fundamentally signaling membership in a particular tribe, that is to conflate an account of the nature of the practice overall with the nature and justification of applications of the practice. If the competitor theories of blame Shoemaker and Vargas criticize mean to be focused just on the latter, there is reason to worry that they have missed their target in giving a theory of the former.

A.3 Weighing Comparative Advantages and Burdens

In closing, contrary to Shoemaker and Vargas's contention, the conversational theory as I set it out in earlier work (2012) is able to handle cases of blame such as overtly blaming in the absence of the blamed. It is as well able to handle cases

[12] Thanks to David Shoemaker who noted this in comments on an earlier draft.

[13] Of course, it is true that functionalist theories do not promise to show that every instance in their extension serves the pertinent function. The function of a clock is to tell time, even if it is broken. But the present criticism is not thereby the result of any misunderstanding of what a functionalist theory is. It remains the burden of any such theory to explain cases wherein the pertinent function is not served.

[14] Thanks to Randy Clarke for suggesting this. Thanks also to Derk Pereboom with help in formulating it.

like private blame, blaming the dead, and even self-blame. (See Chapter 6 for a full treatment of self-blame.) It does so by attending most fundamentally to directed blame and then considers how these exemplar cases can help us to understand the other cases. As for the signaling theory, it does not pose a threat to the conversational theory. If appropriately qualified, it is consistent with the conversational theory. Indeed, I endorse it. *One* function of blame surely is to signal one's commitments to various norms. In many interesting cases, this will be costly. But not always. Regardless, without supplementation from a theory such as the conversational theory, the signaling account of blame's fundamental nature is ill-suited for the normative justifications offered for appropriate instances of it. Perhaps fully accounting for blame's entire extension, at least in the accountability sense, does require some fancy dancing on behalf of conversational theorists. The same is true for every other theory, including Shoemaker and Vargas's. In any event, if we are invited to weigh the advantages and costs of these different theories, as Shoemaker and Vargas claim we should, the conversational theory fares well.

Bibliography

Adams, Marilyn McCord. 1999. *Horrendous Evils and the Goodness of God.* Ithaca, NY: Cornell University Press.

Adams, Robert Merrihew. 1985. "Involuntary Sins." *Philosophical Review* 94: 3–31.

Alicke, Mark D. 2000. "Culpable Control and the Psychology of Blame." *Psychology Bulletin* 126: 556–74.

Alicke, Mark D., Teressa L. Davis, and Mark V. Pezzo. 1994. "A Posteriori Adjustment of a Priori Decision Criteria." *Social Cognition* 8: 286–305.

Alicke, Mark D., David Rose, and Dori Bloom. 2012. "Causation, Norm Violation and Culpable Control." *Journal of Philosophy* 106: 587–612.

Annas, Julia. 2011. *Intelligent Virtue.* New York: Oxford University Press.

Aristotle. 1954. *The Rhetoric and Poetics of Aristotle.* Transl. by W. Rhys Robert. New York: The Modern Library.

Arneson, R. 2003. "The Smart Theory of Moral Responsibility and Desert." In S. Olsaretti, ed., *Desert and Justice*, 233–58. Oxford: Clarendon Press.

Arpaly, Nomy. 2006. *Merit, Meaning, and Human Bondage.* Princeton, NJ: Princeton University Press.

Austin, J. L. 1956–1957. "A Plea for Excuses." *Proceedings of the Aristotelian Society* 57: 1–30.

Ayer, A. J. 1954. "Freedom and Necessity." In his *Philosophical Essays*, 3–20. New York: St. Martin's Press.

Baier, Annette. 1985. *Postures of the Mind. Essays on Mind and Morals.* Minneapolis: University of Minnesota Press.

Baumeister, R. F., A. M. Stillwell, and T. F. Heatherton. 1994. "Guilt: An Interpersonal Approach." *Psychological Bulletin* 115: 243–67.

Bell, MacAlester. 2013. *Hard Feelings: The Moral Psychology of Contempt.* New York: Oxford University Press.

Bennett, Christopher. 2008. *The Apology Ritual.* Cambridge, UK: Cambridge University Press.

Bennett, Christopher. 2002. "The Varieties of Retributive Experience." *Philosophical Quarterly* 52 (207): 145–63.

Bennett, Jonathan. 1980. "Accountability." In Zak van Straaten, ed. 1980. *Philosophical Subjects: Essays Presented to P.F. Stawson.* Oxford, UK: Clarendon Press.

300 BIBLIOGRAPHY

Bergson, Henri. 1889/1910. *Essai sur les donnes immediates de la conscience*. Paris: F. Alcan, 1889; translated as *Time and Free Will* by F. L. Pogson. London: Allen and Urwin, 1910.

Bird, R. B., E. Smith, and D. W. Bird. 2001. "The Hunting Handicap: Costly Signaling in Human Foraging Strategies." *Behavioral Ecology and Sociobiology* 50: 9–19.

Björnsson, Gunnar. 2022. "Blame, Deserved Guilt, and Harms to Standing." In Andreas Brekke Carlsson, ed., *Self-Blame and Moral Responsibility*, 198–216. Cambridge, UK: Cambridge University Press.

Björnsson, Gunnar. 2017. "Explaining (Away) the Epistemic Condition on Moral Responsibility." In Philip Robichaud and Jan Willem Wieland, eds., *Responsibility: The Epistemic Condition*, 146–62. New York: Oxford University Press.

Bok, Hilary. 1998. *Freedom and Responsibility*. Princeton, NJ: Princeton University Press.

Brandenburg, Daphne. 2017. "The Nurturing Stance: Making Sense of Responsibility without Blame." *Pacific Philosophical Quarterly* 99 (5): 5–22.

Briggs, Jean. 1970. *Never in Anger: Portrait of an Eskimo Family*. Cambridge, MA: Harvard University Press.

Brink, David. O. 2021. *Fair Opportunity and Responsibility*. Oxford, UK: Oxford University Press.

Brink, David O., and Dana Nelkin. 2022. "The Nature and Significance of Blame." In M. Vargas and J. Doris, eds., *The Oxford Handbook of Moral Psychology*, 176–96. New York: Oxford University Press.

Brink, David O., and Dana Nelkin. 2013. "Fairness and the Architecture of Responsibility." In David Shoemaker, ed., *Oxford Studies in Agency and Responsibility*, vol. 1, 284–313. New York: Oxford University Press.

Bronson, J., J. Stroop, S. Zimmer, and M. Berzofsky. June 2017. "Drug Use, Dependence, and Abuse Among State Prisoners and Jail Inmates, 2007–2009." US Department of Justice, NCJ 250546. Accessed on November 30, 2020, at, https://www.bjs.gov/content/pub/pdf/dudaspji0709.pdf.

Buss, Sarah. 2005. "Valuing Autonomy and Respecting Persons: Manipulation, Seduction, and the Basis of Moral Constraints." *Ethics* 11 (5): 195–35.

Calhoun, Cheshire. 1989. "Responsibility and Reproach." *Ethics* 99: 389–406.

Campbell, C. A. 1951. "Is Free Will a Pseudo Problem?" *Mind* 60: 446–65.

Carlsson, Andreas Brekke. 2022. "Deserved Guilt and Blameworthiness Over Time." In Andreas Brekke Carlson, ed., *Self-Blame and Moral Responsibility*, 175–97. Cambridge, UK: Cambridge University Press.

Carlsson, Andreas Brekke. 2019. "Shame and Attributability." In D. Shoemaker, ed., *Oxford Studies in Agency and Responsibility*, vol. 6, 112–39. New York: Oxford University Press.

Carlsson, Andreas Brekke. 2017. "Blameworthiness as Deserved Guilt." *Journal of Ethics* 21: 89–115.

BIBLIOGRAPHY 301

Caruso, G. 2020. "Justice Without Retribution: An Epistemic Argument Against Retributive Criminal Punishment." *Neuroethics* 13 (1): 13–28.

Caruso, Greg. 2012. *Free Will and Consciousness: A Determinist Account of the Illusion of Free Will.* Lanham, MD: Lexington Books.

Caruso, Greg, and Derk Pereboom. 2022. *Moral Responsibility Reconsidered.* Cambridge: Cambridge University Press.

Chisholm, Roderick. 1968. "The Defeat of Good and Evil." *Proceedings of the American Philosophical Association* 42: 21–38.

Chisholm, Roderick. 1964. "Human Freedom and the Self." *The Lindley Lectures.* Lawrence: Department of Philosophy, University of Kansas Press.

Christman, Johnathan. 2004. "Relational Autonomy, Liberal Individualism, and the Social Constitution of Selves." *Philosophical Studies* 117: 143–64.

Ciurria, Michelle. 2022. "Responsibility's Double Binds: The Reactive Attitudes in Conditions of Oppression." *Journal of Applied Philosophy* 40 (1): 35–48.

Clarke, Randolph. 2016. "Moral Responsibility, Guilt, and Retribution." *Journal of Ethics* 20: 121–37.

Clarke, Randolph. 2013. "Some Theses on Desert." *Philosophical Explorations* 16: 153–64.

Clarke, Randolph. 2003. *Libertarian Accounts of Free Will.* New York: Oxford University Press.

Clarke, Randolph, and Justin Capes. 2015. "Incompatibilist (Nondeterministic) Theories of Free Will." In *Stanford Encyclopedia of Philosophy.* Stanford, CA: Stanford University Press. https://plato.stanford.edu/entries/incompatibilism-theories/.

Clarke, Randolph, and Piers Rawling. 2022. "Reason to Feel Guilty." In Andreas Brekke Carlsson, ed., *Self-Blame and Moral Responsibility*, 217–36. Cambridge, UK: Cambridge University Press.

Coates, D. J., and N. A. Tognazzini, eds. 2013. *Blame: Its Nature and Norms.* New York: Oxford University Press.

D'Arms, Justin, and Daniel Jacobson. 2023. *Rational Sentimentalism.* Oxford, UK: Oxford University Press.

D'Arms, Justin, and Daniel Jacobson. 2003. "The Significance of Recalcitrant Emotions (Or, Antiquasijudgmentalism)." *Royal Institute of Philosophy Supplement* 52: 127–45.

D'Arms, Justin, and Daniel Jacobson. 2000. "The Moralistic Fallacy: On the 'Appropriateness' of the Emotions." *Philosophy and Phenomenological Research* 61: 65–90.

Darwall, Stephen. 2011. "Justice and Retaliation." *Philosophical Papers* 39 (3): 315–41.

Darwall, Stephen. 2006. *The Second-Person Standpoint: Morality, Respect, Accountability.* Cambridge, MA.: Harvard University Press.

302 BIBLIOGRAPHY

Dennett, Daniel. 1984. *Elbow Room: Varieties of Free Will Worth Wanting.* Cambridge, MA: MIT Press.

Doris, J. 2002. *Lack of Character.* Cambridge, MA.: Cambridge University Press.

Driver, Julia. 1992. "The Suberogatory." *Australian Journal of Philosophy* 70: 286–95.

Duff, Anthony. 2001. *Punishment, Communication, and Community.* Ithaca, NY: Cornell University Press.

Duggan, Austin P. 2020. "A Genealogy of Retributive Intuitions." ms. https://www.academia.edu/31758493/A_Genealogy_of_Retributive_Intuitions

Duggan, P. Austin. 2018. "Moral Responsibility as Guiltworthiness." *Ethical Theory and Moral Practice* 21 (2): 291–309.

Emmons, N. 1860/1987. *The Works of Nathaniel Emmons,* DD, ed. Jacob Ide DD, Boston: Congregational Board of Publication, 1860; reprinted New York and London: Garland, 1987.

Feinberg, Joel. 1986. *Harm to Others.* New York: Oxford University Press.

Feinberg, Joel. 1970. *Doing and Deserving.* Princeton, NJ: Princeton University Press.

Feinberg, Joel. 1963. "Justice and Personal Desert." In Carl J. Friedrich and John W. Chapman, eds., *Nomos VI: Justice,* 69–97. New York: Atherton Press.

Fischer, John Martin. 1994. *The Metaphysics of Free Will.* Oxford: Blackwell Publishers.

Fischer, J. M., R. Kane, D. Pereboom, and M. Vargas. 2007. *Four Views on Free Will.* Malden, MA: Blackwell Publishers.

Fischer, John Martin, and Mark Ravizza. 1998. *Responsibility and Control: An Essay on Moral Responsibility.* Cambridge: Cambridge University Press.

Fischer, John Martin, and Mark Ravizza, eds. 1993. *Perspectives on Moral Responsibility.* Ithaca, NY: Cornell University Press.

Fischer, John Martin, and Neal Tognazinni. 2011. "The Physiognomy of Responsibility." *Philosophy and Phenomenological Research* 82 (2): 381–417.

Flanagan, Owen. 2016. *The Geography of Morals: Varieties of Moral Possibility.* New York: Oxford University Press.

Forster, E. M. 1910/1986. *Howards End.* New York: Penguin Books.

Fricker, Amanda. 2014. "What's the Point of Blame? A Paradigm Based Explanation." *Noûs* 50 (1): 165–83.

Fricker, Miranda. 2007. *Epistemic Injustice: Power and the Ethics of Knowing.* New York: Oxford University Press.

Friedman, Marilyn. 1997. "Autonomy and Social Relationships: Rethinking the Feminist Critique." In D. T. Meyers, ed., *Feminists Rethink the Self,* 40–61. Boulder, CO: Westview.

Frijda, Nico. 1987. "Emotion, Cognitive Structure, and Action Tendency." *Journal of Cognition and Emotion* 1 (2): 115–43.

Gandhi, Mahatma. 1996. *Mahatma Gandhi Selected Political Writings.* Dennis Dalton, ed., Indianapolis: Hackett.

BIBLIOGRAPHY 303

Ginet, Carl. 1990. *On Action.* Cambridge: Cambridge University Press.

Glover, Jonathan. 1970. *Responsibility.* New York: Humanities Press.

Goldberg, Julie H., Jennifer S. Lerner, and Phillip E. Tetlock. 1999. "Rage and Reason: The Psychology of the Intuitive Prosecutor." *European Journal of Social Psychology* 29: 781–95.

Graham, Peter. 2014. "A Sketch of a Theory of Blameworthiness." *Philosophy and Phenomenological Research* 88 (2): 388–409.

Greenspan, Patricia. 1995. *Practical Guilt: Moral Dilemmas, Emotions, and Social Norms.* Oxford: Oxford University Press.

Grice, Paul H. 1957. "Meaning." *Philosophical Review* 66 (3): 377–88.

Haji, Ishtiyaque. 1998. *Moral Appraisability.* New York: Oxford University Press.

Hart, H. L. A. 1968. *Punishment and Responsibility.* Oxford: Oxford University Press.

Hieronymi, Pamela. 2004. "The Force and Fairness of Blame." *Philosophical Perspectives* 18 (1): 115–48.

Hieronymi, Pamela. 2001. "Articulating an Uncompromising Forgiveness." *Philosophy and Phenomenological Research* 62: 529–55.

Hinton, E., L. Henderson, and C. Reed. 2018. *An Unjust Burden: The Disparate Treatment of Black Americans in the Criminal Justice System.* New York: Vera Institute of Justice. Accessed on November 30, 2020, at https://www.vera.org/downloads/publications/for-the-record-unjust-burden-racial-disparities.pdf.

Hobart, R. E. 1934. "Free Will as Involving Indeterminism and Inconceivable Without It." *Mind* 43: 1–27.

Horgan, Terry, and Mark Timmons. 2023. "The Expected, the Contra-Expected, the Supererogatory, and the Suberogatory." In David Heyd, ed., *Supererogation,* 119–30. New York: Springer.

Horgan, Terry, and Mark Timmons. 2022. "Expressing Gratitude as What's Morally Expected: A Phenomenological Approach." *Ethical Theory and Moral Practice* 25: 139–155. https://doi.org/10.1007/s10677-021-10261-w.

Howard, Christopher. 2018. "Fittingness." *Philosophy Compass.* https://doi.org/10.1111/phc3.12542

Hutchison, Katrina, Catriona Mackenzie, and Marina Oshana, eds. 2018. *Social Dimensions of Moral Responsibility.* New York: Oxford University Press.

Jackson, Frank. 2010. "Conceptual Analysis for Representationalists." *Grazer Philosophische Studien* 81 (1): 173–88.

James, Doris J., and L. E. Glaze. 2006. *Mental Health Problems of Prison and Jail Inmates.* U.S. Department of Justice, NCJ 213600. Accessed on November 30, 2020, at https://www.bjs.gov/content/pub/pdf/mhppji.pdf

Jefferson, A. 2019. "Instrumentalism about Moral Responsibility Revisited." *Philosophical Quarterly* 69: 555–73.

304 BIBLIOGRAPHY

Kant, I. 1797/2017. *The Metaphysics of Morals*. L. Denis, ed., M. Gregor, trans. Cambridge: Cambridge University Press.

Kelly, E. 2018. *The Limits of Blame: Rethinking Punishment and Responsibility*. Cambridge, MA: Harvard University Press.

Kennett, Jeanette, and Wolfendale, Jessica. 2019. "Self-Control and Moral Security." In D. Shoemaker, N. A. Tognazzini, and J. D. Coates, eds., *Oxford Studies in Agency and Responsibility*. Oxford: Oxford University Press.

King, Martin Luther, Jr. 1986. *A Testament of Hope: The Essential Writings of Martin Luther King, Jr.* James Melvin Washington, ed. New York: Harper Collins.

Kogelmann, Brian, and Wallace, Robert H. 2018. "Moral Diversity and Moral Responsibility." *Journal of the American Philosophical Association* 4 (3): 371–89.

Korsgaard, Christine. 1983. "Two Distinctions in Goodness." *Philosophical Review* 92: 169–95.

Krishnamurthy, Meena. n.d. "Meena Krishnamurthy on Martin Luther King Jr." *History of Philosophy Without Any Gaps*, Transcript 98. https://historyofphilosophy.net/transcript/king-krishnamurthy

Lenman, J. 2006. "Compatibilism and Contractualism: The Possibility of Moral Responsibility." *Ethics* 117: 7–31.

Levy, Neil. 2011. *Hard Luck*. Oxford: Oxford University Press.

Macnamara, Coleen. 2015. "Reactive Attitudes as Communicative Entities." *Philosophy and Phenomenological Research* 90 (3): 546–69.

Manne, Kate. 2018. *Down Girl*. New York: Oxford University Press.

Martin, Adrienne. 2010. "Owning Up and Lowering Down: The Power of Apology." *Journal of Philosophy* 107 (10): 534–53.

McCormick, Kelly. 2022. *The Problem of Blame: Making Sense of Moral Anger*. Cambridge: Cambridge University Press.

McGeer, Victoria. 2019. "Scaffolding Agency: A Proleptic Account of the Reactive Attitudes." *European Journal of Philosophy* 27: 303–23.

McGeer, Victoria. 2015. "Building a Better Theory of Responsibility." *Philosophical Studies* 172: 2635–49.

McGeer, Victoria. 2014. "P. F. Strawson's Consequentialism." In D. Shoemaker and N. Tognazzini, eds., *Oxford Studies in Agency and Responsibility: "Freedom and Resentment" at 50*, vol. 2: 64–92. Oxford: Oxford University Press.

McGeer, Victoria. 2013. "Civilizing Blame." In D. Justin Coates and N. A. Tognazzini, eds., *Blame: Its Nature and Norms*, 162–88. New York: Oxford University Press.

McKenna, Michael. 2022a. "Fittingness as a Pitiful Intellectualist Trinket." In C. Howard and R. Rowland, eds., *Fittingness*, 329–55. Oxford: Oxford University Press.

BIBLIOGRAPHY 305

McKenna, Michael. 2022b. "Guilt and Self-Blame within a Conversational Theory of Moral Responsibility." In A. B. Carlsson, ed., *Self-Blame and Moral Responsibility*, 151–74. Cambridge: Cambridge University Press.

McKenna, Michael. 2021. "Wimpy Retributivism and the Promise of Moral Influence Theories." *The Monist* 104 (4): 510–25.

McKenna, Michael. 2020. "Punishment and the Value of Deserved Suffering." *Public Affairs Quarterly* 34 (2): 97–123.

McKenna, Michael. 2019a. "Basically Deserved Blame and Its Value." *Journal of Ethics and Social Philosophy* 15 (3): 255–82.

McKenna, Michael. 2019b. "The Free Will Debate and Basic Desert." *Journal of Ethics* 23: 241–55.

McKenna, Michael. 2018. "Power, Social Inequities, and the Conversational Theory of Moral Responsibility." In K. Hutchison, C. Mackenzie, and M. Oshana, eds., *Social Dimensions of Moral Responsibility*, 38–58. New York: Oxford University Press.

McKenna, Michael. 2016. "Quality of Will, Private Blame and Conversation: Reply to Driver, Shoemaker, and Vargas." *Criminal Law and Philosophy* 10 (2): 243–63.

McKenna, Michael. 2014. "Resisting the Manipulation Argument: A Hard-Liner Takes It on the Chin." *Philosophy and Phenomenological Research* 89: 467–84.

McKenna, Michael. 2013a. "Directed Blame and Conversation." In Justin Coates and Neal Tognazinni, eds., *Blame: Its Nature and Norms*, 119–40. New York: Oxford University Press.

McKenna, Michael. 2013b. "Reasons-Responsiveness, Agents, and Mechanisms." In David Shoemaker, ed., *Oxford Studies in Agency and Responsibility*, vol. 1: 151–84. New York: Oxford University Press.

McKenna, Michael. 2012. *Conversation and Responsibility*. New York: Oxford University Press.

McKenna, Michael. 2008. "A Hard-line Reply to Pereboom's Four-Case Argument." *Philosophy and Phenomenological Research* 77 (1): 142–59.

McKenna, Michael, and Justin Coates. 2014. "Compatibilism." *Stanford Encyclopedia of Philosophy*. https://plato.stanford.edu/entries/compat ibilism/

McKenna, M., and Warmke, B. 2017. "Does Situationism Threaten Free Will and Moral Responsibility?" *Journal of Moral Philosophy* 14 (6): 698–733.

McNaughton, David. 1988. *Moral Vision*. New York: Blackwell.

Meldon, A. I. 1961. *Free Action*. New York: Routledge and Kegan Paul.

Mele, Alfred. 2006. *Free Will and Luck*. New York: Oxford University Press.

Mele, Alfred. 1995. *Autonomous Agents*. New York: Oxford University Press.

Mele, Alfred, and Steven Sverdlik. 1996. "Intention, Intentional Action, and Moral Responsibility." *Philosophical Studies* 82: 265–87.

306 BIBLIOGRAPHY

Menges, Leonhard. 2023. "Responsibility, Free Will, and the Concept of Basic Desert." *Philosophical Studies.* https://doi.org/10.1007/s11098-022-01912-4

Meyers, Diana Teitjens. 1989. *Self, Society and Personal Choice.* New York: Columbia University Press.

Milam, Per-Erik. 2021. "Get Smart: An Act Consequentialist Account of Moral Responsibility." *The Monist* 104 (4): 443–57.

Miller, D. 1999. *Principles of Social Justice.* Cambridge, MA: Harvard University Press.

Mills, Charles. 2007. "White Ignorance." In Sharon Sullivan and Nancy Tuana, eds., *Race and Epistemologies of Ignorance*, 11–38. Albany: State University of New York Press.

Moore, G. E. 1903. *Principia Ethica.* New York: Cambridge University Press.

Moore, Michael S. 1987. "The Moral Worth of Retribution." In F. Schoeman, ed., *Responsibility, Character, and the Emotions*, 179–219. Cambridge: Cambridge University Press.

Morris, Herbert. 1976. "Guilt and Suffering." In H. Morris, ed., *On Guilt and Innocence: Essays in Legal and Moral Psychology*, 95–125. Berkeley: University of California Press.

Nadelhoffer, Thomas. 2006. "Bad Acts, Blameworthy Agents, and Intentional Actions: Some Problems for Jury Impartiality." *Philosophical Explorations* 9: 203–20.

Nadelhoffer, Thomas, and Daniela Toccehetto. 2013. "The Potential Dark Side of Believing in Free Will (and Related Concepts." In Gregg D. Caruso, ed., *Exploring the Illusion of Free Will and Moral Responsibility*, 121–40. Lanham, MD: Lexington Books.

Nelkin, Dana. 2019a. "Desert, Free Will, and Our Moral Responsibility Practices." *Journal of Ethics* 23: 265–75.

Nelkin, Dana. 2019b. "Guilt, Grief, and the Good." *Social Philosophy and Policy* 36 (1): 173–91.

Nelkin, Dana. 2018. "Responsibility and Ignorance of the Self." *Social Theory and Practice* 44: 267–78.

Nelkin, Dana. 2016. "Accountability and Desert." *Journal of Ethics* 20: 173–89.

Nelkin, Dana. 2014. "Moral Responsibility, Conversation, and Desert: Comments on Michael McKenna's *Conversation and Responsibility*." *Philosophical Studies* 171 (1): 63–72.

Nelkin, Dana Kay. 2013. "Desert, Fairness, and Resentment." *Philosophical Explorations* 16: 117–32.

Nelkin, Dana Kay. 2011. *Making Sense of Freedom and Responsibility.* New York: Oxford University Press.

Nichols, Shaun. 2015. *Bound.* Oxford: Oxford University Press.

Nichols, Shaun. 2013. "Brute Retributivism." In Thomas Nadelhoffer, ed., *The Future of Punishment*, 65–88. New York: Oxford University Press.

BIBLIOGRAPHY 307

Nichols, Shaun. 2007. "After Incompatibilism: A Naturalistic Defense of the Reactive Attitudes." *Philosophical Perspectives* 21: 405–28.

Nietzsche, Friedrich. 1887/1967. *On the Genealogy of Morals*, trans. Walter Kaufman. New York: Random House.

Nietzsche, Friedrich. 1886/1966. *Beyond Good and Evil*, trans. Walter Kaufmann. New York: Random House.

Nussbaum, Martha C. 2016. *Anger and Forgiveness: Resentment, Generosity, Justice*. New York: Oxford University Press.

Oshana, Marina. 2006. *Personal Autonomy in Society*. Aldershot, UK: Ashgate.

Oshana, Marina. 2004. "Moral Accountability." *Philosophical Topics* 32: 255–74.

Oshana, Marina. 1997. "Ascriptions of Responsibility." *American Philosophical Quarterly* 34: 71–83.

Pereboom, Derk. 2021. *Wrongdoing and the Moral Emotions*. Oxford: Oxford University Press.

Pereboom, Derk. 2019. "What Makes the Free Will Debate Substantive?" *Journal of Ethics* 23: 257–64.

Pereboom, Derk. 2014. *Free Will, Agency, and Meaning in Life*. New York: Oxford University Press.

Pereboom, Derk. 2013. "Free Will Skepticism, Blame, and Obligation." In D. J. Coates and N. A. Tognazzini, eds., *Blame: Its Nature and Norms*, 189–206. New York: Oxford University Press.

Pereboom, Derk. 2009. "Free Will, Love and Anger." *Ideas y Valores* 141: 169–89.

Pereboom, Derk. 2008. "A Hard-Line Reply to the Multiple-Case Manipulation Argument." *Philosophy and Phenomenological Research* 77 (1): 160–70.

Pereboom, Derk. 2001. *Living Without Free Will*. Cambridge: Cambridge University Press.

Pereboom, Derk (with J. M. Fischer, R. Kane, and M. Vargas). 2007. *Four Views on Free Will*. Malden, MA: Blackwell Press.

Pettit, Philip. 2001. *A Theory of Freedom: From the Psychology to the Politics of Agency*. New York: Oxford University Press.

Pickard, Hannah. 2013. "Responsibility without Blame: Philosophical Reflections on Clinical Practice." In K.W.M. Fulford, et al., eds., *Oxford Handbook on Philosophy of Psychiatry*, 1134–54. New York: Oxford University Press.

Pickard, Hannah. 2011. "Responsibility without Blame: Empathy and the Effective Treatment of Personality Disorder." *Philosophy, Psychiatry, and Psychology* 18 (3): 209–24.

Pojman, L. 1997. "Equality and Desert." *Philosophy* 72: 549–70.

Prinz, J. J., and Nichols, S. 2010. "Moral Emotions." In J. Doris, ed., *The Moral Psychology Handbook Oxford University Press*, 111–46. New York: Oxford University Press.

308 BIBLIOGRAPHY

Rawls, John. 1971. *A Theory of Justice*. Cambridge, MA: Harvard University Press.

Raz, Joseph. 1977. "Promises and Obligations." In P. M. S. Hacker and J. Raz, eds., *Law, Morality, and Society: Essays in Honor of H. L. A. Hart*, 210–28. Oxford: Clarendon Press.

Ramsey, William. 1992. "Prototypes and Conceptual Analysis." *Topoi* 11: 95–70.

Roberts, Robert. 2003. *Emotions: An Essay in Aid of Moral Psychology*. Cambridge: Cambridge University Press.

Russell, Paul. 2017. *The Limits of Free Will*. New York: Oxford University Press.

Russell, Paul. 2013. "Responsibility, Naturalism, and the 'Morality System.'" In D. Shoemaker, ed., *Oxford Studies in Agency and Responsibility*, vol. 1: 184–204. New York: Oxford University Press.

Russell, Paul. 2004. "Responsibility and the Condition of Moral Sense." *Philosophical Topics* 32: 287–306.

Russell, Paul. 1995. *Freedom and Moral Sentiment*. New York: Oxford University Press.

Russell, Paul. 1992. "Strawson's Way of Naturalizing Responsibility." *Ethics* 102: 287–302.

Sartorio, Carolina. 2016. *Causation and Free Will*. New York: Oxford University Press.

Sartre, Jean-Paul. 1948. *Being and Nothingness*, trans. Hazel E. Barnes. New York: Philosophical Library.

Scanlon, T. M. 2013. "Giving Desert Its Due." *Philosophical Explorations* 16: 101–16.

Scanlon, T. M. 2008. *Moral Dimensions: Permissibility, Meaning, Blame*. Cambridge, MA: Belknap Harvard Press.

Scanlon, T. M. 1998. *What We Owe to Each Other*. Cambridge, MA: Harvard University Press.

Scanlon, T.M. 1988. "The Significance of Choice." In Sterling M. McMurrin, ed., *The Tanner Lectures on Human Values*, 1–35. Cambridge University Press.

Scarantino, Andrea, and De Sousa, Ronald. 2018. "Emotion." In Ed Zalta, ed., *Stanford Encyclopedia of Philosophy*, Stanford, CA: Stanford University Press: https://plato.stanford.edu/entries/emotion/.

Schlick, Moritz. 1939. "When Is a Man Responsible?" In his *Problems of Ethics*, 143–56. Englewood Cliffs, NJ: Prentice-Hall.

Schoeman, Ferdinand, ed. 1987. *Responsibility, Character, and the Emotions: New Essays in Moral Psychology*. Cambridge: Cambridge University Press.

Seneca, Lucius Annaeus. 1928. "On anger." In *Moral Essays*, trans. John W. Basore, vol. 1: 106–355. London: Heinemann.

Sher, George. 2006. *In Praise of Blame*. New York: Oxford University Press.

Shoemaker, David. 2017a. "Hurt Feelings." *Journal of Philosophy* 116 (3): 125–48.

BIBLIOGRAPHY 309

Shoemaker, David. 2017b. "Response-Dependent Responsibility." *Philosophical Review* 126: 481–527.

Shoemaker, David. 2015. *Responsibility from the Margins*. Oxford: Oxford University Press.

Shoemaker, David. 2011. "Attributability, Answerability, and Accountability: Toward a Wider Theory of Moral Responsibility." *Ethics* 121: 602–32.

Shoemaker, David, and Manuel Vargas. 2019. "Moral Torch Fishing: A Signaling Theory of Blame." *Nous* 55: 581–602.

Sidgwick, Henry. 1874. *The Methods of Ethics*. London: Macmillan.

Smart, J. J. C. 1963. "Free Will, Praise, and Blame." *Mind* 70: 291–306.

Smith, Angela. 2013. "Moral Blame and Moral Protest." In D. J. Coates and N. A. Tognazzini, eds., *Blame: Its Nature and Norms*, 27–48. New York: Oxford University Press.

Smith, Angela. 2007. "On Being and Holding Responsible." *Journal of Ethics* 11: 465–84.

Smith, Angela. 2006. "Control, Responsibility, and Moral Assessment." *Philosophical Studies* 138: 367–92.

Smith, Angela. 2005. "Responsibility for Attitudes: Activity and Passivity in Mental Life." *Ethics* 115: 236–71.

Sosis, R. 2001. "Costly Signaling and Torch Fishing on Ifaluk Atoll." *Evolution and Human Behavior* 21: 223–44.

Srinivasan, Amia. 2017. "The Aptness of Anger." *Journal of Political Philosophy* 26 (22): 123–44.

Stout, Nathan. 2016. "Conversation, Responsibility, and Autism Spectrum Disorder." *Philosophical Psychology* 29 (7): 1015–28.

Strawson, Galen. 1994. "The Impossibility of Moral Responsibility." *Philosophical Studies* 75: 5–24.

Strawson, Galen. 1986. *Freedom and Belief*. Oxford: Clarendon Press.

Strawson, P. F. 1962. "Freedom and Resentment." *Proceedings of the British Academy* 48: 187–211.

Tadros, Victor. 2011. *The Ends of Harm: The Moral Foundations of Criminal Law*. Oxford: Oxford University Press.

Talbert, Matthew. 2012. "Moral Competence, Moral Blame, and Protest." *Journal of Ethics* 16: 89–109.

Taylor, Richard. 1966. *Action and Purpose*. Engelwood Cliffs, NJ: Prentice-Hall.

Tierney, Hannah. 2022. "Don't Suffer in Silence: A Self-Help Guide for Self-Blame." In Andreas Brekke Carlsson, ed., *Self-Blame and Moral Responsibility*, 117–33. Cambridge: Cambridge University Press: 117–133.

Vacarezza, Maria-Silvia. 2017. "The Unity of the Virtues Reconsidered: Competing Accounts in Philosophy and Positive Psychology." *Review of Philosophy and Psychology* 8: 637–51.

van Inwagen, Peter. 2017. *Thinking about Free Will*. Cambridge: Cambridge University Press.

310 BIBLIOGRAPHY

van Inwagen, Peter. 2008. "How to Think about the Problem of Free Will." *Journal of Ethics* 12 (3–4): 327–41.

van Straaten, Zak, ed. 1980. *Philosophical Subjects: Essays Presented to P. F. Strawson.* Oxford: Clarendon.

Vargas, Manuel. 2022. "Instrumentalist Theories of Moral Responsibility." In D. Nelkin and D. Pereboom, eds., *Oxford Handbook on Moral Responsibility*, 3–26. New York: Oxford University Press.

Vargas, Manuel. 2019. "Responsibility, Methodology, and Desert." *Journal of Information Ethics* 28 (1): 131–47.

Vargas, Manuel. 2013. *Building Better Beings: A Theory of Moral Responsibility.* New York: Oxford University Press.

Vihvelin, Kadri. 2015. "How Not to Think about Free Will." *Journal of Cognition and Neuroethics* 3 (1): 393–403.

Vihvelin, Kadri. 2013. *Causes, Laws, and Free Will: Why Determinism Doesn't Matter.* New York: Oxford University Press.

Vilhauer, B. 2009. "Free Will and Reasonable Doubt." *American Philosophical Quarterly* 46: 131–40.

Walen, A. 2020. "Retributive Justice." *Stanford Encyclopedia of Philosophy.* Stanford, CA: Stanford University Press. https://plato.stanford.edu/entries/justice-retributive/.

Wallace, R. Jay. 2019. *The Moral Nexus.* Princeton, NJ: Princeton University Press.

Wallace, R. Jay. 1994. *Responsibility and the Moral Sentiments.* Cambridge, MA.: Harvard University Press.

Waller, Bruce. 2015. *The Stubborn System of Moral Responsibility.* Cambridge, MA: MIT Press.

Waller, Bruce. 2011. *Against Moral Responsibility.* Cambridge, MA: MIT Press.

Wang, Shaun, T. 2021. "The Communication Argument and the Pluralist Challenge." *Canadian Journal of Philosophy* 51 (5) 384–99.

Watson, Gary. 2014. "Peter Strawson on Responsibility and Sociality." In David Shoemaker and Neal A. Tognazzini, eds., *Oxford Studies in Agency and Responsibility, 2: "Freedom and Resentment" at 50*, 15–32. Oxford: Oxford University Press.

Watson, Gary. 2004. *Agency and Answerability.* New York: Oxford University Press.

Watson, Gary, ed. 2003. *Free Will.* 2nd ed. New York: Oxford University Press.

Watson, Gary. 1996. "Two Faces of Responsibility." *Philosophical Topics* 24 (2): 227–48.

Watson, Gary. 1987. "Responsibility and the Limits of Evil: Variations on a Strawsonian Theme." In F. Schoeman, ed., *Responsibility, Character, and the Emotions*, 256–86. Cambridge: Cambridge University Press.

White, Morton. 1979. "Oughts and Cans." In Alan Ryan, ed., *The Idea of Freedom: Essays in Honor of Isiah Berlin*, 211–19. Oxford: Oxford University Press.

BIBLIOGRAPHY 311

Wolf, Susan. 1990. *Freedom within Reason*. Oxford: Oxford University Press.
Zimmerman, Michael. 2022. *Ignorance and Moral Responsibility*. Oxford: Oxford University Press.
Zimmerman, Michael. 2011. *The Immorality of Punishment*. Toronto: Broadview Press.
Zimmerman, Michael. 1988. *An Essay on Moral Responsibility*. Totowa, NJ: Rowman and Littlefield.

Index of Authors

For the benefit of digital users, indexed terms that span two pages (e.g., 52–53) may, on occasion, appear on only one of those pages.

Adams, Marilyn McCord, 72–73
Alicke, Mark D., 200–1
Annas, Julia, 214, 216–17
Aristotle, 215
Arneson, Richard, 263n.5, 264n.8
Arpaly, Nomy, 15–16
Austin, J. L., 163–64
Ayer, A. J., 36n.14

Baier, Annette, 229n.5
Baumeister, R. F., 173–74
Bell, Macalester, 197, 198, 217n.16
Bennett, Christopher, 32n.13, 36–37, 37n.15, 49, 50, 61n.9, 79n.1, 255
Bennett, Jonathan, 32–33, 197, 201–2, 213–14, 225n.1, 228n.3
Bergson, Henri, 145–46
Bird, R. B., 291
Björnsson, Gunnar, 15n.1, 18n.2, 21n.5, 94n.10
Bok, Hilary, 119–20, 126
Brandenburg, Daphne, 200–1, 221–23
Briggs, Jean, 209n.10
Brink, David O., 15n.*, 15–16, 15n.1, 32–33, 41–44, 288n.1
Bronson, J., 261
Buss, Sarah, 238–39

Calhoun, Cheshire, 231–35, 240–43

Campbell, C. A., 145–46
Capesv, Justin, 205n.5
Carlsson, Andreas Brekke, 9, 137, 157, 161n.21, 172, 177–78, 188–92, 204n.3, 211
Caruso, Gregg, 197, 214n.14, 262
Chisholm, Roderick, 72–73, 145–46
Christman, Johnathan, 229n.5
Ciurria, Michelle, 241n.13
Clarke, Randolph, 61n.9, 87–89, 133, 137, 156, 173–74, 177–78, 187, 192n.6, 289n.2, 294n.10, 296n.14

D'Arms, Justin, 138, 192n.6
Darwall, Stephen, 23, 87, 225n.1
Dennett, Daniel, 36–37, 101, 117
Doris, John, 260–61
Driver, Julia, 23
Duff, Anthony, 1–2, 6–7, 81–82, 84n.4, 89–94
Duggan, Austin P., 172

Emmons, Nathaniel, 79–80, 101–2

Feinberg, Joel, 1–2, 3, 8, 35–36, 45–47, 48, 57, 90–91, 135–71, 186, 275–76
Fischer, J. M., 15–16, 32–33, 45–46, 107n.1, 133, 148–49, 167n.25, 213–14, 228n.4, 230n.7, 249

314 INDEX OF AUTHORS

Flanagan, Owen, 197
Forster, E. M., 244, 245
Fricker, Amanda, 15n.*, 17, 40, 41–
    43, 230n.6
Friedman, Marilyn, 229n.5
Frijda, Nico, 213–14

Gandhi, Mahatma, 200–1, 217–19
Ginet, Carl, 133
Goldberg, Julie H., 200–1
Graham, Peter, 168n.26, 210
Greenspan, Patricia, 173–74
Grice, Paul H., 1–2, 148, 236–37

Haji, Ishtiyaque, 17, 22n.7, 31–32,
    107n.1, 110, 133, 228n.4
Hieronymi, Pamela, 15–16, 19n.3,
    28, 168n.26, 172, 210, 219
Hinton, E., L., 259–60
Hobart, R. E., 36n.14
Horgan, Terry, 23–24, 50n.3
Howard, Christopher, 137n.1, 155n.16

Jackson, Frank, 38n.17
Jacobson, Daniel, 138
James, Doris J., 261
Jefferson, Anneli, 169–70n.27,
    263n.5, 264–65, 266–67

Kant, Immanuel, 37n.15, 95–96,
    223n.20, 254–55, 257n.4
Kelly, Erin, 259–60
Kennett, Jeanette, 200–1, 213–14,
    223n.20
King, Martin Luther, Jr., 200–
    1, 217–19
Kogelmann, Brian, 292n.4
Korsgaard, Christine, 65–66
Krishnamurthy, Meena, 218n.17

Lenman, James, 36n.14, 55n.6, 62,
    120–22, 126
Levy, Neil, 197

Macnamara, Coleen, 86–87, 172
Martin, Adrienne, 26n.11
McCormick, Kelly, 54n.5, 137,
    154n.15, 170n.28
McGeer, Victoria, 169–70n.27,
    208n.9, 208–9, 214–15n.15, 223,
    263n.5, 264–65, 266–67
McNaughton, David, 50n.3
Meldon, A. I., 145–46
Mele, Alfred, 45–46, 110, 133, 215–16
Menges, Leonhard, 51n.4
Meyers, Diana Teitjens, 229n.5
Milam, Per-Erik, 263n.7
Miller, D., 162
Mills, Charles, 230n.6
Moore, G. E., 72–73
Moore, Michael S., 93n.9
Morris, Herbert, 173–74

Nadelhoffer, Thomas, 197, 200–1
Nelkin, Dana, 32–33, 41–44, 51–54,
    71–73, 120–22, 127–30, 137,
    157, 158n.19, 172, 177–78, 190–
    91, 228n.4, 293n.8
Nichols, Shaun, 173–74, 219n.18, 255
Nietzsche, Friedrich, 246
Nussbaum, Martha C., 199, 200–1,
    213–14, 215

Oshana, Marina, 225n.1, 229n.5

Pereboom, Derk, 7–8, 28, 37, 38n.17,
    45–47, 54, 57n.8, 65, 67–71, 79–
    80, 105–6, 108, 111–12, 113–20,
    127–28, 130–33, 137, 153–54,
    158n.19, 161n.21, 162, 170,
    180–81, 197, 199–202, 204n.4,
    207, 209n.10, 213–15, 218n.17,
    219n.18, 219–20, 221, 228,
    235n.11, 261–62, 296n.15
Pettit, Philip, 229
Pickard, Hannah, 200–1, 213–14, 220–21
Pojman, Louis, 162

INDEX OF AUTHORS 315

Prinz, J. J., 173–74

Ramsey, William, 38n.17
Ravizza, Mark, 45–46, 107n.1, 133, 148–49, 167n.25, 213–14, 228n.4, 230n.7
Rawling, Piers, 156, 177–78, 192n.6
Rawls, John, 55n.6, 115n.4
Raz, Joseph, 157–58
Roberts, Robert, 180–81
Russell, Paul, 178, 225n.1, 228n.3, 267–68n.11

Sartorio, Carolina, 45–46, 107n.1, 133, 167n.25, 228n.4, 292n.3
Sartre, Jean-Paul, 145–46
Scanlon, T. M., 3, 16, 17, 36–37, 38n.17, 39–40, 45–47, 48–49, 50–51, 56–57, 62, 74, 106–7, 108–9, 112–13, 120, 122–24, 126, 137, 159n.20, 203, 225n.1, 252, 255, 271–72
Schlick, Moritz, 36n.14, 124, 126, 143, 261–62
Seneca, Lucius Annaeus, 200
Sher, George, 15–16, 37n.15
Shoemaker, David, 4, 15n.*, 16, 17, 26n.11, 32–33, 39–40, 87, 137, 153–54, 168–70, 173–74, 177–78, 197, 198, 201–2, 210–11, 212, 225n.1, 228n.3, 229n.5, 252–53, 270n.13, 287–97
Smart, J. J. C., 3, 5, 11–12, 15–16, 36–37, 55–56, 119–20, 124, 126, 143, 263, 264–65
Smith, Angela, 15–16, 28, 87, 168n.26, 210
Sosis, R., 288–89
Srinivasan, Amia, 200
Stout, Nathan, 212
Strawson, Galen, 10, 59–60, 75–76, 77–79, 101, 109n.2, 170, 228, 254–55

Strawson, P. F. passim
on demand for good, 10–11, 191–92, 225–27, 237–38, 278–79
on desert, 150–52
on fittingness, 8, 135–36, 140–41, 143–51, 154, 274–76
on libertarian's mistake, 144–47, 156–54
on quality of will, 20
on reactive attitudes, 32–33, 178, 198, 201–2
on wrong kinds of reasons, 139, 148–49, 293–94

Tadros, Victor, 89n.6, 90n.7, 98–99
Talbert, Matthew, 16, 28
Taylor, Richard, 146
Tierney, Hannah, 182n.3
Timmons, Mark, 23–24, 50n.3
Tocchetto, Daniela, 200–1
Tognazinni, Neal, 17

Vacarezza, Maria-Silvia, 216–17
van Inwagen, Peter, 7–8
Vargas, Manuel, 3, 11–12, 15–16, 26n.11, 36–37, 39–40, 55n.6, 62, 114–16, 153–54, 169–70n.27, 223, 225–26, 235–36, 247n.17, 263–67, 280, 287–97
Vihvelin, Kadri, 7–8, 133
Vilhauer, Benjamin, 262

Walen, Alec, 253–54
Wallace, R. Jay, 3, 5, 23, 25–26, 31–33, 49–50, 55n.6, 62, 74, 106–9, 112–14, 124–26, 127–29, 136–37, 149–50, 157–58, 178, 197, 198, 201–2, 206n.7, 213–14, 225–26
Wallace, Robert H., 292n.4
Waller, Bruce, 197, 199, 200–1, 213–14, 215

316 INDEX OF AUTHORS

Warmke, Brandon, 260–61
Watson, Gary, 1–2, 4, 17, 22–23,
    26–27, 28–29, 32–33, 39–40,
    86, 150n.11, 173, 175–76,
    200–1, 203n.2, 213–14, 217–19,
    225n.1, 226–27

White, Morton, 121n.5
Wolf, Susan, 228n.4

Zimmerman, Michael, 15–16, 17,
    22n.7, 31–32, 38n.17, 39–40,
    295n.11

Index of Topics

For the benefit of digital users, indexed terms that span two pages (e.g., 52–53) may, on occasion, appear on only one of those pages.

accountability, 4, 7–8, 17, 191–92, 250
active dispositions (of intelligent creatures), 214, 216–17
agent meaning, passim, 2, 28–31, 81–82
anger, passim, 9, 10, 12, 26–27, 38–39, 148, 149–51, 152–54, 166–68, 173–75, 183–86, 197–224, 250, 258–59
appropriateness, as a generic form of appraisal, 47, 136–37
axiological desert thesis, 49–57, 73–75, 84, 88, 97–98, 252, 272–73

basic desert, passim, 1, 5, 7–8, 36–37, 45–76, 84–85, 105–34, 167, 250–54, 265–66
blame passim
    attenuated by compassion, 220–24
    for definition, 17–18
    directed blame, 15–44
    as distinct from punishment, 57–59, 90–94, 252–53
    ethics of, 38–39, 213–17
    harm in, 35–36, 58–59
    overt blame, 17–18
    private blame, 17–18
    without anger, 31–32, 178–79, 202–10
blameworthiness passim
    conditions of, 20–23, 228–31
    grounds of, 109–11, 127, 133–34

communicative theory, 4, 28–29, 81–82, 84n.4, 172–75
compatibilism, 80–81, 101–2, 106, 167
consequentialist justifications, 3, 7–8, 11–12, 36–37, 110–11, 116, 139, 214n.14, 248–49, 263–68
contractualist justifications, 3, 36–37, 55–56, 55n.6, 107, 110–11
    Lenman's nonbasic desert version, 120–22
    Scanlon's non-desert-based proposal, 122–24
control condition (for moral responsibility), 1, 21–22, 39, 109–11, 133, 164–66, 228–29. *See also* freedom condition
conversational theory, passim, 1–2, 15–44, 59–64, 77–102, 173–76, 225–47, 287–97
crime, 90–97, 253, 259–60

deontological desert thesis, 18–19, 50–54, 74–75
desert passim
    basic desert, 1, 5, 7–8, 36–37, 45–76
    nonbasic desert, 36–37, 55–56, 62, 120–22, 264n.8
    post-institutional desert, 55n.6, 115n.4
    as species of fittingness, 8, 135–71, 183–88

318 INDEX OF TOPICS

determinism, 7–8, 78–79, 100–1, 105–6, 124–25, 143, 144, 261–62, 285

dropping acid, 180

epistemic condition (for moral responsibility), 21–22, 228–31

essentialist thesis, 10, 198, 202–10, 211–12, 281–82

etiquette (as it pertains to moral responsibility), 237–39

expected, as distinct deontic category, 23–24, 50n.3

expressive theories of punishment, 1–2, 90–91

extrinsic goodness, 65–66, 67–73, 254
  defeating the bad, 72–73
  instrumental goodness, 45–46, 55–56, 65–67, 68–69
  intrinsic goodness, 55–57, 64–67
  Korsgaard's two distinctions in, 65–67
  noninstrumental goodness, 5, 65–66, 98–99, 129–30, 133–34, 157
  outweighing the bad, 72–73

fairness, 3, 5, 36–37, 45–46, 55n.6, 107–8, 137, 149–50, 211
  as involving a robust freedom condition, 124–26, 127–33

fittingness, 8, 47, 49, 54n.5, 135–71, 176–78, 274–77, 282
  desert as species of, 8, 154–62, 183–88
  as distinct basis for a theory of responsibility, 61–62, 166–70, 210
  as distinct from desert, 141–42, 166–70, 192–93

free will, 1, 7–8, 11–12, 37, 45–46, 54, 75–76, 77–81, 100–2, 105–34, 135–36, 140–41, 145–47,
164–66, 167, 192–93, 248–49, 260–62

freedom condition (for moral responsibility), 21–22, 77–78, 116, 122, 133, 164–68, 274–75. *See also* control condition

good(ness), 46, 48, 49, 50–52, 54–57, 64–73. *See* also value

grief, harm in as noninstrumental good, 70–73, 157

guilt (as an emotion), 6–7, 9, 23n.8, 51–52, 86–89, 92–99, 137–38, 172–93, 204n.3, 272–73
  as distinct from self-blame, 180–81
  pain of as noninstrumentally good, 88–89, 185, 186, 191–92

guilty (for committing a crime), 90

harm as set back to interests, 35–36

hostility Thesis, 10, 198–202, 210–20, 277–78

incompatibilism, 79–80, 116, 117

indignation, 1, 8, 12, 24, 25–28, 86–89, 148, 160–61, 170n.28, 173, 176, 178, 201–2, 206n.7

justice, 59–60, 155–57, 192–93

ledger theory, 31–32

libertarian(ism), 80–81, 101–2, 135, 140–41, 144–47, 152–54, 166–67, 274–75, 281
  agent causation, 145–46
  noncausal theories, 145–46

Look, The (Nelkin's thought experiment), 52–53

manipulation argument for incompatibilism, 79–81

INDEX OF TOPICS   319

moral address. *See* moral
    responsibility exchange
moral contribution. *See* moral
    responsibility exchange
moral influence theories, 11–12,
    248–49, 263–68
moral reply. *See* moral responsibility
    exchange
moral responsibility passim
    different kinds of, 17
    as distinct from other kinds of
        responsibility, 16, 17
    as substantive responsibility (ala
        Scanlon), 122–24
moral responsibility exchange, 29
    stages of (contribution, address,
        reply), 29

naturalism about responsibility (ala
    Strawson), 148–50
Nietzschean critique (of moral
    responsibility), 246
nondesert-based theories, 36–37,
    62, 122–24
nonnatural condition for
    responsibility, 146–47
nonnatural meaning (Gricean), 1–2
nurturing stance, 221–24

organic unity, 72–73

praise, 1–3, 46, 135–36, 140–41,
    154–55, 159–60, 162–63, 226,
    274–75, 284
proportionality of punishment, 59–
    60, 95–97, 98, 253–54, 255–57
protest theory of blame, 15–16, 28, 287
punishment, 1–2, 4, 6–7, 11–12, 15,
    57–48, 59–60, 62–63, 77–102,
    120–66, 199, 248–70, 271, 279–
    80, 281–82, 283
    as distinct from blame, 57–59, 90–
        94, 252–53

quality of will, 2, 4, 20–24, 26, 28–29,
    58–59, 90–92, 226–31, 240–
    42, 274–75
    as a distinct condition for moral
        responsibility, 26, 47, 230–31

reactive attitudes, 8, 9, 10, 24, 25–29,
    31–32, 86–87, 120–22, 142,
    144, 147–51, 153–54, 169–70,
    173, 178–83, 187, 197–202, 204,
    208–20, 223–24, 225, 237, 250,
    276–77, 281–82
reasonableness, as a condition of
    fairness, 125–26, 128–30
reasons passim
    discounting, 157–62
    exclusionary, 157–58
    favoring, 50–54, 159–60, 256–
        57, 258–59
    outweighing, 157–59
    requiring, 159–60
    silencing, 157–62
    wrong kind of, 54n.5, 138–39, 143,
        146, 148–49, 293–94
reasons-responsiveness, 108
resentment, 1–3, 8, 24–28, 86–87,
    141–42, 150n.12, 160–61, 173–
    76, 178, 182–83, 198, 201–2,
    206n.7, 226, 274–75, 276–
    77, 281–82
retributivism, 6–7, 11–12, 49, 77,
    89–90, 95–96, 97–99, 107, 248–
    70, 279–80
    hard-ass, 249–50, 257, 258–
        59, 269–70
    minimal, 11–12, 254–62, 266–68
    wimpy, 11–12, 248–50, 258–
        62, 265–70

self-blame, 9, 172–93, 279–80
    as distinct from guilt, 179–80
sentence meaning, 2, 236–37
signaling theory of blame, 287–97

320 INDEX OF TOPICS

skepticism (about free will or moral responsibility), 10, 11–12, 45–46, 77–81, 100–2, 116, 193, 221, 260–62
speaker meaning, 236–37
standing to blame, 19–20
state, the (role in punishment), 90–91, 100
Strawsonian theory, 8, 10–11, 20–21, 26–27, 144–51
  dispositionalist interpretation of, 148–49
  normative interpretation of, 148–51
suberogatory action, 23

value, 20–21, 22, 45–76, 51n.4, 97–98, 254
  extrinsic value, 67–68, 69–70, 254
  instrumental value, 67, 68, 69, 214n.14
  intrinsic value, 64–65, 69
  noninstrumental value, 66, 69–70
  See also good(ness)

welfare interests, 35–36, 58, 60, 252–53, 267
wrongdoing, as a requirement for blameworthiness, 23–24